# Christmas

## Taste of Home
### BOOKS

RDA ENTHUSIAST BRANDS, LLC
MILWAUKEE, WI

# Taste of Home

## EDITORIAL

Editor-in-Chief **CATHERINE CASSIDY**
Vice President, Content Operations **KERRI BALLIET**
Creative Director **HOWARD GREENBERG**

Managing Editor/Print & Digital Books **MARK HAGEN**
Associate Creative Director **EDWIN ROBLES JR.**

Editor **MICHELLE ROZUMALSKI**
Associate Editors **MOLLY JASINSKI, DANA MEREDITH**
Art Director **JESSIE SHARON**
Layout Designer **NANCY NOVAK**
Editorial Production Manager **DENA AHLERS**
Editorial Production Coordinator **JILL BANKS**
Copy Chief **DEB WARLAUMONT MULVEY**
Copy Editor **CHRIS MCLAUGHLIN**
Contributing Copy Editors **KRISTIN SUTTER, VALERIE PHILLIPS**
Content Director **JULIE BLUME BENEDICT**
Food Editor **JAMES SCHEND**
Recipe Editors **SUE RYON (LEAD); MARY KING; IRENE YEH**
Business Architect, Publishing Technologies **AMANDA HARMATYS**
Solutions Architect, Publishing Technologies **JOHN MOSEY**
Junior Business Analyst **SHANNON STROUD**
Editorial Services Administrator **MARIE BRANNON**

Test Kitchen & Food Styling Manager **SARAH THOMPSON**
Test Cooks **NICHOLAS IVERSON (LEAD), MATTHEW HASS, LAUREN KNOELKE**
Food Stylists **KATHRYN CONRAD (LEAD), SHANNON ROUM, LEAH REKAU**
Prep Cooks **BETHANY VAN JACOBSON (LEAD), MELISSA HANSEN, ARIA C. THORNTON**
Culinary Team Assistant **MEGAN BEHR**

Photography Director **STEPHANIE MARCHESE**
Photographers **DAN ROBERTS, JIM WIELAND**
Photographer/Set Stylist **GRACE NATOLI SHELDON**
Set Stylists **MELISSA FRANCO (LEAD), STACEY GENAW, DEE DEE JACQ**
Set Stylist Assistant **STEPHANIE CHOJNACKI**
Contributors **MARK DERSE (PHOTOGRAPHY); MEGHAN HURLEY (SET STYLING); PAM STASNEY, KAREN PONTERI (SET STYLING, CRAFTS); SUZANNE HARPER, STEPHANIE SLIWINSKI, DELANIE FORD (CRAFTS)**
Editorial Business Manager **KRISTY MARTIN**
Rights & Permissions Associate **SAMANTHA LEA STOEGER**
Editorial Business Associate **ANDREA HEEG POLZIN**
Editor, *Taste of Home* **EMILY BETZ TYRA**
Associate Creative Director, *Taste of Home* **ERIN TIMMONS**
Art Director, *Taste of Home* **KRISTIN BOWKER**

## BUSINESS

Vice President, Group Publisher **KIRSTEN MARCHIOLI**
Publisher, *Taste of Home* **DONNA LINDSKOG**
Business Development Director, Taste of Home Live **LAUREL OSMAN**
Promotional Partnerships Manager, Taste of Home Live **JAMIE PIETTE ANDRZEJEWSKI**

## TRUSTED MEDIA BRANDS, INC.

President and Chief Executive Officer **BONNIE KINTZER**
Chief Financial Officer **DEAN DURBIN**
Chief Marketing Officer **C. ALEC CASEY**
Chief Revenue Officer **RICHARD SUTTON**
Chief Digital Officer **VINCE ERRICO**
Senior Vice President, Global HR & Communications **PHYLLIS E. GEBHARDT, SPHR; SHRM-SCP**
General Counsel **MARK SIROTA**
Vice President, Magazine Marketing **CHRISTOPHER GAYDOS**
Vice President, Operations **MICHAEL GARZONE**
Vice President, Consumer Marketing Planning **JIM WOODS**
Vice President, Digital Content & Audience Development **DIANE DRAGAN**
Vice President, Financial Planning & Analysis **WILLIAM HOUSTON**
Publishing Director, Books **DEBRA POLANSKY**

## COVER PHOTOGRAPHY

Photographer **JIM WIELAND**
Food Stylist **KATHRYN CONRAD**
Set Stylist **STACEY GENAW**

**PICTURED ON THE BACK COVER:**
Garlic Herbed Beef Tenderloin (p. 55), Italian Sausage Bruschetta (p.20), Gingerbread People (p. 75), Gingerbread Hot Cocoa (p. 69) and Santa Fe Chipotle Chili (p. 38).

**ADDITIONAL ART:**
alicedaniel/Shutterstock (endpapers).

FROZEN GRASSHOPPER TORTE, P. 47

MALLOW CRANBERRY CHEESECAKE, P. 73

TURTLE TART WITH CARAMEL SAUCE, P. 176

# Contents

# Make holidays merry and bright with
## TASTE OF HOME CHRISTMAS

*Set the table for an unforgettable season with the appetizers, entrees and desserts in this fantastic collection of Christmas favorites. Whether you're planning the perfect cookie platter or decking the halls with striking homemade decor, this collection of holiday ideas promises to be a yuletide keepsake for years to come.*

**PARTY STARTERS & BEVERAGES.** Let the party begin! Celebrate the season with more than 2 dozen savory bites, frosty beverages and holiday hostess tips.

**WINTER SOUPS & BREADS.** Simmer a hearty pot of soup and bake up golden loaves for a winter warm-up. Whether served alone or added to a menu, this classic pairing always brings comfort and joy.

**CHRISTMAS FEASTS.** If a ham dinner, turkey feast or hearty beef menu is in your future, these three Christmas meals will have mouths watering on the big day.

**THE MERRIEST OF THE MERRY.** Looking for the flakiest biscuit? The cheesiest side dish? The cutest cookies? Look no further! The best-of-the-best recipes are here!

**SOUTHERN CHRISTMAS.** Mix things up with a bit of Southern flair. Fried chicken, Memphis ribs and bourbon pecan pie are a just a few finger-licking options.

**SEASONAL GET-TOGETHERS.** From a cute breakfast with Santa to a sophisticated Chinese New Year appetizer buffet, these party ideas make holiday get-togethers sparkle. Check out the change-of-pace ideas!

**ENTERTAINING IN 30.** It can be difficult to host a gathering during the busy Christmas season. Turn here for 20 impressive half-hour dishes. What could be easier?

**A TWIST OF CITRUS.** Gorgeous oranges, lemons and limes are true gems in the produce department this time of year. Spruce up menus with a few sweet-savory specialties.

**MAKE-AHEAD COOKIES.** There's always time for Christmas cookies! Keep these treats at the ready for drop-in guests, last-minute gifts and merry munching all season.

**SWEET SENSATIONS.** From impressive Rum Raisin Creme Brulee to luscious Cheesecake Layered Red Velvet Cake, these 22 alluring desserts are simply unforgettable. Try one and see!

**GIFTS FROM THE KITCHEN.** Ideal presents for anyone on your list, mixes, marmalades and more are tasty ways to stir up some memories that say "Happy Holidays!"

**HOMEMADE GIFTS & DECOR.** Create a little holiday magic when you quickly spruce up your home or surprise a friend with the 29 no-fuss crafts in this popular section.

# PARTY STARTERS & BEVERAGES

## Cheesy BBQ Beef Dip

Barbecued beef dip is a holiday staple in our house. My husband can't get enough!

**—SELENA SWAFFORD** DALTON, GA

**START TO FINISH:** 30 MIN.
**MAKES:** 8 SERVINGS

- 1 **package (8 ounces) cream cheese, softened**
- 1 **package (15 ounces) refrigerated fully cooked barbecued shredded beef**
- 1 **cup (4 ounces) shredded cheddar cheese**
- ½ **cup chopped red onion**
- ¾ **cup french-fried onions**

**Optional toppings: chopped tomatoes, chopped red onion and minced fresh cilantro**
**Tortilla chips**

**1.** Preheat the oven to 350°. Spread the cream cheese onto the bottom of a greased 9-in. pie plate. Spread evenly with the barbecued shredded beef. Sprinkle with cheddar cheese and red onion. Bake 15-20 minutes or until heated through.

**2.** Sprinkle with french-fried onions; bake 5 minutes longer. If desired, top dip with tomatoes, onion and cilantro. Serve with tortilla chips.

### Holiday Helper

Have lots of leftover tortilla chips after the party? Here's how to give them new life! Sprinkle crushed chips over casseroles before baking as a tasty topping. Finely crush them to use in place of dry bread crumbs as a coating for poultry or fish. Or try a garnish of coarsely crushed chips on your favorite chili or Mexican-style soup.

## Mexican Shrimp Cocktail

It's up to you how to enjoy this cocktail—eat it with a spoon as a chilled soup, or use tortilla chips or crackers for scooping.
—**ERIN MORENO** ARCADIA, WI

**PREP:** 20 MIN. + CHILLING • **MAKES:** 12 SERVINGS (¾ CUP EACH)

- 2 medium tomatoes, seeded and finely chopped
- 1 medium onion, finely chopped
- ½ cup chopped fresh cilantro
- 1 tablespoon grated lime peel
- 1 teaspoon salt
- 1 bottle (12½ ounces) mandarin natural flavor soda
- 1½ cups Clamato juice
- ¼ cup lime juice
- ¼ cup ketchup
- 1½ pounds peeled and deveined cooked shrimp (100–150 per pound)
- 2 avocados, finely chopped
  Tortilla chips

**1.** In a large bowl, combine the first five ingredients. Stir in the soda, Clamato juice, lime juice and ketchup. Add shrimp. Refrigerate, covered, at least 2 hours.
**2.** Just before serving, add avocados. Serve with a slotted spoon and tortilla chips.

## Roasted Red Pepper Tapenade

When entertaining, I often rely on my pepper tapenade recipe because it takes only 15 minutes to whip up and pop in the fridge. Sometimes I swap out the almonds for walnuts or pecans.
—**DONNA MAGLIARO** DENVILLE, NJ

**PREP:** 15 MIN. + CHILLING • **MAKES:** 2 CUPS

- 3 garlic cloves
- 2 cups roasted sweet red peppers, drained
- ½ cup blanched almonds
- ⅓ cup tomato paste
- 2 tablespoons olive oil
- ¼ teaspoon salt
- ¼ teaspoon pepper
  Minced fresh basil
  Toasted French bread baguette slices or water crackers

**1.** In a small saucepan, bring 2 cups water to a boil. Add the garlic; cook, uncovered, 6-8 minutes or just until tender. Drain and pat dry. Place the red peppers, almonds, tomato paste, oil, garlic, salt and pepper in a small food processor; process until blended. Transfer to a small bowl. Refrigerate at least 4 hours to allow flavors to blend.
**2.** Sprinkle with basil. Serve with bread slices or crackers.

## Sweet & Spicy Curried Nuts

The bowl is soon empty after I set out this zippy mix. You may want to make extra!
—**GINNY CARMEN** PEARL RIVER, NY

**PREP:** 15 MIN. • **BAKE:** 1½ HOURS
**MAKES:** 8 CUPS

- 1 large egg white
- 2 cups pecan halves
- 2 cups salted cashews
- 2 cups salted roasted almonds
- ¾ cup packed dark brown sugar
- 2 tablespoons mild curry powder
- 2 teaspoons garlic salt
- 1 teaspoon dried rosemary, crushed
- ½ to 1 teaspoon cayenne pepper
- ½ teaspoon ground cinnamon

**1.** Preheat oven to 250°. In a large bowl, whisk the egg white until frothy. Add nuts; stir gently to coat. In a small bowl, combine the brown sugar and seasonings. Sprinkle over nut mixture and toss to coat. Spread into a greased 15x10x1-in. baking pan.
**2.** Bake for 1½-2 hours or until the nuts are dry and crisp, stirring every 15 minutes. Cool completely; store in an airtight container.

## Sensational Crab Fondue

We entertain a lot, and luxurious crab fondue makes guests feel indulged.
—**DEBBIE OBERT** MIDDLEBURG, FL

**START TO FINISH:** 30 MIN.
**MAKES:** 8 CUPS

- ½ cup butter, cubed
- 3 green onions, finely chopped
- 2 packages (8 ounces each) imitation crabmeat, coarsley chopped
- 2 cups whole milk
- ½ cup white wine or chicken broth
- ¼ teaspoon pepper
- 2 cups (8 ounces) shredded Monterey Jack cheese
- 2 cups (8 ounces) shredded Swiss cheese
- 2 cups shredded Gruyere cheese or additional shredded Swiss cheese
- 1 cup cubed process cheese (Velveeta)
  Cubed French bread

**1.** In a 6-qt. stockpot, cook butter over medium-high heat. Add green onions; cook and stir until tender. Add crab; cook 2-3 minutes longer or until heated through. Stir in milk, wine and pepper; heat until bubbles form around sides of pan.
**2.** Reduce the heat to medium-low. Add ½ cup cheese; stir constantly until almost completely melted. Continue adding cheese, ½ cup at a time, allowing cheese to almost melt completely between additions. Cook and stir until the mixture is thickened and smooth.
**3.** Transfer to a heated fondue pot; keep the fondue bubbling gently. Serve with bread cubes.

# Pork Meatballs with Chimichurri Sauce

If you've never had chimichurri sauce with meatballs, it's time to give it a try!

**—AMY CHASE** VANDERHOOF, BC

**PREP:** 20 MIN. • **BAKE:** 15 MIN.
**MAKES:** 5 DOZEN (⅔ CUP SAUCE)

- ½ cup dry bread crumbs
- ½ cup 2% milk
- 2 tablespoons grated onion
- 1 tablespoon ground cumin
- 1 tablespoon dried oregano
- 1 tablespoon lemon juice
- 2 teaspoons salt
- ¼ teaspoon coarsely ground pepper
- 2 pounds ground pork

**CHIMICHURRI SAUCE**

- 3 garlic cloves, peeled
- 1 cup packed Italian flat leaf parsley
- ¼ cup packed fresh cilantro leaves
- 1 teaspoon salt
- ¼ teaspoon coarsely ground pepper
- 2 tablespoons red wine vinegar
- ½ cup extra virgin olive oil

**1.** Preheat oven to 450°. In a large bowl, combine first eight ingredients. Add pork; mix lightly but thoroughly. Shape into 1-in. meatballs. Place on a greased rack in a 15x10x1-in. baking pan. Bake 15-20 minutes or until the meatballs are cooked through. Let stand 5 minutes.

**2.** Meanwhile, place garlic in a small food processor; pulse until chopped. Add parsley, cilantro, salt and pepper; pulse until finely chopped. Add the vinegar. While processing, gradually add oil in a steady stream.

**3.** In a large bowl, toss meatballs with half of the chimichurri sauce. Transfer to a platter. Serve with the remaining sauce for dipping.

 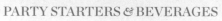

# Little Pigs in a Hammock

Pigs in a blanket aren't just for children anymore! Enjoy a version for grown-ups.
—**CRYSTAL SCHLUETER** NORTHGLENN, CO

**START TO FINISH:** 30 MIN.
**MAKES:** 1½ DOZEN

- 1 package (17.3 ounces) frozen puff pastry, thawed
- 3 tablespoons seedless raspberry jam
- 1 tablespoon Dijon mustard
- 1 round (8 ounces) Camembert cheese
- 18 miniature smoked sausages
- 1 large egg
- 1 tablespoon water

**1.** Preheat oven to 425°. Unfold the puff pastry. Cut each pastry into nine squares. Cut each square into two triangles. In a small bowl, mix the jam and mustard; spread over the triangles. Cut cheese in half crosswise; cut each half into nine wedges.

**2.** Top each triangle with a cheese piece and a sausage. Fold pastry over sausage and cheese; press to seal. Place on a parchment paper-lined baking sheet. In a small bowl, whisk the egg with water. Brush over pastries. Bake 15-17 minutes or until golden brown.

# Christmas Cranberry Punch

Every year, my grandma made her zingy punch for our Christmas Eve feast.
—**HELEN ROLAND** MIAMI, FL

**PREP:** 20 MIN. + FREEZING
**MAKES:** 16 SERVINGS (¾ CUP EACH)

- 2 cups fresh or frozen cranberries
- 2 cups sugar
- 2 cups water
- ½ teaspoon ground cinnamon
- ¼ teaspoon ground cloves
- 1 liter ginger ale, chilled
- 4 cups cold water
- 2 cups unsweetened pineapple juice, chilled
- 1 cup lemon juice
  Mint leaves and additional fresh or frozen cranberries, optional

**1.** In a large saucepan, combine the first five ingredients. Bring to a boil. Reduce heat; simmer, uncovered, 4-6 minutes or until the berries are softened. Remove from the heat; cool slightly. Transfer to a blender; process until smooth. If desired, strain through a fine-mesh strainer. Pour into a 6-cup ring mold. Freeze until solid.

**2.** Just before serving, wrap the bottom of the ring mold in a hot damp dishcloth; invert onto a baking sheet and lift off the mold. Place the ice ring in a punch bowl. Gently stir in the ginger ale, cold water, unsweetened pineapple juice and lemon juice. If desired, serve with mint leaves and additional cranberries.

## Texas Red River Margaritas

When I lived in Texas, I decided to create a cocktail that represented my new home. I've found that blood orange juice works just as well as the grapefruit juice.
—**DANNY SCHNEIDER** OMAHA, NE

**PREP:** 15 MIN. + STANDING
**MAKES:** 2 SERVINGS

- 4 ounces tequila
- 2 jalapeno peppers, quartered and seeded
- 1 tablespoon kosher salt
- 1 teaspoon coarse sugar
- 1 cup ruby red grapefruit juice
- ½ cup simple syrup

**1.** Place the tequila and jalapenos in a small bowl. Let stand 2-3 hours.

**2.** Using water, moisten the rims of four margarita or cocktail glasses. Mix salt and sugar on a plate; hold each glass upside down and dip rim into salt mixture. Set aside. Discard remaining salt mixture on plate.

**3.** Strain tequila into a small bowl, discarding the jalapenos. Stir in the grapefruit juice and simple syrup. Serve in prepared glasses over ice.

**NOTE** *Wear disposable gloves when cutting hot peppers; the oils can burn skin. Avoid touching your face.*

## Chili-Lime Roasted Chickpeas

**PREP:** 10 MIN. • **BAKE:** 40 MIN.
**MAKES:** 2 CUPS

- 2 cans (15 ounces each) garbanzo beans or chickpeas, rinsed, drained and patted dry
- 2 tablespoons extra virgin olive oil
- 1 tablespoon chili powder
- 2 teaspoons ground cumin
- 1 teaspoon grated lime peel
- 1 tablespoon lime juice
- ¾ teaspoon sea salt

**1.** Preheat the oven to 400°. Line a 15x10x1-in. baking sheet with foil. Spread beans in a single layer over foil. Remove any loose skins. Bake 40-45 or until very crunchy, stirring every 15 minutes.

**2.** Meanwhile, in a small bowl, whisk the extra virgin olive oil, chili powder, cumin, grated lime peel, lime juice and salt. Remove the beans from the oven; let cool 5 minutes. Drizzle the beans with the oil mixture; shake pan to coat. Cool completely. Store in an airtight container.

*"Looking for a lighter snack that's still a crowd-pleaser? You've found it! Chili-Lime Roasted Chickpeas will have everyone happily munching."*

— **JULIE RUBLE** CHARLOTTE, NC

## Holiday Helper

When serving veggies and dip, add Christmasy color to your table by making little pepper bowls. Just cut off the tops of red or green bell peppers and remove the membranes and seeds. Then spoon the cold dip into the pepper cups.

—**EMMA K.** CLAXTON, GA

## Aunt Grace's Eggnog

When I was growing up, I couldn't get enough of the nonalcoholic eggnog my aunt always prepared for us kids. Now I enjoy the adult version.

**—SUSAN HEIN** BURLINGTON, WI

**PREP:** 15 MIN. • **COOK:** 15 MIN. + CHILLING
**MAKES:** 20 SERVINGS (¾ CUP EACH)

- 8 **cups 2% milk, divided**
- 6 **large eggs**
- 1 **cup plus 2 tablespoons sugar, divided**
- ½ **cup rum**
- ½ **cup brandy**
- ½ **teaspoon ground nutmeg**
- 3 **cups heavy whipping cream**
  **Cinnamon sticks and additional ground nutmeg, optional**

**1.** In a large saucepan, heat 4 cups of milk until bubbles form around sides of pan. Meanwhile, in a large bowl, whisk the eggs and 1 cup sugar until blended. Slowly stir in the hot milk; return all to saucepan.

**2.** Cook mixture over medium-low heat 6-8 minutes or until slightly thickened and a thermometer reads at least 160°, stirring constantly (do not allow to boil). Immediately transfer to a large bowl.

**3.** Stir in rum, brandy, nutmeg and remaining milk. Refrigerate, covered, several hours or until cold.

**4.** In a large bowl, beat cream until it begins to thicken. Add the remaining sugar; beat until soft peaks form. Fold into the egg mixture. (Mixture may separate; stir before serving.) Serve with cinnamon sticks and additional nutmeg, if desired.

# Sun-Dried Tomato Spinach-Artichoke Dip

Fresh veggies and crackers will disappear quickly when they're next to this cheesy slow-cooked dip. With smoked Gouda, it has an extra level of flavor that keeps everyone guessing.

**—KATIE STANCZAK** HOOVER, AL

**PREP:** 10 MIN. • **COOK:** 2 HOURS
**MAKES:** 3 CUPS

- 1 package (10 ounces) frozen chopped spinach, thawed and squeezed dry
- 1 package (8 ounces) cream cheese, softened
- 1 cup (4 ounces) shredded smoked Gouda cheese
- ½ cup shredded fontina cheese
- ½ cup chopped water-packed artichoke hearts
- ¼ to ½ cup soft sun-dried tomato halves (not packed in oil), chopped
- ⅓ cup finely chopped onion
- 1 garlic clove, minced
  Assorted fresh vegetables and crackers

In a 1½-qt. slow cooker, mix spinach, cheeses, artichoke hearts, sun-dried tomatoes, onion and garlic. Cook, covered, on low 2-3 hours or until cheese is melted. Stir before serving. Serve with vegetables and crackers.

**NOTE** *This recipe was tested with sun-dried tomatoes that can be used without soaking. When using other sun-dried tomatoes that are not oil-packed, cover them with boiling water and let them stand until soft. Drain before using.*

## The Perfect Lemon Martini

Time to relax with a refreshing cocktail! The combination of tart lemon and sweet liqueur will tingle your taste buds.

—**MARILEE ANKER** CHATSWORTH, CA

**START TO FINISH:** 5 MIN.
**MAKES:** 1 SERVING

- 1 lemon slice
  Sugar
  Ice cubes
- 2 ounces vodka
- 1½ ounces limoncello
- ½ ounce lemon juice

**1.** Using lemon slice, moisten rim of a chilled cocktail glass; set lemon aside. Sprinkle sugar on a plate; hold the glass upside down and dip the rim into sugar. Discard the remaining sugar on plate.

**2.** Fill a shaker three-fourths full with ice. Add the vodka, limoncello and lemon juice; cover and shake for 10-15 seconds or until condensation forms on outside of shaker. Strain into the prepared glass. Garnish with the lemon slice.

## Spicy Sweet Chicken Bacon Bites

I've been serving these for many years. Guests love dipping the bacon-wrapped chicken tidbits into blue cheese salad dressing or barbecue sauce.

—**JACQULYN FLETCHER**
SPOKANE VALLEY, WA

**PREP:** 35 MIN. • **BAKE:** 10 MIN.
**MAKES:** 2 DOZEN

- ¾ pound thick-sliced peppered bacon strips
- 1 pound boneless skinless chicken breasts, cut into 1-inch cubes
- ¼ cup packed brown sugar
- ½ teaspoon onion powder
- ½ teaspoon chili powder
- ¼ teaspoon garlic powder
- ¼ teaspoon salt
- ⅛ teaspoon cayenne pepper
- ⅛ teaspoon pepper
  Blue cheese salad dressing and barbecue sauce

**1.** Preheat oven to 350°. Cut bacon strips crosswise into thirds. In a large skillet, cook bacon over medium heat until partially cooked but not crisp. Remove to paper towels to drain; keep warm.
**2.** Wrap a bacon piece around each chicken piece; secure with a toothpick. In a shallow bowl, mix brown sugar and seasonings. Add wrapped chicken, a few pieces at a time, and toss to coat.
**3.** Place on 15x10x1-in. baking pans. Bake 10-12 minutes or until bacon is crisp and chicken is no longer pink. Serve with blue cheese salad dressing and barbecue sauce.

# Thai Curry Meatballs

A little bit of Thai flavor spices up the party. Serve these chicken meatballs with the accompanying dipping sauce of coconut milk and curry.

**—MARISA RAPONI** VAUGHAN, ON

**PREP:** 25 MIN. + CHILLING • **BAKE:** 20 MIN.
**MAKES:** ABOUT 3½ DOZEN (⅔ CUP SAUCE)

- 1 cup shredded zucchini (about 1 small)
- ⅓ cup seasoned bread crumbs
- 1 large egg, lightly beaten
- 1 tablespoon minced fresh cilantro leaves
- 1 tablespoon yellow curry paste
- 1 teaspoon paprika
- ½ teaspoon garlic powder
- ½ teaspoon pepper
- 1 pound ground chicken

**DIPPING SAUCE**

- 4 teaspoons red curry paste
- 1 cup coconut milk
  Chopped fresh cilantro leaves and paprika, optional

**1.** Preheat oven to 350°. In a large bowl, combine first eight ingredients. Add the ground chicken; mix lightly but thoroughly. Refrigerate, covered, for 1 hour. Shape into 1-in. meatballs. Place the meatballs on a greased rack in a 15x10x1-in. baking pan. Bake for 20-25 minutes or until cooked through and golden brown.

**2.** Meanwhile, in a small saucepan, heat curry paste over medium-high heat. Add the coconut milk. Bring to a boil; cook and stir 5-7 minutes or until slightly thickened. Serve the sauce with meatballs; sprinkle with additional cilantro and paprika if desired.

# Cranberry Brie Pie

Now you don't have to wait for dessert to have pie! Give everyone a thin slice of this extra-special appetizer that joins tart cranberries with rich Brie.

**—MARIE PARKER** MILWAUKEE, WI

**PREP:** 30 MIN. • **BAKE:** 30 MIN. + COOLING
**MAKES:** 12 SERVINGS

- 3 cups fresh or frozen cranberries
- 1 cup packed brown sugar
- 1 cup orange juice
- ⅓ cup all-purpose flour
- 1 teaspoon balsamic vinegar
- 1 sheet refrigerated pie pastry
- 4 ounces Brie cheese, finely chopped
- 1 teaspoon vanilla extract
- 2 tablespoons butter

**TOPPING**

- ½ cup all-purpose flour
- ¼ cup packed brown sugar
- ¼ cup cold butter, cubed

**1.** Preheat oven to 450°. In a small saucepan, combine the cranberries, brown sugar, orange juice, flour and vinegar. Cook over medium heat until berries pop, about 15 minutes.

**2.** Meanwhile, unroll the pastry into a 9-in. metal pie plate; flute the edges. Sprinkle with cheese; bake 8 minutes or until cheese begins to melt. Reduce oven temperature to 350°.

**3.** Remove cranberry mixture from heat; stir in vanilla. Pour into crust. Dot with butter.

**4.** For the topping, in a small bowl, combine the flour and brown sugar; cut in butter until crumbly. Sprinkle over filling.

**5.** Bake 30-35 minutes or until crust is golden brown and filling is bubbly (cover edges with foil during the last 20 minutes to prevent overbrowning if necessary). Serve warm or at room temperature. Refrigerate leftovers.

## Walnut & Fig Goat Cheese Log

Here's a simple spread that calls for only a handful of ingredients. The tablespoon of honey is optional, but I think that touch of sweetness really complements the tang of the goat cheese.
**—ANA-MARIE CORRELL** HOLLISTER, CA

**PREP:** 10 MIN. + CHILLING
**MAKES:** 1⅓ CUPS

- **2  logs (4 ounces each) fresh goat cheese**
- **8  dried figs, finely chopped**
- **½  cup finely chopped walnuts, toasted, divided**
- **¾  teaspoon pepper**
- **1  tablespoon honey, optional
  Assorted crackers**

In a small bowl, crumble the goat cheese. Stir in the dried figs, ¼ cup toasted walnuts, pepper and, if desired, honey. Shape the cheese mixture into a log, about 6 in. long. Roll the log in the remaining walnuts. Refrigerate for 4 hours or overnight. Serve with assorted crackers.

### Holiday Helper

Crystallization is the natural process by which liquid honey becomes solid. If honey has crystallized, place the jar in warm water and stir until the crystals dissolve. Or place the honey in a microwave-safe container and microwave on high, stirring every 30 seconds, until the crystals dissolve.

# Marinated Almond-Stuffed Olives

Marinated stuffed olives go over so well with company that I try to keep a batch of them in the fridge at all times.

**—LARISSA DELK** COLUMBIA, TN

**PREP:** 15 MIN. + MARINATING • **MAKES:** 8 CUPS

- 1  cup blanched almonds, toasted
- 3  cans (6 ounces each) pitted ripe olives, drained
- 3  jars (7 ounces each) pimiento-stuffed olives, undrained
- ½  cup white balsamic vinegar
- ½  cup dry red wine
- ½  cup canola oil
- 1  medium garlic clove, minced
- ½  teaspoon sugar
- 1  teaspoon dried oregano
- 1  teaspoon pepper
- ½  teaspoon dill weed
- ½  teaspoon dried basil
- ½  teaspoon dried parsley flakes

Insert an almond into each ripe olive; place in a large bowl. Add pimiento-stuffed olives with olive juice. In a small bowl, whisk the balsamic vinegar, dry red wine, oil, garlic, sugar and seasonings. Pour mixture over the olives. Refrigerate, covered, 8 hours or overnight, stirring occasionally. Transfer to a serving bowl.

# Santa's Orange-Kissed Cocktail

Refreshing but not overly sweet, this drink is a festive choice for Christmas get-togethers. Serve it during cocktail hour, at dinner or even for brunch in place of mimosas.

**—CLAIRE BEATTIE** TORONTO, ON

**START TO FINISH:** 5 MIN. • **MAKES:** 1 SERVING

- Ice cubes
- ¼  cup light rum
- ¼  cup unsweetened pineapple juice
- 1  tablespoon lime juice
- 2  tablespoons orange juice
- 1  teaspoon grenadine syrup
- 3  tablespoons lemon-lime soda

**1.** Fill a shaker three-fourths full with ice. Add rum, juices and grenadine syrup.
**2.** Cover and shake for 10-15 seconds or until condensation forms on outside of the shaker. Strain into a chilled glass. Top with lemon-lime soda.

## Pickled Green Beans with Smoked Salmon Dip

I came up with this appetizer for my son, who's big on delicious but healthy food. The lighter beans-and-dip combo has won over even finicky eaters.

—**DINAH HALTERMAN** HARMONY, NC

**PREP:** 30 MIN. + MARINATING
**MAKES:** 1½ POUNDS BEANS (2⅓ CUPS DIP)

- 1½ pounds fresh green beans, trimmed
- 2 tablespoons dill seed
- 3 garlic cloves, coarsely chopped
- 4 cups water
- 1¼ cups white wine vinegar
- 2 tablespoons sea salt

**DIP**
- 1 package (8 ounces) reduced-fat cream cheese or non-dairy imitation cream cheese
- ¾ cup plain yogurt
- 2 tablespoons chopped fresh parsley
- 1 tablespoon minced chives
- 1 teaspoon horseradish
- ½ teaspoon grated lemon peel
- ½ teaspoon lemon juice
- ½ teaspoon dill weed
- ¼ teaspoon sea salt
- 1½ cups flaked smoked salmon fillets
  Fresh dill sprig, optional
  Assorted crackers

**1.** Place green beans in a 13x9-in. dish. Add the dill seed and garlic. In a large saucepan, combine water, vinegar and salt. Bring to a boil; cook and stir until salt is dissolved. Pour hot brine over beans. Cool completely. Refrigerate, covered, for 2 days.

**2.** For the dip, in a small bowl, beat cream cheese and yogurt until smooth. Stir in the parsley, chives, horseradish, grated lemon peel, lemon juice, dill weed and salt. Stir in smoked salmon. Refrigerate, covered, 1 hour to allow flavors to blend.

**3.** To serve, drain the green beans; arrange on a serving platter. If desired, top dip with dill sprig. Serve dip with beans and crackers.

## Spiced Cranberry Glogg

Years ago, a friend of mine shared her easy recipe for glogg. Simmered on the stove, it'll warm up everyone from head to toe on a blustery day.

—**JUNE LINDQUIST** HAMMOND, WI

**START TO FINISH:** 30 MIN.
**MAKES:** 8 SERVINGS

- 6 whole cloves
- 2 cinnamon sticks (3 inches)
- 4 cardamom pods, crushed
- 4 cups cranberry juice, divided
- 1 cup raisins
- ¼ cup sugar
- 2 cups ruby port wine
  Additional raisins, optional

**1.** Place the cloves, cinnamon and cardamom on a double thickness of cheesecloth. Gather the corners of cloth to enclose the seasonings; tie securely with string. Place in a large saucepan. Add 2 cups cranberry juice, raisins and sugar. Bring to a simmer; cook, uncovered, 10 minutes.

**2.** Discard the spice bag. Add port wine and remaining cranberry juice; bring just to a simmer (do not boil). Serve warm in mugs with additional raisins if desired.

## Italian Sausage Bruschetta

Sometimes I garnish each slice of this bruschetta with a sprig of fresh basil.

**—TERESA RALSTON** NEW ALBANY, OH

**START TO FINISH:** 20 MIN.
**MAKES:** 2 DOZEN

- 1 **pound bulk Italian sausage**
- 8 **ounces mascarpone cheese, softened**
- 3 **tablespoons prepared pesto**
- 24 **slices French bread baguette (½ inch thick)**
- 3 **tablespoons olive oil**
- ¾ **cup finely chopped seeded plum tomatoes**
- 3 **tablespoons chopped fresh parsley**
- 3 **tablespoons shredded Parmesan cheese**

**1.** In a large skillet, cook sausage over medium heat 6-8 minutes or until no longer pink, breaking into crumbles; drain. In a small bowl, combine the mascarpone cheese and pesto.

**2.** Preheat broiler. Place the bread slices on ungreased baking sheets. Brush bread slices on one side with the olive oil. Broil 3-4 in. from the heat 30-45 seconds on each side or until golden brown. Spread with the mascarpone mixture. Top each with sausage, tomatoes, parsley and Parmesan cheese. Serve warm.

# WINTER
# SOUPS & BREADS

# Sour Cream Cut-Out Biscuits

After trying different ways to make biscuits without being completely satisfied, I decided to incorporate buttermilk and sour cream. Success! Split while warm, butter and enjoy.

**—LORRAINE CALAND** SHUNIAH, ON

**START TO FINISH:** 30 MIN.
**MAKES:** 10 BISCUITS

- 2 **cups all-purpose flour**
- 2 **tablespoons sugar**
- 3 **teaspoons baking powder**
- ½ **teaspoon salt**
- ½ **teaspoon baking soda**
- 1 **cup (8 ounces) sour cream**
- 1 **tablespoon butter, melted**

**1.** Preheat oven to 425°. In a large bowl, whisk the flour, sugar, baking powder, salt and baking soda. Stir in sour cream just until moistened.

**2.** Turn dough onto a lightly floured surface; knead gently 8-10 times. Pat or roll dough to ½-in. thickness; cut with a floured 2¼-in. biscuit cutter. Place 1 in. apart on an ungreased baking sheet. Bake 10-12 minutes or until golden brown. Brush the biscuits with butter; serve warm.

## Holiday Helper

To make biscuits in a hurry, I pat or roll the dough into a rectangle and cut out square biscuits using a pizza cutter. The dough only needs to be rolled out once because there are no leftover pieces, making it a great time-saver.

**—KONNIE L.** GROVE, OK

3. Stir in the water, sweet potatoes, bay leaves, curry, salt, cinnamon, paprika and pepper. Bring to a boil. Reduce the heat; simmer, covered, 10-15 minutes or until the vegetables are tender. Discard the bay leaves. Stir in the cream and sour cream just until blended. Cool.

4. Meanwhile, in a small bowl, combine the mint, oil, sugar, salt, pepper flakes and pepper. Let oil stand 5-10 minutes.

5. Process the bisque in batches in a blender until smooth; return all to the pan. Heat through (do not boil). Ladle bisque into bowls; drizzle with minted chili oil.

## Vintage-Style Soup Can Gifts

Recycle your empty soup cans! Start by gluing solid red paper around a clean can, then glue a vintage postcard or strip of vintage-pattern paper around the center. For the inside, sew a hem around the edges of a fabric square or cut a square with pinking shears. Then just gather the fabric around a bag of soup mix or another treat, tie the fabric with ribbon and place your gift in the can.

## Sweet Potato Bisque

I love to serve this bright orange bisque for special occasions in fall and winter. The recipe includes a minted chili oil to drizzle on top. It's well worth the few extra minutes it takes to make!
—**LILY JULOW** LAWRENCEVILLE, GA

**PREP:** 30 MIN. • **COOK:** 40 MIN.
**MAKES:** 8 SERVINGS (2 QUARTS)

- 8 bacon strips, finely chopped
- 6 medium carrots, chopped (2 cups)
- 1 medium onion, chopped (1 cup)
- 3 garlic cloves, minced
- 3 cups water
- 1¾ pounds sweet potatoes (about 4 medium), peeled and cubed
- 3 bay leaves
- 2½ teaspoons curry powder
- ¾ teaspoon salt
- ½ teaspoon ground cinnamon
- ½ teaspoon smoked paprika
- ½ teaspoon pepper
- 1½ cups heavy whipping cream
- 1 cup (8 ounces) sour cream

**MINTED CHILI OIL**
- 18 mint sprigs, chopped
- 3 tablespoons olive oil
- ¼ teaspoon sugar
- ¼ teaspoon salt
- ¼ teaspoon crushed red pepper flakes
- ¼ teaspoon pepper

1. In a large saucepan, cook chopped bacon over medium heat until crisp, stirring occasionally. Remove bacon with a slotted spoon; drain on paper towels. Discard drippings, reserving 2 tablespoons in pan.

2. Add the carrots and onion to the bacon drippings; cook and stir over medium-high heat until tender. Add garlic; cook 1 minute longer.

## So-Easy-Yet-Delicious Onion Soup

Topped with a slice of cheesy toast hot from the broiler, homemade onion soup is guaranteed to please. Add a green side salad for a complete meal.

**—HILDY SCHLEGEL** ADDISON, NY

**PREP:** 40 MIN. • **COOK:** 35 MIN.
**MAKES:** 6 SERVINGS

- **3 tablespoons butter**
- **1 tablespoon canola oil**
- **3 medium red onions, halved and thinly sliced (about 4 cups)**
- **6 garlic cloves, minced**
- **8 cups beef broth**
- **½ cup Madeira wine or additional beef broth**
- **½ teaspoon dried basil**
- **½ teaspoon coarsely ground pepper**
- **¼ teaspoon dried oregano**
- **¼ teaspoon dried thyme**
- **⅛ teaspoon crushed red pepper flakes**
- **6 slices Italian bread (¾ inch thick)**
- **½ cup shredded part-skim mozzarella cheese**
- **½ cup shredded provolone cheese**

**1.** In a 6-qt. stockpot, heat the butter and oil over medium heat. Add the onions; cook and stir until softened. Reduce the heat to medium-low; cook 30 minutes or until deep golden brown, stirring occasionally. Add the garlic; cook 1 minute longer.

**2.** Add the broth, wine, basil, ground pepper, oregano, thyme and pepper flakes. Bring to a boil. Reduce heat; cook, uncovered, 20-30 minutes or until liquid is reduced to about 6 cups.

**3.** Place the bread on a baking sheet. Broil 4 in. from the heat 2 minutes on each side or until toasted. Sprinkle with cheeses; broil 2 minutes longer or until cheese is melted. Ladle soup into bowls; top each with a cheese toast. Serve immediately.

## Honey Beer Bread

It's true—this amazing bread requires just four ingredients! Simply combine self-rising flour, sugar, honey and beer, pour the batter into the pan and bake. For a twist, try one of the fun variations listed at the end of the recipe.
—**CAK MARSHALL** SALEM, OR

**PREP:** 5 MIN. • **BAKE:** 45 MIN. + COOLING
**MAKES:** 1 LOAF (12 SLICES)

> 3 **cups self-rising flour**
> 3 **tablespoons sugar**
> ⅓ **cup honey**
> 1 **bottle (12 ounces) beer**

**1.** Preheat oven to 350°. In a large bowl, whisk the self-rising flour and sugar. Stir in the honey and beer just until moistened.

**2.** Transfer the batter to a greased 8x4-in. loaf pan. Bake 45-50 minutes or until a toothpick inserted in the center comes out clean. Cool in the pan for 10 minutes before removing to a wire rack to cool.

**CRANBERRY-ORANGE BEER BREAD**
*Add 1 cup dried cranberries or Craisins and 1 teaspoon orange extract to batter.*

**CHERRY-ALMOND BEER BREAD**
*Add 1 cup dried cherries and ¾ teaspoon almond extract to batter.*

### Holiday Helper

Self-rising flour contains a leavening agent. Don't have self-rising flour? Make your own with pantry staples. For each cup, place 1½ teaspoons baking powder and ½ teaspoon salt in a measuring cup, then add enough all-purpose flour to measure 1 cup. Stir or sift.

# Cherry Tomato & Basil Focaccia

When I had 80 pounds of tomatoes, I got creative incorporating them into meals. Sometimes I slice this loaf into squares to make sandwiches with fresh mozzarella cheese and deli meats.
—KATIE FERRIER HOUSTON, TX

**PREP:** 45 MIN. + RISING • **BAKE:** 15 MIN.
**MAKES:** 24 SERVINGS

- 1 package (¼ ounce) active dry yeast
- 2 cups warm 2% milk (110° to 115°)
- ¼ cup canola oil
- 4½ teaspoons sugar
- 1 teaspoon salt
- 5 to 5½ cups all-purpose flour
- 2 cups cherry tomatoes
- ⅓ cup olive oil
- 2 tablespoons cornmeal
- 3 tablespoons thinly sliced fresh basil
- 1 teaspoon coarse salt
- ⅛ teaspoon pepper

**1.** In a small bowl, dissolve yeast in warm milk. In a large bowl, combine canola oil, sugar, salt, yeast mixture and 2 cups flour; beat on medium speed until smooth. Stir in enough remaining flour to form a stiff dough (dough will be sticky).

**2.** Turn dough onto a floured surface; knead until smooth and elastic, about 6-8 minutes. Place dough in a greased bowl, turning once to grease the top. Cover with plastic wrap and let rise in a warm place until doubled, about 45 minutes.

**3.** Meanwhile, fill a large saucepan two-thirds full with water; bring to a boil. Cut a shallow "X" on the bottom of each tomato. Using a slotted spoon, place the tomatoes, a cup at a time, in boiling water for 30 seconds or just until skin at the "X" begins to loosen.

**4.** Remove tomatoes and immediately drop into ice water. Pull off and discard skins. Place tomatoes in a small bowl; drizzle with oil.

**5.** Preheat oven to 425°. Sprinkle two greased baking sheets with cornmeal; set aside. Punch the down dough. Turn onto a lightly floured surface.

Cover with a kitchen towel; let rest for 10 minutes. Divide dough in half. Shape each into a 12x8-in. rectangle and place on prepared baking sheets.

**6.** Using fingertips, press several dimples into the dough. Pour tomato mixture over the dough; sprinkle with basil, coarse salt and pepper. Let rise in a warm place until doubled, about 30 minutes.

**7.** Bake for 15-18 minutes or until golden brown.

# Hearty Pasta Fajioli

Here's an Italian favorite. Spaghetti sauce and canned broth form the flavorful base.
—CINDY GARLAND LIMESTONE, TN

**PREP:** 40 MIN. • **COOK:** 40 MIN.
**MAKES:** 24 SERVINGS (7½ QUARTS)

- 2 pounds ground beef
- 6 cans (14½ ounces each) beef broth
- 2 cans (28 ounces each) diced tomatoes, undrained
- 2 jars (26 ounces each) spaghetti sauce
- 3 large onions, chopped
- 8 celery ribs, diced
- 3 medium carrots, sliced
- 2 cups canned white kidney or cannellini beans, rinsed and drained
- 2 cups canned kidney beans, rinsed and drained
- 3 teaspoons minced fresh oregano or 1 teaspoon dried oregano
- 2½ teaspoons pepper
- 1½ teaspoons hot pepper sauce
- 8 ounces uncooked medium pasta shells
- 5 teaspoons minced fresh parsley

**1.** In a large stockpot, cook ground beef over medium heat until the meat is no longer pink, breaking meat into crumbles; drain. Add the beef broth, tomatoes, spaghetti sauce, onions, celery, carrots, beans, oregano, pepper and pepper sauce.

**2.** Bring to a boil. Reduce the heat; simmer, covered, 30 minutes. Add pasta and parsley; simmer, covered, 10-14 minutes or until pasta is tender.

# Anaheim Chicken Tortilla Soup

Want to put a little spice in your holiday season? Anaheim peppers, jalapenos and cayenne will do just that!

—**JOHNNA JOHNSON** SCOTTSDALE, AZ

**PREP:** 30 MIN. + STANDING • **COOK:** 45 MIN.
**MAKES:** 10 SERVINGS (2¾ QUARTS)

- 6 **Anaheim peppers**
- 3 **tablespoons canola oil, divided**
- 8 **corn tortillas (6 inches), cut into ½-inch strips**
- 2 **medium onions, chopped**
- 8 **garlic cloves, peeled**
- 7 **cups chicken broth**
- 1 **can (29 ounces) tomato puree**
- 2 **tablespoons minced fresh cilantro**
- 1 **tablespoon ground cumin**
- 1 **teaspoon ground coriander**
- 1 **bay leaf**
- 2 **jalapeno peppers, seeded and finely chopped, optional**
- 1 **pound boneless skinless chicken breasts, cut into ½-inch cubes**
- 2 **tablespoons lemon juice**
- ½ **teaspoon salt**
- ¼ **teaspoon pepper**
  **Dash cayenne pepper**
- 1½ **cups (6 ounces) shredded cheddar cheese**
- 1 **medium ripe avocado, peeled and chopped**

**1.** Place the peppers on a foil-lined baking sheet. Broil the peppers 4 in. from heat until the skins blister, about 5 minutes. With tongs, rotate peppers a quarter turn. Broil and rotate until all sides are blistered and blackened. Immediately place peppers in a large bowl; let stand, covered, 20 minutes.

**2.** Peel off and discard charred skin. Remove stems and seeds. Coarsely chop peppers; set aside.

**3.** In a large skillet, heat 2 tablespoons canola oil. Fry the corn tortilla strips in batches until crisp and browned. Remove with a slotted spoon; drain on paper towels.

**4.** In a Dutch oven, heat 2 teaspoons oil over medium-high heat. Add the onions; cook and stir until tender. Add the garlic; cook and stir 1 minute longer. Add the broth, tomato puree, cilantro, cumin, coriander, bay leaf, half of the fried tortilla strips, reserved peppers and, if desired, jalapenos. Bring to a boil. Reduce the heat; simmer, uncovered, 35 minutes.

**5.** Remove soup from the heat; cool slightly. Discard the bay leaf. Process in batches in a blender until blended. Return to the Dutch oven.

**6.** In a large skillet, heat remaining oil over medium-high heat. Add chicken; cook and stir 4-5 minutes or until no longer pink. Add chicken, lemon juice, salt, pepper and cayenne to the soup; heat through. Serve with the cheese, avocado and remaining tortilla strips.

**NOTE** *Wear disposable gloves when cutting hot peppers; the oils can burn skin. Avoid touching your face.*

## Italian Herb and Cheese Breadsticks

Thanks to convenient frozen dough, these delectable breadsticks are oven-ready in 20 minutes. The cheesy bites are so good dipped in warm marinara sauce.

**—REBEKAH BEYER** SABETHA, KS

**PREP:** 20 MIN. • **BAKE:** 20 MIN.
**MAKES:** 2 DOZEN

- **1 loaf (1 pound) frozen bread dough, thawed**
- **⅓ cup butter, softened**
- **1 tablespoon Italian seasoning**
- **1 garlic clove, minced**
- **¾ cup shredded part-skim mozzarella cheese**
- **½ cup grated Parmesan cheese, divided**
- **Marinara sauce, warmed, optional**

**1.** On a lightly floured surface, roll dough into a 12-in. square. In a small bowl, mix butter, Italian seasoning and minced garlic; spread over dough. Sprinkle the mozzarella cheese and ¼ cup Parmesan cheese over butter mixture. Fold the dough in thirds over filling; pinch seams to seal.

**2.** Cut crosswise into twenty-four ½-in.-wide strips. Twist each strip 2-3 times. Place 2 in. apart on greased baking sheets. Cover and let rise until almost doubled, about 30 minutes.

**3.** Preheat oven to 375°. Sprinkle the breadsticks with remaining Parmesan cheese. Bake 20-22 minutes or until golden brown. If desired, serve with warmed marinara sauce.

## Garlic Potato Bread

If you love the convenience of using a bread machine, keep this easy loaf in mind. It's wonderful for sandwiches, with soup or all by itself.

—**SHILAH KOSTER** RAPID RIVER, MI

**PREP:** 10 MIN. • **BAKE:** 3 HOURS
**MAKES:** 1 LOAF (1½ POUNDS, 16 SLICES)

- 1 **cup plus 2 tablespoons water (70° to 80°)**
- 4½ **teaspoons butter, softened**
- ½ **cup plus 2 tablespoons mashed potato flakes**
- 4½ **teaspoons sugar**
- 1 **tablespoon nonfat dry milk powder**
- 1 **teaspoon minced garlic**
- ½ **teaspoon salt**
- ½ **teaspoon onion salt**
- 3 **cups bread flour**
- 1 **package (¼ ounce) active dry yeast**

**1.** In bread machine pan, place all ingredients in the order suggested by manufacturer. Select basic bread setting. Choose crust color and loaf size if available.

**2.** Check the dough after 5 minutes of mixing; add 1-2 tablespoons of additional water or flour if needed. Bake the loaf according to the bread machine directions.

**NOTE** *We recommend you do not use a bread machine's time-delay feature for this recipe.*

> *"When I'm making a pot of Smoky Cheddar Corn Chowder, no one misses dinner. Smoked cheese brings the flavor to another level."*
>
> —**DANIELLE CRAWFORD** PELZER, SC

## Holiday Helper

For food safety, the experts in the *Taste of Home* Test Kitchen recommend not using the time-delay feature of a bread machine for recipes like Garlic Potato Bread that contain dairy products or other fresh ingredients where bacteria can grow.

## Smoky Cheddar Corn Chowder

**PREP:** 20 MIN. • **COOK:** 30 MIN.
**MAKES:** 6 SERVINGS (2 QUARTS)

- 1 **fully cooked boneless ham steak (1½ pounds), cubed**
- 2 **large baking potatoes, peeled and cubed**
- 2 **cups 2% milk**
- 1 **can (15¼ ounces) whole kernel corn, drained**
- 1 **can (14¾ ounces) cream-style corn**
- 1 **medium onion, finely chopped**
- 1½ **cups (6 ounces) shredded smoked cheddar cheese**

**1.** In a Dutch oven, cook and stir the ham over medium-high heat until browned. Add the potatoes, milk, corn and onion. Bring to a boil. Reduce heat; simmer, uncovered, 20-25 minutes or until the potatoes are tender.

**2.** Remove from the heat; stir in the cheddar cheese until melted.

## Savory Corn Bread

Want to serve your favorite chili or stew with an equally amazing corn bread? Look no further than this simply perfect recipe. It's the best! I've brought it to potlucks many times.
—**KRISTA KLAUS** ROUND ROCK, TX

**START TO FINISH:** 30 MIN. • **MAKES:** 9 SERVINGS

- 1 cup yellow cornmeal
- ½ cup all-purpose flour
- 3 teaspoons baking powder
- 1 teaspoon salt
- ½ teaspoon baking soda
- 1 large egg
- 1 cup buttermilk
- ½ cup 2% milk
- ¼ cup canola oil

**1.** Preheat oven to 450°. In a small bowl, whisk cornmeal, flour, baking powder, salt and baking soda. In another bowl, whisk egg, buttermilk, milk and oil until blended. Add to the flour mixture; stir just until moistened.

**2.** Transfer the batter to a greased 8-in.-square baking pan. Bake 15-18 minutes or until a toothpick inserted in center comes out clean. Serve warm.

## Hearty Turkey 'n' Rice Soup

Use the leftover cooked turkey in the fridge to speed up dinner. You'll be ladling up bowlfuls of goodness in only 30 minutes.
—**MAGGIE BREWER** CANANDAIGUA, NY

**START TO FINISH:** 30 MIN. • **MAKES:** 6 SERVINGS

- 1 teaspoon butter
- 1 celery rib, sliced
- 1 medium carrot, sliced
- ½ cup chopped fresh mushrooms
- 2 cups chicken or turkey broth
- ¾ pound process cheese (Velveeta), cubed
- 1½ cups cubed cooked turkey
- 1½ cups cooked rice
- 2 teaspoons chicken bouillon granules
- ½ teaspoon celery salt
- ¼ teaspoon pepper

In a large saucepan, melt the butter over medium-high heat. Add celery, carrot and mushrooms; cook and stir 6-8 minutes or until tender. Stir in broth, cheese, turkey, rice, bouillon, celery salt and pepper. Cook and stir until cheese is melted and soup is heated through.

## Honey-Squash Dinner Rolls

Dinner rolls take on a rich, gorgeous color when you stir mashed winter squash into the dough. Any variety of squash will do. You can also substitute cooked carrots.

—**MARCIA WHITNEY** GAINESVILLE, FL

**PREP:** 40 MIN. + RISING • **BAKE:** 20 MIN.
**MAKES:** 2 DOZEN

- 2 **packages (¼ ounce each) active dry yeast**
- 2 **teaspoons salt**
- ¼ **teaspoon ground nutmeg**
- 6 **to 6½ cups all-purpose flour**
- 1¼ **cups 2% milk**
- ½ **cup butter, cubed**
- ½ **cup honey**

- 1 **package (12 ounces) frozen mashed winter squash, thawed (about 1⅓ cups)**
- 1 **large egg, lightly beaten**
  **Poppy seeds, salted pumpkin seeds or pepitas, or sesame seeds**

**1.** In a large bowl, mix the yeast, salt, nutmeg and 3 cups of flour. In a small saucepan, heat milk, butter and honey to 120°-130°. Add to dry ingredients; beat on medium speed for 2 minutes. Add squash; beat on high 2 minutes. Stir in enough remaining flour to form a soft dough (dough will be sticky).

**2.** Turn dough onto a floured surface; knead until smooth and elastic, about 6-8 minutes. Place in a greased bowl, turning once to grease the top. Cover with plastic wrap; let rise in a warm place until doubled, about 1 hour.

**3.** Punch down dough. Turn onto a lightly floured surface; divide and shape into 24 balls. Divide between two greased 9-in. round baking pans. Cover with kitchen towels; let rise in a warm place until doubled, about 45 minutes.

**4.** Preheat oven to 375°. Brush tops with beaten egg; sprinkle with seeds. Bake 20-25 minutes or until dark golden brown. Cover loosely with foil during the last 5-7 minutes if needed to prevent overbrowning. Remove from pans to wire racks; serve warm.

# Lentil Soup with Sausage

Chunks of smoked kielbasa, lentils and veggies—they all add up to one satisfying soup! A side dish is definitely optional.

—**PEARL HARDEN** JAMESTOWN, CA

**PREP:** 15 MIN. • **COOK:** 45 MIN.
**MAKES:** 12 SERVINGS (3 QUARTS)

- 1 **pound smoked kielbasa or Polish sausage**
- 1 **tablespoon canola oil**
- 3 **medium carrots, chopped**
- 3 **celery ribs, chopped**
- 1 **medium onion, chopped**
- 2 **garlic cloves, minced**
- 3 **cans (14¼ ounces each) reduced-sodium beef broth**
- ¾ **cup water**
- 1½ **cups dried lentils, rinsed**
- 1 **bay leaf**
- 2 **cans (14½ ounces each) no-salt-added diced tomatoes, undrained**
- ½ **cup ketchup**
- ¼ **cup lemon juice**
- 2 **tablespoons Worcestershire sauce**
- 1 **tablespoon brown sugar**
- ½ **teaspoon pepper**

**1.** Remove casings from sausage; cut the sausage into ½-in. slices. In a 6-qt. stockpot, heat the oil over medium-high heat. Add the sausage, carrots, celery, onion and garlic in batches; cook and stir until the vegetables are crisp-tender.
**2.** Add the broth, water, lentils and bay leaf; bring to a boil. Reduce heat; simmer, covered, for 20-25 minutes or until lentils are almost tender.
**3.** Stir in the remaining ingredients. Bring to a boil. Reduce heat; simmer, covered, 15 minutes or until lentils are tender. Remove bay leaf.

# Shrimp & Cod Stew

I love coming inside on a cold day and smelling this comforting seafood stew simmering in the kitchen.

—**LYDIA JENSEN** KANSAS CITY, MO

**PREP:** 20 MIN. • **COOK:** 25 MIN.
**MAKES:** 8 SERVINGS (3 QUARTS)

- 2 **tablespoons olive oil**
- 1 **large onion, chopped**
- 3 **garlic cloves, minced**
- 1 **tablespoon minced fresh thyme or 1 teaspoon dried thyme**
- ¼ **teaspoon saffron threads or 1 teaspoon ground turmeric**
- 2 **bay leaves**
- 2 **cans (14½ ounces each) no-salt-added diced tomatoes**
- 1 **pound cod fillet, cut into 1-inch cubes**
- 1 **pound uncooked large shrimp, peeled and deveined**
- 2 **cups water**
- 1 **can (14½ ounces) vegetable broth**
- 1 **cup whole kernel corn**
- ¼ **teaspoon pepper**
- 1 **package (6 ounces) fresh baby spinach**
  **Lemon wedges, optional**

**1.** In a 6-qt. stockpot, heat olive oil over medium heat. Add the onion; cook and stir until tender. Add the garlic, thyme, saffron and bay leaves. Cook and stir 1 minute longer. Add tomatoes, fish, shrimp, water, broth, corn and pepper.
**2.** Bring to a boil. Reduce the heat; simmer, uncovered, 8-10 minutes or until shrimp turn pink and fish flakes easily with a fork, adding the spinach during the last 2-3 minutes of cooking. Discard the bay leaves. If desired, serve with lemon wedges.

## Hearty Beef & Vegetable Soup

When you need to feed a crowd, consider this beefy favorite loaded with both fresh and frozen veggies.

**—SUE STRAUGHAN** PRATTVILLE, AL

**PREP:** 1¾ HOURS • **COOK:** 2¼ HOURS
**MAKES:** 26 SERVINGS (1½ CUPS EACH)

- 2 to 4 tablespoons canola oil
- 4 pounds beef stew meat
- 8 medium onions (2¼ pounds), halved and thinly sliced
- 12 cups water
- 1 can (28 ounces) diced tomatoes, undrained
- 1 can (15 ounces) tomato sauce
- 1⅓ cups Worcestershire sauce
- ½ cup beef bouillon granules
- 12 medium red potatoes (about 3½ pounds), cubed
- ½ large head cabbage, chopped
- 1 pound carrots, thinly sliced
- 6 celery ribs, thinly sliced (3 cups)
- 3 cups (about 15 ounces) frozen corn
- 3 cups (about 12 ounces) frozen peas
- 3 cups (about 12 ounces) frozen cut green beans
- 1½ cups (about 15 ounces) frozen lima beans
- 1 bay leaf
- 3 teaspoons dried marjoram
- 3 teaspoons dried thyme
- 1 teaspoon salt
- 1 teaspoon pepper
- 1½ cups (6 ounces) frozen sliced okra

**1.** In a large stockpot, heat 1 tablespoon oil over medium heat. Brown beef stew meat in batches, adding additional oil as necessary. Remove with a slotted spoon. Add onions to drippings; cook and stir until tender. Discard drippings; return beef to pan. Stir in water, tomatoes, tomato sauce, Worcestershire sauce and bouillon. Bring to a boil. Reduce heat; simmer, covered, 45 minutes.

**2.** Stir in potatoes, cabbage, carrots, celery, corn, peas, green beans, lima beans and seasonings. Return to a boil. Reduce heat; simmer, covered, 35 minutes. Stir in okra; cook 15-20 minutes longer or until beef and vegetables are tender. Discard bay leaf.

## Tender Whole Wheat Muffins

Simple whole wheat muffins are wonderful paired with soup or spread with a little jam for breakfast.

**—KRISTINE CHAYES** SMITHTOWN, NY

**START TO FINISH:** 30 MIN. • **MAKES:** 10 MUFFINS

- 1 cup all-purpose flour
- 1 cup whole wheat flour
- 2 tablespoons sugar
- 2½ teaspoons baking powder
- 1 teaspoon salt
- 1 large egg
- 1¼ cups milk
- 3 tablespoons butter, melted

**1.** Preheat oven to 400°. In a large bowl, whisk the flours, sugar, baking powder and salt. In another bowl, whisk the egg, milk and melted butter until blended. Add to the flour mixture; stir just until moistened.

**2.** Fill greased muffin cups three-fourths full. Bake for 15-17 minutes or until a toothpick inserted in the center comes out clean. Cool 5 minutes before removing from the pan to a wire rack. Serve warm.

## Easy Pork Posole

Looking for a meal in a bowl? Sit down to a Mexican classic full of cubed pork, sliced sausage, hominy and more. It all goes into the slow cooker, so you can come home at night to a table-ready dinner.

**—GREG FONTENOT** THE WOODLANDS, TX

**PREP:** 30 MIN. • **COOK:** 6 HOURS
**MAKES:** 8 SERVINGS (2 QUARTS)

- 1 tablespoon canola oil
- ½ pound boneless pork shoulder butt roast, cubed
- ½ pound fully cooked andouille sausage links, sliced
- 6 cups reduced-sodium chicken broth
- 2 medium tomatoes, seeded and chopped
- 1 can (16 ounces) hominy, rinsed and drained
- 1 cup minced fresh cilantro
- 1 medium onion, chopped
- 4 green onions, chopped
- 1 jalapeno pepper, seeded and chopped
- 2 garlic cloves, minced
- 1 tablespoon chili powder
- 1 teaspoon ground cumin
- ½ teaspoon cayenne pepper
- ½ teaspoon coarsely ground pepper
  Optional ingredients: corn tortillas, chopped onion, minced fresh cilantro and lime wedges

**1.** In a large skillet, heat the canola oil over medium-high heat. Brown the cubed pork roast and sliced andouille sausage; drain. Transfer the meat to a 4-qt. slow cooker.

**2.** Stir in the chicken broth, tomatoes, hominy, cilantro, onion, green onions, jalapeno pepper, garlic, chili powder, cumin, cayenne and pepper. Cook, covered, on low 6-8 hours or until the meat is tender.

**3.** If desired, serve the soup with corn tortillas, chopped onion, minced fresh cilantro and lime wedges.

**NOTE** *Wear disposable gloves when cutting hot peppers; the oils can burn skin. Avoid touching your face.*

## Slow Cooker Cheeseburger Soup

When my mother-in-law gave me her recipe for cheeseburger soup, I changed it a bit to make it my own.

**—CHRISTINA ADDISON** BLANCHESTER, OH

**PREP:** 20 MIN. • **COOK:** 7 HOURS
**MAKES:** 6 SERVINGS (2¼ QUARTS)

- 1 pound lean ground beef (90% lean)
- 1 small onion, chopped
- 1¾ pounds potatoes (about 3-4 medium), peeled and cut into ½-inch pieces
- 3 cups chicken broth
- 1½ cups whole milk
- 2 medium carrots, shredded
- 1 celery rib, finely chopped
- 1 tablespoon dried parsley flakes
- ½ teaspoon salt
- ½ teaspoon dried basil
- ¼ teaspoon pepper
- 1 package (8 ounces) process cheese (Velveeta), cubed
- ¼ cup sour cream
  Chopped fresh parsley, optional

**1.** In a large skillet, cook the beef and onion over medium heat 6-8 minutes or until the beef is no longer pink, breaking up beef into crumbles; drain. Transfer to a 4- or 5-qt. slow cooker. Add the potatoes, chicken broth, milk, carrots, celery and seasonings. Cook, covered, on low 7-9 hours or until the vegetables are tender.

**2.** Stir in the cheese until melted. Stir in the sour cream. If desired, sprinkle with parsley.

## Christmas White Chili

Dreaming of a white Christmas? Try this chili decked with red and green veggies!

**—CATHERINE NICKELSON** SCANDIA, MN

**PREP:** 25 MIN. • **COOK:** 30 MIN.
**MAKES:** 8 SERVINGS (3½ QUARTS)

- 2 tablespoons olive oil
- 2 pounds boneless skinless chicken breasts, cut into ½-inch cubes
- 2 medium onions, chopped
- 2 garlic cloves, minced
- 4 cans (15½ ounces each) great northern beans, rinsed and drained
- 2 cans (14½ ounces each) chicken broth
- 4 cans (4 ounces each) chopped green chilies
- 2 jars (8 ounces each) roasted sweet red peppers, drained and finely chopped
- 2 teaspoons salt
- 2 teaspoons ground cumin
- 2 teaspoons dried oregano
- 1 teaspoon pepper
- ½ teaspoon hot pepper sauce
- 2 cups (16 ounces) sour cream
- 1 cup heavy whipping cream
  Chopped roasted sweet red peppers, ripe avocado and green onions, optional

**1.** In a 6-qt. stockpot, heat oil over medium-high heat. Add the chicken and onions in batches; cook and stir 4-5 minutes or until the chicken is no longer pink and the onions are tender. Add the garlic; cook 1 minute longer. Stir in the beans, broth, green chilies, red peppers, seasonings and pepper sauce. Bring to a boil. Reduce heat; simmer, uncovered, 25-30 minutes or until thickened.

**2.** Remove from heat. Stir in the sour cream and whipping cream. If desired, serve with toppings.

## Santa Fe Chipotle Chili

Sausage and ground beef make this spiced-up chili a meat lover's delight. I can freeze and reheat it later without sacrificing any of the flavor.

—**ANGELA SPENGLER** TAMPA, FL

**PREP:** 15 MIN. • **COOK:** 35 MIN.
**MAKES:** 8 SERVINGS (3 QUARTS)

- 1 **pound ground beef**
- 1 **pound bulk pork sausage**
- 1 **medium onion, chopped**
- 2 **cans (14½ ounces each) diced tomatoes, undrained**
- 2 **cans (15 ounces each) tomato sauce**
- 2 **cans (16 ounces each) kidney beans, rinsed and drained**
- 1 **cup frozen corn**
- ¼ **cup canned diced jalapeno peppers**
- ¼ **cup chili powder**
- 1 **chipotle pepper in adobo sauce, finely chopped**
- 1 **teaspoon salt**
  **Optional toppings: sour cream, shredded Monterey Jack cheese and crushed tortilla chips**

**1.** In a 6-qt. stockpot, cook the beef, sausage and onion over medium heat 8-10 minutes or until meat is no longer pink and onion is tender, breaking up meat into crumbles; drain.

**2.** Add the tomatoes, tomato sauce, beans, corn, jalapeno peppers, chili powder, chipotle pepper and salt. Bring to a boil. Reduce heat; simmer, covered, 20-25 minutes or until heated through. If desired, serve with toppings.
**NOTE** *Wear disposable gloves when cutting hot peppers; the oils can burn skin. Avoid touching your face.*

## Christmas Eve Clam Chowder

Our Christmas Eve is all about fabulous seafood and classic movies. We have our clam chowder while watching *Holiday Inn*.
—**PAMELA STEPP** LOUISVILLE, TN

**PREP:** 15 MIN. • **COOK:** 35 MIN.
**MAKES:** 8 SERVINGS (2 QUARTS)

- 1¾ pounds medium Yukon Gold potatoes, peeled and cut into ½-inch cubes
- ¼ cup butter, cubed
- 2 celery ribs, chopped
- 2 medium carrots, chopped
- ½ cup chopped sweet onion
- ½ cup all-purpose flour
- 4 cups heavy whipping cream
- 2 cans (6½ ounces each) chopped clams, undrained
- ½ teaspoon salt
- ½ teaspoon pepper
- Dash ground nutmeg

**1.** Place potatoes in a large saucepan; add water to cover. Bring to a boil. Reduce the heat; cook, uncovered, 7-9 minutes or until tender. Drain, reserving ½ cup potato water.

**2.** Meanwhile, in another large saucepan, heat butter over medium heat. Add celery, carrots and sweet onion; cook and stir for 6-8 minutes or until tender.

**3.** Stir in the flour until blended; gradually stir in the whipping cream and reserved potato water. Bring to a boil; cook 2-3 minutes or until slightly thickened, stirring occasionally. Add the clams, seasonings and potatoes; heat through.

## Scottish Oatmeal Rolls

My family likes rolls that can hold up to scooping gravies, sauces and more. This recipe is a favorite. The oatmeal in the dough gives it a Scottish touch.
—**PEGGY GOODRICH** ENID, OK

**PREP:** 30 MIN. + RISING • **BAKE:** 20 MIN.
**MAKES:** 2 DOZEN

- 1½ cups boiling water
- 1½ cups old-fashioned oats
- ⅓ cup packed brown sugar
- 1½ teaspoons salt
- 1 tablespoon canola oil
- 1 package (¼ ounce) active dry yeast
- ¼ cup warm water (110° to 115°)
- 2¾ to 3¼ cups all-purpose flour
- Butter and honey, optional

**1.** Pour the boiling water over the oats in a large bowl. Add the brown sugar, salt and oil. Cool to 110°-115°, stirring occasionally. Meanwhile, in a small bowl, dissolve the yeast in warm water; let stand 5 minutes. Add to oat mixture. Beat in enough flour to form a stiff dough (the dough will be sticky).

**2.** Turn dough onto a floured surface; knead until smooth and elastic, about 6-8 minutes. Place in a greased bowl, turning once to grease the top. Cover with plastic wrap; let rise in a warm place until doubled, about 1 hour.

**3.** Punch the dough down. Turn onto a lightly floured surface; divide and shape into 24 balls. Place in a greased 13x9-in. baking pan. Cover dough with a kitchen towel and let rise in a warm place until doubled, about 30 minutes.

**4.** Preheat oven to 350°. Bake for 20-25 minutes or until lightly browned. Remove from the pan to a wire rack to cool. If desired, served with butter and honey.

## Creamy Cauliflower & Goat Cheese Soup

Here's an elegant choice for a first course or even a meatless dinner. Goat cheese adds an extra-special touch.

—**ROXANNE CHAN** ALBANY, CA

**PREP:** 20 MIN. • **COOK:** 30 MIN.
**MAKES:** 6 SERVINGS

- 1 tablespoon olive oil
- 1 small onion, chopped
- 1 medium head cauliflower, broken into florets
- 1 small potato, peeled and cubed
- 2 cans (14½ ounces each) vegetable broth
- 1 tablespoon Dijon mustard
- ½ teaspoon white pepper
- 2 cups half-and-half cream
- 1 log (4 ounces) fresh goat cheese, crumbled
- 2 tablespoons snipped fresh dill
  Minced chives and lemon peel strips, optional

**1.** In a large saucepan, heat the oil over medium-high heat. Add the onion; cook and stir until tender. Stir in cauliflower and potato; cook and stir 4-5 minutes.

**2.** Stir in broth, mustard and white pepper. Bring to a boil. Reduce heat; simmer, covered, 15-20 minutes or until vegetables are tender. Remove from heat; stir in cream and cheese. Cool slightly.

**3.** Process the soup in batches in a blender until smooth. Return all to pan. Stir in the dill; heat through. If desired, top with minced chives and lemon peel strips.

### Holiday Helper

Made from the milk of goats, distinctively tangy goat cheese is soft and easy to spread. It's frequently found in Middle Eastern and Mediterranean cuisines. Common varieties include chevre and feta.

## Italian Flatbread

Pair wedges of this chewy flatbread with a tomato-based soup and start dunking!

—**CYNTHIA BENT** NEWARK, DE

**PREP:** 20 MIN. + RISING
**BAKE:** 15 MIN. + COOLING
**MAKES:** 2 LOAVES (8 WEDGES EACH)

- 1 package (¼ ounce) active dry yeast
- 1 cup warm water (110° to 115°)
- ¼ cup plus 3 tablespoons olive oil, divided
- 2 teaspoons sugar
- ¼ teaspoon salt
- 2½ to 3 cups all-purpose flour
- ¼ cup shredded Parmesan cheese
- ½ teaspoon garlic salt
- ½ teaspoon dried rosemary, crushed

**1.** In a small bowl, dissolve yeast in warm water. In a large bowl, combine ¼ cup oil, sugar, salt, yeast mixture and 2 cups of flour; beat on medium speed until smooth. Stir in enough remaining flour to form a soft dough.

**2.** Turn dough onto a floured surface; knead until smooth and elastic, about 5 minutes. Place dough in a greased bowl, turning once to grease the top. Cover with plastic wrap and let rise in a warm place until doubled, about 40 minutes.

**3.** Punch the dough down. Turn onto a lightly floured surface; divide in half. Pat each piece flat. Let rest 5 minutes. Roll out each piece into an 11-in. circle; place on greased baking sheets. Cover with kitchen towels and let dough rise in a warm place until almost doubled, about 40 minutes.

**4.** Preheat oven to 425°. Using the end of a wooden spoon handle, make several ¼-in. indentations in the dough. Brush with remaining oil. In a small bowl, combine shredded Parmesan cheese, garlic salt and rosemary; sprinkle over the dough. Bake 12-15 minutes or until golden brown. Remove from pans to wire racks to cool. Cut into wedges.

# CHRISTMAS FEASTS

# Citrus-Molasses Glazed Ham

We're always trying to think of new ways to enjoy Florida citrus, which is plentiful during the holidays. Here's one of our best creations.

—**CHARLENE CHAMBERS** ORMOND BEACH, FL

**PREP:** 15 MIN. • **BAKE:** 2 HOURS
**MAKES:** 12 SERVINGS

- 1 **fully cooked bone-in ham (7 to 9 pounds)**

**GLAZE**
- ½ **cup grapefruit juice**
- ½ **cup orange juice**
- ¼ **cup molasses**
- 3 **tablespoons honey**
- 1 **tablespoon packed brown sugar**
- 1 **tablespoon Dijon mustard**
- 3 **teaspoons coarsely ground pepper**

1. Preheat oven to 325°. Place ham on a rack in a shallow roasting pan. Using a sharp knife, score surface of ham with ¼-in.-deep cuts in a diamond pattern. Cover and bake 1¾-2¼ hours or until a thermometer reads 130°.
2. Meanwhile, in a large saucepan, combine grapefruit and orange juices. Bring to a boil; cook 6-8 minutes or until liquid is reduced by half. Stir in remaining ingredients; return to a boil. Reduce heat; simmer, uncovered, 12-15 minutes or until thickened.
3. Remove ham from oven. Brush with ⅓ cup glaze. Bake ham, uncovered, 15-20 minutes longer or until a thermometer reads 140°, basting occasionally with the remaining glaze.

# Scalloped Sweet Corn Casserole

I grew up enjoying my grandmother's sweet corn casserole. Now a grandmother myself, I still serve that comforting, delicious side dish.

—**LONNIE HARTSTACK** CLARINDA, IA

**PREP:** 25 MIN. • **BAKE:** 50 MIN.
**MAKES:** 8 SERVINGS

- 4 **teaspoons cornstarch**
- ⅔ **cup water**
- ¼ **cup butter, cubed**

- 3 **cups fresh or frozen corn**
- 1 **can (5 ounces) evaporated milk**
- ¾ **teaspoon plus 1½ teaspoons sugar, divided**
- ½ **teaspoon plus ¾ teaspoon salt, divided**
- 3 **large eggs**
- ¾ **cup 2% milk**
- ¼ **teaspoon pepper**
- 3 **cups cubed bread**
- 1 **small onion, chopped**
- 1 **cup crispy rice cereal, slightly crushed**
- 3 **tablespoons butter, melted**

1. Preheat oven to 350°. In a small bowl, mix cornstarch and water until smooth. In a large saucepan, heat butter over medium heat. Stir in corn, evaporated milk, ¾ teaspoon sugar and ½ teaspoon salt; bring just to a boil. Stir in cornstarch mixture; return to a boil, stirring constantly.

Cook and stir 1-2 minutes or until thickened; cool slightly.
2. In a large bowl, whisk eggs, milk, pepper and the remaining sugar and salt until blended. Stir in the bread, onion and corn mixture. Transfer to a greased 8-in. square or 1½-qt. baking dish.
3. Bake, uncovered, 40 minutes. In a small bowl, toss cereal with melted butter; sprinkle over casserole. Bake 10-15 minutes longer or until golden brown.

**FREEZE OPTION** *Cool unbaked casserole, reserving cereal topping for baking; cover and freeze. To use, partially thaw in the refrigerator overnight. Remove from refrigerator 30 minutes before baking. Preheat oven to 350°. Bake casserole as directed, increasing time as necessary to heat through and for a thermometer inserted into center to read 165°.*

## Icebox Potato Rolls

Some years, we have more than 20 people around our holiday table. A big batch of rolls is a must! I love that I can make this dough the night before and bake before mealtime.

**—BARB LINNERUD** BOILING SPRINGS, SC

**PREP:** 1 HOUR + RISING • **BAKE:** 15 MIN.
**MAKES:** ABOUT 2½ DOZEN

- 1¼ **pounds potatoes, peeled and cubed (about 3½ cups)**
- ¾ **cup sugar**
- 2 **teaspoons salt**
- 1 **package (¼ ounce) active dry yeast**
- 5½ **to 6 cups bread flour**
- 1 **cup 2% milk**
- ½ **cup water**
- ½ **cup shortening**
- 3 **large eggs**
- ⅓ **cup butter, melted**

**1.** Place potatoes in a saucepan; add water to cover. Bring to a boil. Reduce heat; cook, uncovered, 10-15 minutes or until tender. Drain; return to pan. Mash potatoes (you should have about 2 cups). Cool slightly.

**2.** In a large bowl, mix sugar, salt, yeast and 2 cups flour. In a small saucepan, heat milk, water and shortening to 120°-130°. Add to dry ingredients; beat on medium speed 2 minutes. Add eggs and potatoes; beat on high 2 minutes. Stir in enough remaining flour to form a soft dough (dough will be very sticky).

**3.** Do not knead. Place dough in a large greased bowl. Cover with greased plastic wrap; refrigerate overnight.

**4.** Punch down dough. Using a tablespoon dipped in melted butter, drop three spoonfuls of dough into a greased muffin cup. Repeat, redipping spoon in butter.

**5.** Cover with greased plastic wrap; let rise in a warm place until almost doubled, about 45 minutes. Preheat oven to 375°.

**6.** Brush tops with remaining melted butter. Bake 12-15 minutes or until golden brown. Cool in pans 5 minutes. Remove to wire racks; serve warm.

## Twice-Baked Cheddar Potato Casserole

Bacon, cheddar and sour cream turn ordinary potatoes into an extraordinary casserole. It's one of our family's most beloved holiday dishes.

—**KYLE COX** SCOTTSDALE, AZ

**PREP:** 70 MIN. • **BAKE:** 15 MIN.
**MAKES:** 12 SERVINGS (⅔ CUP EACH)

- 8 medium baking potatoes (about 8 ounces each)
- ½ cup butter, cubed
- ⅔ cup sour cream
- ⅔ cup 2% milk
- 1 teaspoon salt
- ¾ teaspoon pepper
- 10 bacon strips, cooked and crumbled, divided
- 2 cups (8 ounces) shredded cheddar cheese, divided
- 4 green onions, chopped, divided

**1.** Preheat oven to 425°. Scrub potatoes; pierce several times with a fork. Bake 45-60 minutes or until tender. Remove from oven; reduce oven setting to 350°.

**2.** When potatoes are cool enough to handle, cut each potato lengthwise in half. Scoop out pulp and place in a large bowl; discard shells. Mash pulp with butter; stir in sour cream, milk, salt and pepper.

**3.** Reserve ¼ cup crumbled bacon for topping. Gently fold remaining bacon, 1 cup cheese and half of the green onions into potato mixture (do not overmix).

**4.** Transfer to a greased 11x7-in. baking dish. Top with the remaining cheese and green onions; sprinkle with the reserved bacon. Bake for 15-20 minutes or until heated through and cheese is melted.

## Bacon and Fontina Stuffed Mushrooms

These are also known as my "piled-high cheesy stuffed mushrooms." They're an instant hit no matter where I serve them. Just six ingredients go into the yummy filling.

**—TAMMY REX** NEW TRIPOLI, PA

**PREP:** 30 MIN. • **BAKE:** 10 MIN. • **MAKES:** 2 DOZEN

- 4 ounces cream cheese, softened
- 1 cup (4 ounces) shredded fontina cheese
- 8 bacon strips, cooked and crumbled
- 4 green onions, chopped
- ¼ cup chopped oil-packed sun-dried tomatoes
- 3 tablespoons minced fresh parsley
- 24 large fresh mushrooms (about 1¼ pounds), stems removed
- 1 tablespoon olive oil

**1.** Preheat oven to 425°. In a small bowl, mix the first six ingredients until blended. Arrange mushroom caps in a greased 15x10x1-in. baking pan, stem side up. Spoon about 1 tablespoon filling into each.

**2.** Drizzle tops with oil. Bake, uncovered, 9-11 minutes or until golden brown and mushrooms are tender.

## Overnight Layered Lettuce Salad

Here's a tried-and-true salad we've enjoyed for more than 40 years. I think the key is the bacon—it adds savory flavor and crunch.

**—MARY BREHM** CAPE CORAL, FL

**PREP:** 20 MIN. + CHILLING • **MAKES:** 16 SERVINGS (1 CUP EACH)

- 1 medium head iceberg lettuce, torn
- 1 medium green pepper, chopped
- 1 small sweet red pepper, chopped
- 1 medium onion, sliced and separated into rings
- 2 cups frozen peas (about 10 ounces)
- 1 cup mayonnaise
- 2 tablespoons sugar
- 1 cup (4 ounces) shredded cheddar cheese
- 12 bacon strips, cooked and crumbled
- ¾ cup dried cranberries

**1.** In a 4-qt. or 13x9-in. glass dish, layer the first five ingredients. In a small bowl, mix mayonnaise and sugar; spoon over salad, spreading to cover.

**2.** Sprinkle top with cheese, bacon and cranberries. Refrigerate, covered, overnight.

### Holiday Helper

Overnight Layered Lettuce Salad is a Christmas time-saver because it sets up in the fridge the day before. Beat the clock on Bacon and Fontina Stuffed Mushrooms by preparing the filling the day before as well and storing it in the fridge.

## Frozen Grasshopper Torte

This cool chocolate-mint dessert was a hit when I served it at a ladies' meeting at our church. If you prefer, use chopped candy canes instead of Oreos on top.

**—ELMA PENNER** OAK BLUFF, MB

**PREP:** 25 MIN. + FREEZING
**MAKES:** 12 SERVINGS

- **4 cups crushed Oreo cookies (about 40 cookies)**
- **¼ cup butter, melted**

- **1 pint (2 cups) vanilla ice cream, softened if necessary**
- **2 cups heavy whipping cream**
- **1 jar (7 ounces) marshmallow creme**
- **¼ cup 2% milk**
- **¼ to ½ teaspoon peppermint extract**
- **3 drops green food coloring, optional**

**1.** In a large bowl, combine crushed cookies and melted butter; toss until coated. Reserve ¼ cup mixture for topping. Press remaining mixture onto bottom of a 9-in. springform pan or 13x9-in. dish. Freeze 10 minutes. Spread ice cream over crust. Freeze, covered, until firm.

**2.** In a bowl, beat cream until soft peaks form. In a large bowl, mix marshmallow creme, milk, extract and, if desired, food coloring until blended. Fold in whipped cream.

**3.** Spread over ice cream. Sprinkle with reserved cookie mixture. Freeze, covered, until firm.

## Make-Ahead Turkey and Gravy

Ease the holiday time crunch with a done-in-advance turkey that's ready to serve when you are. It's a great choice for potlucks, too.

—MARIE PARKER MILWAUKEE, WI

**PREP:** 4¼ HOURS + FREEZING • **BAKE:** 50 MIN.
**MAKES:** 16 SERVINGS (2½ CUPS GRAVY)

### TURKEY
- 1 turkey (14 to 16 pounds)
- 2 teaspoons poultry seasoning
- 1 teaspoon pepper
- 3 cups chicken broth
- ½ cup minced fresh parsley
- ¼ cup lemon juice
- 1 tablespoon minced fresh thyme or 1 teaspoon dried thyme
- 1 tablespoon minced fresh rosemary or 1 teaspoon dried rosemary, crushed
- 2 teaspoons grated lemon peel
- 2 garlic cloves, minced

### FOR SERVING
- 1½ cups chicken broth
- 1 tablespoon butter
- 1 tablespoon all-purpose flour

**1.** Preheat oven to 325°. Sprinkle turkey with poultry seasoning and pepper. Tuck wings under turkey; tie drumsticks together. Place on a rack in a shallow roasting pan, breast side up.

**2.** Roast, uncovered, 30 minutes. In a 4-cup measuring cup, mix remaining turkey ingredients; carefully pour over turkey. Roast, uncovered, for 3-3½ hours longer or until a thermometer inserted into thigh reads 180°, basting occasionally with broth mixture. Cover loosely with foil if turkey browns too quickly.

**3.** Remove turkey from pan; let stand at least 20 minutes before carving. Skim fat from cooking juices.

**4.** Carve turkey; place in shallow freezer containers. Pour strained juices over turkey; cool completely. Freeze, covered, up to 3 months.

**TO SERVE** *Partially thaw turkey in refrigerator overnight. Preheat oven to 350°. Transfer turkey and cooking juices to a baking dish; pour broth over turkey. Bake, covered, 50-60 minutes or until a thermometer reads 165°.*

**5.** Remove turkey from baking dish, reserving cooking liquid; keep warm. In a small saucepan, melt butter; stir in flour until smooth. Gradually whisk in reserved cooking liquid. Bring to a boil, stirring constantly; cook and stir 2 minutes or until thickened. Serve with turkey.

**NOTE** *It is best not to use a prebasted turkey for this recipe.*

## Braised & Creamy Vidalia Onions

Here in Georgia, sweet Vidalia onions are king. I use them in my creamy side dish, which goes well with poultry and beef.

—ELAINE OPITZ MARIETTA, GA

**PREP:** 10 MIN. • **COOK:** 40 MIN.
**MAKES:** 6 SERVINGS

- 2 tablespoons butter
- 3 tablespoons honey
- 10 cups sliced Vidalia or other sweet onions (about 5 onions)
- ¼ cup chicken broth
- ½ teaspoon salt
- ⅛ teaspoon white pepper
- ⅛ teaspoon ground mace
- ½ cup heavy whipping cream

**1.** In a Dutch oven, melt butter over medium heat; stir in honey until blended. Add onions, broth and seasonings. Bring to a boil. Reduce heat; simmer, covered, 15-18 minutes or until onions are tender.

**2.** Cook, uncovered, over medium-high heat 15-20 minutes or until the liquid is almost evaporated, stirring occasionally. Stir in cream; cook 3-5 minutes longer or until sauce is thickened.

## Classic Make-Ahead Mashed Potatoes

Tired of quickly mashing potatoes while hungry guests wait? Save time on the day of your holiday feast with this convenient make-ahead recipe.

—MARTY RUMMEL TROUT LAKE, WA

**PREP:** 40 MIN. + CHILLING • **BAKE:** 55 MIN.
**MAKES:** 12 SERVINGS (¾ CUP EACH)

- **5 pounds potatoes, peeled and cut into wedges**
- **1 package (8 ounces) reduced-fat cream cheese, cubed**
- **2 large egg whites, beaten**
- **1 cup (8 ounces) reduced-fat sour cream**
- **2 teaspoons onion powder**
- **1 teaspoon salt**
- **½ teaspoon pepper**
- **1 tablespoon butter, melted**

**1.** Place potatoes in a Dutch oven and cover with water. Bring to a boil. Reduce heat; cover and cook for 15-20 minutes or until tender. Drain.

**2.** In a large bowl, mash potatoes with cream cheese. Combine the egg whites, sour cream, onion powder, salt and pepper; stir into potatoes until blended. Transfer to a greased 3-qt. baking dish. Drizzle with butter. Cover and refrigerate overnight.

**3.** Remove from the refrigerator 30 minutes before baking. Preheat oven to 350°. Cover and bake for 50 minutes. Uncover; bake another 5-10 minutes or until a thermometer reads 160°.

## Spiced Ambrosia Punch

It's so convenient to serve warm beverages from the slow cooker. The flavor of chai tea inspired this twist on a basic cider punch.

**—AYSHA SCHURMAN** AMMON, ID

**PREP:** 15 MIN. • **COOK:** 3 HOURS
**MAKES:** 10 SERVINGS (¾ CUP EACH)

- 3½ cups apple cider or juice
- 3 cups apricot nectar
- 1 cup peach nectar or additional apricot nectar
- ¼ cup water
- 3 tablespoons lemon juice
- ½ teaspoon ground cardamom
- ½ teaspoon ground nutmeg
- 2 cinnamon sticks (3 inches each)
- 1 teaspoon finely chopped fresh gingerroot
- 1 teaspoon grated orange peel
- 8 whole cloves
  Lemon or orange slices, optional

**1.** In a 3- or 4-qt. slow cooker, combine the first seven ingredients. Place cinnamon sticks, ginger, orange peel and cloves on a double thickness of cheesecloth. Gather corners of the cloth to enclose seasonings; tie securely with string. Place bag in slow cooker.

**2.** Cook, covered, on low 3-4 hours or until heated through. Remove and discard spice bag. Serve warm, with fruit slices, if desired.

### Holiday Helper

Want to serve Spiced Ambrosia Punch from a serving bowl instead of your slow cooker? Avoid shattering the bowl by making sure it's heat-resistant. Warm the bowl with warm water before adding the hot punch.

## Warm Tasty Greens with Garlic

When I had kale and other ingredients I needed to use up, I combined them for a new side dish. It goes well with a variety of main courses.

—**MARTHA NETH** AURORA, CO

**START TO FINISH:** 30 MIN.
**MAKES:** 4 SERVINGS

- 1 pound kale, trimmed and torn (about 20 cups)
- 2 tablespoons olive oil
- ¼ cup chopped oil-packed sun-dried tomatoes
- 5 garlic cloves, minced
- 2 tablespoons minced fresh parsley
- ¼ teaspoon salt

**1.** In a 6-qt. stockpot, bring 1 in. of water to a boil. Add the kale; cook, covered, 10-15 minutes or until tender. Remove with a slotted spoon; discard cooking liquid.

**2.** In same pot, heat oil over medium heat. Add tomatoes and garlic; cook and stir 1 minute. Add kale, parsley and salt; heat through, stirring occasionally.

## Sausage & Corn Bread Dressing

At our house, we add sausage and a little steak sauce to our corn bread dressing. It warms us up on even the coldest days.

—**MANDY NALL** MONTGOMERY, AL

**PREP:** 30 MIN. • **BAKE:** 40 MIN.
**MAKES:** 12 SERVINGS

- 1 package (19½ ounces) Italian turkey sausage links, casings removed
- 4 medium onions, chopped (about 3 cups)
- ½ cup chopped celery
- 6 cups cubed day-old white or French bread
- 6 cups coarsely crumbled corn bread
- 2 large eggs
- 2 tablespoons steak sauce
- 2 teaspoons onion salt
- 2 teaspoons poultry seasoning
- 2 teaspoons dried parsley flakes
- 1 teaspoon garlic powder
- 1 teaspoon baking powder
- 2½ to 3 cups reduced-sodium chicken broth

**1.** Preheat oven to 350°. In a 6-qt. stockpot, cook sausage over medium heat 6-8 minutes or until no longer pink, breaking into crumbles. Remove with a slotted spoon, reserving drippings in pot.

**2.** Add onions and celery to drippings; cook and stir 6-8 minutes or until tender. Remove from heat; stir in sausage. Add cubed bread and corn bread; toss to combine.

**3.** In a small bowl, whisk eggs, steak sauce, seasonings and baking powder until blended; stir into bread mixture. Stir in enough broth to reach desired moistness.

**4.** Transfer to a greased 13x9-in. or 3-qt. baking dish. Bake 40-50 minutes or until lightly browned.

# Maple Walnut Cake

This wonderful cake reminds me of my grandpa, who made maple syrup when I was a child. Want to get baking ahead of time? Wrap each layer tightly in plastic wrap and then foil before putting it in the freezer. Thaw them in the fridge overnight.
—LORI FEE MIDDLESEX, NY

**PREP:** 45 MIN. • **BAKE:** 15 MIN. + COOLING
**MAKES:** 16 SERVINGS

- ½ cup unsalted butter, softened
- 1½ cups packed light brown sugar
- 3 large eggs
- 1 teaspoon maple flavoring or maple syrup
- 2 cups all-purpose flour
- 1 teaspoon baking powder
- 1 teaspoon baking soda
- ¼ teaspoon salt
- 1 cup buttermilk

**CANDIED WALNUTS**
- 1 tablespoon unsalted butter
- 1½ cups coarsely chopped walnuts
- 1 tablespoon maple syrup
- ¼ teaspoon salt

**FROSTING**
- 2 cups unsalted butter, softened
- 5 cups confectioners' sugar
- 1 teaspoon maple flavoring or maple syrup
- ¼ teaspoon salt
- ¼ to ½ cup half-and-half cream
- 3 tablespoons maple syrup, divided

**1.** Preheat oven to 350°. Line the bottoms of three greased 9-in. round baking pans with parchment paper; grease paper.
**2.** In a large bowl, cream butter and brown sugar until blended. Add eggs, one at a time, beating well after each addition. Beat in maple flavoring. In another bowl, whisk the flour, baking powder, baking soda and salt; add to creamed mixture alternately with buttermilk, beating well after each addition.
**3.** Transfer to prepared pans. Bake 11-13 minutes or until a toothpick inserted in center comes out clean. Cool in pans 10 minutes before removing to wire racks. Cool completely.
**4.** For candied walnuts, in a large skillet, melt butter. Add walnuts; cook and stir over medium heat until nuts are toasted, about 5 minutes. Stir in maple syrup and salt; cook and stir 1 minute longer. Spread on foil to cool completely.
**5.** For frosting, in a large bowl, beat butter until creamy. Beat in confectioners' sugar, maple flavoring, salt and enough cream to reach desired consistency.
**6.** Place one cake layer on a serving plate; spread with 1 cup frosting. Sprinkle with ½ cup candied walnuts and drizzle with 1 tablespoon maple syrup. Repeat layers.
**7.** Top with remaining layer. Frost top and sides of cake. Top with remaining walnuts and syrup.

## Ornament Centerpiece

Put your cupcake stand to good use by using it to create a lovely table setting. Set ornaments in the cupcake holders, then fill with your choice of foliage. Even the kids can help!

# Beef Dinner

## Garlic Herbed Beef Tenderloin

Want your beef tenderloin to really make an impression? A mild blend of rosemary, basil and garlic is all it takes.

**—RUTH ANDREWSON** LEAVENWORTH, WA

**PREP:** 5 MIN. • **BAKE:** 40 MIN. + STANDING
**MAKES:** 12 SERVINGS

- 1 beef tenderloin roast (3 pounds)
- 2 teaspoons olive oil
- 2 garlic cloves, minced
- 1½ teaspoons dried basil
- 1½ teaspoons dried rosemary, crushed
- 1 teaspoon salt
- 1 teaspoon pepper

**1.** Tie tenderloin at 2-in. intervals with kitchen string. Combine oil and garlic; brush over meat. Combine the basil, rosemary, salt and pepper; sprinkle evenly over meat. Place on a rack in a shallow roasting pan.
**2.** Bake, uncovered, at 425° for 40-50 minutes or until meat reaches desired doneness (for medium-rare, a thermometer should read 145°; medium, 160°; well-done, 170°). Let stand for 10 minutes before slicing.

## Caesar Salad in Parmesan Bowls

Edible salad bowls look impressive but are a cinch to make. It can be your little secret!
**—MELISSA WILKES** ST. AUGUSTINE, FL

**PREP:** 20 MIN. • **COOK:** 15 MIN.
**MAKES:** 8 SERVINGS

- 2 cups shredded Parmesan cheese
- ½ teaspoon coarsely ground pepper
- 2 romaine hearts, cut into bite-size pieces (about 6 cups)
- 1 cup grape tomatoes, halved
- ¾ cup Caesar salad croutons, slightly crushed
- ¼ cup creamy Caesar salad dressing

**1.** In a bowl, toss cheese with pepper. Heat a small nonstick skillet over medium heat. Evenly sprinkle ¼ cup cheese mixture into pan to form a 6-in. circle; cook, uncovered, until bubbly and edges are golden brown, about 1-2 minutes. Remove skillet from heat; let stand 15 seconds.
**2.** Using a spatula, remove cheese and drape over an inverted ramekin; press cheese gently to form a bowl. Cool completely. Repeat with remaining cheese, making eight bowls.

**3.** In a bowl, combine romaine, tomatoes and croutons. Just before serving, drizzle with dressing and toss to coat. Serve in Parmesan bowls.

## Parmesan Bowls Made Easy

**1.** Spread shredded Parmesan evenly in heated skillet; add seasonings or nuts to melted cheese if desired.

**2.** Cook over medium-high heat 1-2 minutes until edges are lightly brown; lift out of pan with spatula.

**3.** Invert hot cheese disk over bottom of an inverted glass or ramekin; allow to cool.

## Gorgonzola Pear Tartlets

Whether you serve these simple tartlets as an appetizer or dessert, they're too good to pass up. I leave the peel on the pear to add texture.

**—SUSAN HEIN** BURLINGTON, WI

**START TO FINISH:** 30 MIN. • **MAKES:** 2½ DOZEN

- 1  **large pear, finely chopped**
- 1  **cup (4 ounces) crumbled Gorgonzola cheese**
- ½  **cup finely chopped hazelnuts, toasted**
- 2  **packages (1.9 ounces each) frozen miniature phyllo tart shells**

**1.** In a small bowl, combine the pear, cheese and hazelnuts. Spoon into tart shells. Place on ungreased baking sheets.
**2.** Bake at 350° for 10-12 minutes or until shells are lightly browned. Serve warm.

## Thyme-Roasted Carrots

Cutting carrots lengthwise gives a simple side dish a special look. For an added touch, garnish with sprigs of fresh thyme or parsley.

**—DEIRDRE COX** KANSAS CITY, MO

**START TO FINISH:** 30 MIN.
**MAKES:** ABOUT 12 SERVINGS (2 CARROT HALVES EACH)

- 3  **pounds medium carrots, halved lengthwise**
- 2  **tablespoons minced fresh thyme or 2 teaspoons dried thyme**
- 2  **tablespoons canola oil**
- 1  **tablespoon honey**
- 1  **teaspoon salt**

Preheat oven to 400°. Divide carrots between two greased 15x10x1-in. baking pans. In a small bowl, mix thyme, oil, honey and salt; brush over carrots. Roast 20-25 minutes or until tender.

# Garlic-Mashed Rutabagas & Potatoes

My family absolutely loves garlic mashed potatoes. When I snuck in some cubed rutabagas, they were just as enthusiastic as before.

**—ROSEMARY TATUM** STERLINGTON, LA

**START TO FINISH:** 30 MIN.
**MAKES:** 8 SERVINGS

- 4 medium potatoes, peeled and cubed (about 4 cups)
- 2 medium rutabagas, peeled and cubed (about 5 cups)
- 2 garlic cloves, peeled
- 2 tablespoons butter
- 1 teaspoon salt
- ¼ teaspoon pepper
- ¼ to ⅓ cup warm buttermilk

**1.** Place potatoes, rutabagas and garlic in a Dutch oven; add water to cover. Bring to a boil. Reduce heat; cook, uncovered, 15-20 minutes or until tender.

**2.** Drain; return to pan. Mash potatoes, gradually adding butter, salt, pepper and enough buttermilk to reach desired consistency.

## Holiday Helper

Rutabagas are a great addition to yuletide menus. Select those that are smooth-skinned, heavy, firm and not spongy. Look for rutabagas no larger than 4 inches in diameter. Store them in the refrigerator. Just before using, wash, trim the ends and peel.

## Sparkling Berry Punch

I often serve this refreshing cranberry beverage at Christmastime, but it's a great choice for any special occasion. Add a few cranberries to each glass for extra flair.

**—KAY CURTIS** GUTHRIE, OK

**START TO FINISH:** 10 MIN.
**MAKES:** ABOUT 2 QUARTS

- 6 **cups cranberry juice, chilled**
- 2 **cans (12 ounces each) ginger ale, chilled**
- ¼ **teaspoon almond extract**
  **Ice cubes**

Combine all ingredients in a punch bowl or pitcher. Serve in chilled glasses over ice. Serve immediately.

## Raspberry-Swirled Cheesecake Pie

My dad always said my cheesecake pie was his favorite dessert. He's now gone, but I remember his smile every time I make it. Feel free to use whatever fruit filling suits your family's tastes.

**—PEGGY GRIFFIN** ELBA, NE

**PREP:** 15 MIN. • **BAKE:** 35 MIN. + CHILLING
**MAKES:** 8 SERVINGS

- 1 **package (8 ounces) cream cheese, softened**
- ½ **cup sugar**
- 2 **large eggs, lightly beaten**
- 1 **graham cracker crust (9 inches)**
- 1 **can (21 ounces) raspberry pie filling, divided**

**1.** Preheat oven to 350°. In a large bowl, beat cream cheese and sugar until smooth. Add eggs; beat on low speed just until blended. Pour into crust. Drop ½ cup pie filling by tablespoonfuls over batter. Cut through batter with a knife to swirl.
**2.** Bake 35-45 minutes or until filling is set. Transfer remaining raspberry filling to a covered container; refrigerate until serving.
**3.** Cool pie 1 hour on a wire rack. Refrigerate at least 2 hours, covering when completely cooled. Serve with reserved filling.

# More Choices for Christmas Menus

If you like the three yuletide menus showcased in this chapter but want even more options for entrees, sides and desserts, page through this extra-special section. You'll find bonus recipes that can make wonderful substitutions in any of the featured dinners.

## Fancy Stuffed Pork Chops

These comforting pork chops bake to a perfect golden brown, and the stuffing is incredibly moist. It's one of my favorite dishes to serve guests because I know they'll love it.

—LORRAINE DAROCHA MOUNTAIN CITY, TN

**PREP:** 40 MIN. • **BAKE:** 30 MIN.
**MAKES:** 6 SERVINGS

- 2 celery ribs, diced
- 1 small onion, chopped
- 1 teaspoon olive oil
- 9 slices white bread, cubed
- ¼ cup minced fresh parsley
- ¼ teaspoon salt
- ¼ teaspoon rubbed sage
- ⅛ teaspoon white pepper
- ⅛ teaspoon dried marjoram
- ⅛ teaspoon dried thyme
- ¾ cup reduced-sodium chicken broth

**PORK CHOPS**

- 6 pork rib chops (7 ounces each)
- 2 teaspoons olive oil
- ¼ teaspoon salt
- ¼ teaspoon pepper

**1.** In a large nonstick skillet coated with cooking spray, saute celery and onion in 1 teaspoon oil until tender; remove from the heat. In a large bowl, combine bread and seasonings. Add celery mixture and broth; toss to coat. Set aside.

**2.** Cut a pocket in each pork chop by making a horizontal slice almost to the bone. Coat the same skillet with cooking spray. Cook chops in oil in batches over medium-high heat for 1-2 minutes on each side or until browned. Fill chops with bread mixture; secure with toothpicks if necessary.

**3.** Transfer to a 13x9-in. baking dish coated with cooking spray. Sprinkle with salt and pepper. Cover and bake at 350° for 15 minutes. Uncover; bake 15-20 minutes longer or until a thermometer reads 165° when inserted in center of stuffing and the pork is tender. Discard toothpicks before serving.

## Berry-Beet Salads

Here's a delightfully different salad that balances the earthy flavor of beets with the natural sweetness of berries. If you prefer, substitute crumbled feta for the goat cheese.

—AMY LYONS MOUNDS VIEW, MN

**PREP:** 20 MIN. • **BAKE:** 30 MIN. + COOLING
**MAKES:** 4 SERVINGS

- 1 each red and golden fresh beets
- ¼ cup balsamic vinegar
- 2 tablespoons walnut oil
- 1 teaspoon honey
  - Dash salt
  - Dash pepper
- ½ cup sliced fresh strawberries
- ½ cup fresh raspberries
- ½ cup fresh blackberries
- 3 tablespoons chopped walnuts, toasted
- 1 shallot, thinly sliced
- 4 cups torn mixed salad greens
- 1 ounce fresh goat cheese, crumbled
- 1 tablespoon fresh basil, thinly sliced

**1.** Place beets in an 8-in. square baking dish; add 1 in. of water. Cover and bake at 400° for 30-40 minutes or until tender.

**2.** Meanwhile, in a small bowl, whisk the vinegar, oil, honey, salt and pepper; set aside. Cool beets; peel and cut into thin slices.

**3.** In a bowl, combine the beets, berries, walnuts and shallot. Gently toss with dressing. Divide the salad greens among four serving plates or transfer to a large serving platter. Top with beet mixture; sprinkle with cheese and basil.

## Mushroom, Walnut & Thyme Cheesecake

Cut thin wedges of this appetizer cheesecake to serve as a spread for crackers. With a buttery crumb crust and savory filling, it always impresses guests.
—**ERIKA SZYMANSKI** WAITATI, AE

**PREP:** 35 MIN. + COOLING
**BAKE:** 25 MIN. + CHILLING
**MAKES:** 24 SERVINGS

- 1 **cup dry bread crumbs**
- ¼ **cup butter, melted**

**FILLING**

- 1 **tablespoon butter**
- ½ **pound baby portobello mushrooms, chopped**
- 1 **garlic clove, minced**
- ⅓ **cup chopped walnuts**
- 1 **tablespoon minced fresh thyme or 1 teaspoon dried thyme**
- 1 **teaspoon reduced-sodium soy sauce**
- ¼ **teaspoon white pepper**
- 2 **packages (8 ounces each) cream cheese, softened**
- ½ **cup plain Greek yogurt**
- 2 **large eggs, lightly beaten
  Assorted crackers, baguette slices or sliced apples**

**1.** Preheat oven to 325°. In a small bowl, mix bread crumbs and butter. Press onto bottom of a greased 9-in. springform pan. Place pan on baking sheet. Bake 15-17 minutes or until golden brown. Cool on a wire rack.

**2.** In a large skillet, heat butter over medium-high heat. Add mushrooms; cook and stir until tender. Add garlic; cook 1 minute longer. Stir in walnuts; cook until toasted. Stir in thyme, soy sauce and pepper. Remove from heat; cool completely.

**3.** In a large bowl, beat cream cheese until smooth. Beat in yogurt. Add eggs; beat on low speed just until blended. Fold in mushroom mixture. Pour over crust. Return pan to baking sheet.

**4.** Bake 25-30 minutes or until center of cheesecake is just set and top appears dull. Cool 10 minutes on a wire rack. Loosen sides from pan with a knife. Cool 1 hour longer. Refrigerate overnight.

**5.** Remove rim from pan. Serve with crackers.

## Pomegranate-Cranberry Salad

Juicy pomegranate seeds give cranberry gelatin a refreshing twist. For the crowning touch, top the salad with whipped topping and a sprinkling of pecans.

—**LORIE MCKINNEY** MARION, NC

**PREP:** 15 MIN. + CHILLING • **MAKES:** 8 SERVINGS

- 1 package (.3 ounce) sugar-free cranberry gelatin
- 1 cup boiling water
- ½ cup cold water
- 1⅔ cups pomegranate seeds
- 1 can (14 ounces) whole-berry cranberry sauce
- 1 can (8 ounces) unsweetened crushed pineapple, drained
- ¾ cup chopped pecans
  Frozen whipped topping, thawed, optional
  Additional chopped pecans, optional

In a large bowl, dissolve gelatin in boiling water. Add cold water; stir. Add the pomegranate seeds, cranberry sauce, pineapple and pecans. Pour into a 1½-qt. serving bowl. Refrigerate for 4-5 hours or until firm. If desired, top with whipped topping and additional pecans.

## Spinach-Pesto Spiral Chicken

The homemade pesto sets this main dish apart from the rest. Elegant enough for a special dinner but simple enough for a quiet evening at home, this is an entree you can make anytime.

—**AMY BLOM** MARIETTA, GA

**PREP:** 20 MIN. • **BAKE:** 40 MIN. • **MAKES:** 12 SERVINGS

- 12 boneless skinless chicken thighs (about 3 pounds)
- 2 cups fresh baby spinach
- 1 cup packed basil leaves
- 6 garlic cloves
- 2 teaspoons olive oil
- 2 tablespoons grated Parmesan cheese
- 2 tablespoons chopped walnuts
- 2 tablespoons reduced-sodium chicken broth
- ½ cup chopped oil-packed sun-dried tomatoes
- ⅓ cup chopped water-packed artichoke hearts, rinsed and drained
- ½ teaspoon salt, divided
- ¼ teaspoon pepper, divided

1. Preheat oven to 375°. Pound chicken breasts with a meat mallet to ¼-in. thickness.
2. In a food processor, combine spinach, basil, garlic, oil, cheese, walnuts and broth. Cover and process until blended. Stir in tomatoes, artichoke hearts, ¼ teaspoon salt and ⅛ teaspoon pepper. Spread over chicken. Starting at a short side, roll up and secure with toothpicks.
3. Place in two greased 11x7-in. baking dishes, seam side down. Sprinkle with remaining salt and pepper. Bake 40-45 minutes or until a thermometer reads 170°. Discard toothpicks before serving.

## Sour Cream & Cheddar Biscuits

Here's my go-to recipe for biscuits. Brushing them with the garlic-butter topping before baking seals the deal!
—AMY MARTIN VANCOUVER, WA

**PREP:** 25 MIN. • **BAKE:** 15 MIN.
**MAKES:** 1½ DOZEN

- 2½ cups all-purpose flour
- 3 teaspoons baking powder
- 2 teaspoons sugar
- 1 teaspoon garlic powder
- ½ teaspoon cream of tartar
- ¼ teaspoon salt
- ¼ teaspoon cayenne pepper
- ½ cup cold butter, cubed
- 1½ cups (6 ounces) shredded cheddar cheese
- 1¼ cups 2% milk
- ½ cup sour cream

**TOPPING**
- 6 tablespoons butter, melted
- 1½ teaspoons garlic powder
- 1 teaspoon minced fresh parsley

**1.** Preheat oven to 450°. In a large bowl, whisk the first seven ingredients. Cut in cold butter until mixture resembles coarse crumbs; stir in cheese. Add milk and sour cream; stir just until moistened.
**2.** Drop by ¼ cupfuls 2 in. apart onto greased baking sheets. Mix topping ingredients; brush over tops. Bake 12-15 minutes or until light brown. Serve warm.

### Holiday Helper

Sour Cream & Cheddar Biscuits freeze well. Save time this season by baking up a batch or two early on and stashing them in the freezer. Simply reheat in a microwave or in the oven.

## Citrus Salmon Fillets with Salsa

Take lemony salmon fillets to the next level with a fresh, colorful homemade salsa. Just add a simple side of rice for a complete dinner.
—TIFFANY HARTPENCE LANDER, WY

**START TO FINISH:** 30 MIN.
**MAKES:** 4 SERVINGS

- 2 plum tomatoes, seeded and chopped
- ½ cup cubed fresh pineapple
- ¼ cup minced fresh basil
- ¼ cup lime juice
- 2 shallots, chopped
- 2 tablespoons reduced-sodium soy sauce
- 1 teaspoon brown sugar
- ¼ teaspoon pepper, divided
- 4 salmon fillets (6 ounces each)
- ½ cup reduced-sodium chicken broth
- 2 teaspoons grated lemon peel

**1.** For salsa, in a small bowl, combine the tomatoes, pineapple, basil, lime juice, shallots, soy sauce, brown sugar and ⅛ teaspoon pepper. Cover and chill until serving.
**2.** Place fillets in a greased 13x9-in. baking dish; pour broth into dish. Sprinkle fillets with lemon peel and remaining pepper.
**3.** Bake, uncovered, at 375° for 10-15 minutes or until salmon flakes easily with a fork. Serve with salsa.

> ## "It's easy to create mini
> *pumpkin pies using refrigerated pie pastry and a standard muffin tin. If you like, dollop the finished tarts with whipped cream."*
>
> —JESSIE OLESON SANTA FE, NM

## Pumpkin Tartlets

**PREP:** 20 MIN. • **BAKE:** 40 MIN. + COOLING
**MAKES:** 16 TARTLETS

- 1 **package (15 ounces) refrigerated pie pastry**
- 1 **can (15 ounces) solid-pack pumpkin**
- 1 **can (12 ounces) evaporated milk**
- ¾ **cup sugar**
- 2 **large eggs**
- ½ **teaspoon salt**
- 1 **teaspoon ground cinnamon**
- ½ **teaspoon ground ginger**
- ¼ **teaspoon ground cloves**
  **Miniature marshmallows, optional**

**1.** Preheat oven to 425°. On a work surface, unroll each pastry sheet; roll to ⅛-in. thickness. Using a floured 4-in. round cutter, cut out 16 circles, rerolling scraps if necessary. Press circles into muffin pans coated with cooking spray.

**2.** In a large bowl, whisk pumpkin, milk, sugar, eggs, salt and spices until blended. Pour into pastry cups. Bake 15 minutes. Reduce oven setting to 350°.

**3.** Bake 25-30 minutes or until a knife inserted near center comes out clean. If desired, top with marshmallows and bake 2-3 minutes longer or until marshmallows are lightly browned. Cool 5 minutes.

**4.** Carefully run a knife around sides to loosen tarts. Cool in pans on wire racks before removing. Serve or refrigerate within 2 hours.

## Roasted Garlic Green Beans with Cashews

My mom got a garlic roaster, and she soon started sharing the fruits of her labor with me. This recipe was the result of one of my many experiments.

**—VIRGINIA STURM** SAN FRANCISCO, CA

**PREP:** 40 MIN. • **COOK:** 15 MIN. • **MAKES:** 8 SERVINGS

- 10 **garlic cloves, unpeeled**
- 2 **teaspoons plus ¼ cup olive oil, divided**
- 2 **pounds fresh green beans, trimmed**
- 1 **cup water**
- 1 **cup lightly salted cashews, coarsely chopped**
- ½ **teaspoon salt**
- ¼ **teaspoon pepper**

**1.** Preheat oven to 375°. Cut stem ends off unpeeled garlic cloves. Place cloves on a piece of foil. Drizzle with 2 teaspoons oil; wrap in foil. Bake 25-30 minutes or until cloves are soft. Unwrap and cool slightly. Squeeze garlic from skins; mash with a fork to form a paste.

**2.** In a Dutch oven, heat remaining oil over medium-high heat. Add green beans and garlic; cook and stir 2-3 minutes. Add water; bring to a boil. Reduce heat; simmer beans, uncovered, 7-10 minutes or until beans are crisp-tender and water is almost evaporated, stirring occasionally. Add cashews, salt and pepper; toss to combine.

## Rustic Cranberry Tarts

Bright red cranberries are always perfect for Christmastime. I bundle them up in pie pastry for rustic tarts that are simple but scrumptious.

**—HOLLY BAUER** WEST BEND, WI

**PREP:** 15 MIN. • **BAKE:** 20 MIN./BATCH
**MAKES:** 2 TARTS (6 SERVINGS EACH)

- 1 **cup orange marmalade**
- ¼ **cup sugar**
- ¼ **cup all-purpose flour**
- 4 **cups fresh or frozen cranberries, thawed**
- 1 **package (14.1 ounces) refrigerated pie pastry**
- 1 **large egg white, lightly beaten**
- 1 **tablespoon coarse sugar**

**1.** Preheat oven to 425°. In a large bowl, mix marmalade, sugar and flour; stir in cranberries.

**2.** Unroll one pastry sheet onto a parchment paper-lined baking sheet. Spoon half of the cranberry mixture over pastry to within 2 in. of edge. Fold pastry edge over filling, pleating as you go and leaving a 5-in. opening in the center. Brush folded pastry with egg white; sprinkle with half of the coarse sugar.

**3.** Bake 18-22 minutes or until crust is golden and filling is bubbly. Repeat with remaining ingredients. Transfer tarts to wire racks to cool.

# THE MERRIEST
# OF THE MERRY

## Flaky Cheddar-Chive Biscuits

Dotted with bits of gold and green, these look wonderful—and taste even better!
—**BETSY KING** DULUTH, MN

**START TO FINISH:** 25 MIN.
**MAKES:** 10 BISCUITS

- 2¼ cups all-purpose flour
- 2½ teaspoons baking powder
- 2 teaspoons sugar
- ½ teaspoon baking soda
- ½ teaspoon salt
- ½ cup cold butter, cubed
- 1 cup (4 ounces) shredded cheddar cheese
- 3 tablespoons minced fresh chives
- 1 cup buttermilk

**1.** Preheat oven to 425°. In a large bowl, whisk the first five ingredients. Cut in the cold butter until mixture resembles coarse crumbs; stir in the cheese and chives. Add buttermilk; stir just until moistened. Turn biscuit dough onto a lightly floured surface; knead gently 8-10 times.

**2.** Pat or roll the biscuit dough to ¾-in. thickness; cut with a floured 2½-in. biscuit cutter. Place 2 in. apart on a greased baking sheet. Bake for 10-12 minutes or until golden brown. Serve warm.

## Gingerbread Hot Cocoa

Are you in the Christmas spirit yet? If not, this special cocoa will do the trick. It's like drinking a chocolate gingerbread cookie!

**—ERIKA MONROE-WILLIAMS** SCOTTSDALE, AZ

**START TO FINISH:** 15 MIN. • **MAKES:** 3 SERVINGS

- ¼ cup packed brown sugar
- ¼ cup baking cocoa
- 1 tablespoon molasses
- 1½ teaspoons ground cinnamon
- 1½ teaspoons ground ginger
- ½ teaspoon ground allspice
  Pinch salt
- 3 cups whole milk
- 1 teaspoon vanilla extract
  Whipped cream

In a small saucepan, combine the first seven ingredients; gradually add milk. Cook and stir over medium-heat until heated through. Remove from the heat; stir in the vanilla. Serve with whipped cream.

## Deluxe Baked Macaroni and Cheese

By adding diced ham, tomatoes and a crumb topping, I turned mac and cheese into a comforting meal-in-one.

**—KATHY YAROSH** APOPKA, FL

**PREP:** 30 MIN. • **BAKE:** 25 MIN. • **MAKES:** 12 SERVINGS

- 1 package (16 ounces) elbow macaroni
- ¼ cup all-purpose flour
- 2 cups 2% milk
- ½ cup heavy whipping cream
- 1 package (8 ounces) process cheese (Velveeta), cubed
- 1 cup (4 ounces) shredded cheddar cheese
- ⅔ cup whipped cream cheese
- ¼ cup grated Parmesan cheese
- 1 can (14½ ounces) diced tomatoes, drained
- 1½ cups cubed fully cooked ham
- 1 cup (8 ounces) sour cream
- 1 teaspoon Dijon mustard
**TOPPING**
- 1½ cups soft bread crumbs
- ¼ cup grated Parmesan cheese
- 2 tablespoons butter, melted

**1.** Preheat oven to 350°. Cook the macaroni according to the package directions. In a Dutch oven, whisk the flour, milk and cream until smooth. Bring to a boil; cook and stir 2 minutes or until thickened.

**2.** Stir in the cheeses until melted. Add tomatoes, ham, sour cream and mustard. Drain macaroni; add to cheese mixture and toss to coat.

**3.** Transfer to a greased 13x9-in. baking dish. In a small bowl, mix the topping ingredients; sprinkle over the top. Bake, uncovered, 25-30 minutes or until bubbly and the bread crumbs are lightly browned.

**NOTE** *To make soft bread crumbs, tear bread into pieces and place in a food processor or blender. Cover; pulse until crumbs form. One slice of bread yields ½ to ¾ cup crumbs.*

*Cheesiest*

**Stickiest**

## Cinnamon-Walnut Sticky Buns

Set out oven-warm, finger-licking-good rolls and watch your family come running!
—**DEBBIE BROEKER** ROCKY MOUNT, MO

**PREP:** 1 HOUR + RISING • **BAKE:** 30 MIN.
**MAKES:** 2 DOZEN

- **2 packages (¼ ounce each) active dry yeast**
- **1½ cups warm water (110° to 115°)**
- **1 cup mashed potatoes (without added milk and butter)**
- **½ cup sugar**
- **½ cup butter, softened**
- **2 large eggs**
- **2 teaspoons salt**
- **6 to 6½ cups all-purpose flour**

**TOPPING**
- **¼ cup butter**
- **1 cup packed brown sugar**
- **1 cup honey**
- **1 teaspoon ground cinnamon**
- **1 cup chopped walnuts**

**FILLING**
- **½ cup sugar**
- **2 teaspoons ground cinnamon**
- **2 tablespoons butter, melted**

**1.** In a small bowl, dissolve yeast in warm water. In a large bowl, combine mashed potatoes, sugar, butter, eggs, salt, yeast mixture and 2 cups flour; beat on medium speed until smooth. Stir in enough of the remaining flour to form a soft dough.

**2.** Turn the dough onto a floured surface; knead until smooth and elastic, about 6-8 minutes. Place in a greased bowl, turning once to grease the top. Cover with plastic wrap and let rise in a warm place until doubled, about 1 hour.

**3.** For topping, in a small saucepan, melt butter. Stir in brown sugar, honey and cinnamon. Divide mixture among three greased 9-in. round baking pans, spreading evenly. Sprinkle with nuts.

**4.** For filling, in a small bowl, mix sugar and cinnamon. Punch down dough. Turn onto a lightly floured surface and divide in half. Roll one portion into an 18x12-in. rectangle. Brush with 1 tablespoon melted butter to within ½ in. of the edges; sprinkle with ¼ cup sugar mixture.

**5.** Roll up jelly-roll style, starting with a long side; pinch seam to seal. Cut into 12 slices. Repeat with the remaining dough, butter and sugar mixture. Place eight slices in each pan, cut side down. Cover with kitchen towels; let rise until doubled, about 30 minutes. Preheat oven to 350°.

**6.** Bake 30-35 minutes or until golden brown. Immediately invert onto serving plates. Serve warm.

Naughtiest

## Loaded Smashed Taters

My husband loves these potatoes with a steak. Even my young daughter is a fan! I like to use baby Yukon Golds because the skins are thin and easy to mash.
—**ANDREA QUIROZ** CHICAGO, IL

**PREP:** 20 MIN. • **COOK:** 20 MIN.
**MAKES:** 8 SERVINGS

- 2½ **pounds baby Yukon Gold potatoes**
- 1 **cup 2% milk, warmed**
- ½ **cup spreadable garlic and herb cream cheese**
- 3 **tablespoons butter, softened**
- 1 **pound bacon strips, cooked and crumbled**
- 1 **cup (4 ounces) shredded cheddar cheese**
- ½ **cup shredded Parmesan cheese**
- 3 **green onions, chopped**
- ⅓ **cup oil-packed sun-dried tomatoes, chopped**
- 2 **teaspoons dried parsley flakes**
- ¼ **teaspoon salt**
- ¼ **teaspoon pepper**

**1.** Place the Yukon Gold potatoes in a large saucepan; add water to cover. Bring to a boil. Reduce heat; cook, uncovered, 15-20 minutes or until tender.

**2.** Drain the potatoes; return to pan. Lightly mash the potatoes, gradually adding the milk, cream cheese and butter to reach desired consistency. Stir in the bacon, cheddar cheese, Parmesan cheese, green onions, sun-dried tomatoes, parsley flakes, salt and pepper.

### Holiday Helper

My family is big on mashed potatoes. For quicker prep, I skip peeling the potatoes. I simply clean, cook and mash them—peels and all. Prepared like this, mashed potatoes are more nutritious and quick enough to serve regularly.
—**BARB W.** LAKEWOOD, OH

Cranberriest

# Mallow Cranberry Cheesecake

Tangy cranberry sauce is a tongue-tingling complement to rich, sweet cheesecake. For an extra-special touch, top it off with sugared berries, fresh mint leaves, orange slices or orange peel strips.

**—GLORIA COLTON** RUSSELL, NY

**PREP:** 1 HOUR + CHILLING
**MAKES:** 12 SERVINGS

- ¾ cup graham cracker crumbs
- ½ cup finely chopped macadamia nuts
- 2 tablespoons sugar
- ¼ cup butter, melted
- 1 envelope unflavored gelatin
- ¼ cup cold water
- 2 packages (8 ounces each) cream cheese, softened
- 1 jar (7 ounces) marshmallow creme
- 1 can (14 ounces) whole-berry cranberry sauce
- 1 cup heavy whipping cream

**SUGARED CRANBERRIES**

- 1 envelope unflavored gelatin
- ¼ cup cold water
- 1 package (12 ounces) fresh cranberries or frozen cranberries, thawed
- ⅔ cup superfine sugar
  Fresh mint leaves, thin orange slices and orange peel strips, optional

**1.** In a small bowl, combine the graham cracker crumbs, chopped macadamia nuts and sugar. Stir in the melted butter. Press mixture onto the bottom of a greased 9-in. springform pan for crust. Place on a baking sheet. Bake at 350° for 10 minutes or until the crust is lightly browned. Cool on a wire rack.

**2.** In a small saucepan, sprinkle the gelatin over the cold water and let stand for 1 minute. Heat over low heat, stirring until the gelatin is completely dissolved; cool slightly.

**3.** In a large bowl, beat the cream cheese and marshmallow creme until smooth. Beat in the cranberry sauce. Add cooled gelatin; mix well.

**4.** In a small bowl, beat cream until stiff peaks form. Fold into the cream cheese mixture. Pour over the crust. Refrigerate for 8 hours or overnight.

**5.** In a microwave-safe bowl, sprinkle the gelatin over cold water; let stand for 1 minute. Microwave on high for 1-2 minutes, stirring every 20 seconds, until gelatin is completely dissolved. Whisk until slightly frothy.

**6.** Lightly brush mixture over all sides of cranberries. Place on a wire rack over waxed paper; sprinkle with superfine sugar. Let stand at room temperature for up to 24 hours (do not refrigerate or the sugar will dissolve).

**7.** Just before serving, carefully run a knife around edge of pan to loosen. Spoon the sugared cranberries over cheesecake. If desired, top with mint, orange slices or orange peel strips.

## Making Sugared Cranberries

When sprinkling the superfine sugar on the gelatin-brushed cranberries, don't worry about completely coating the berries. Allowing some of the red berry to peek through adds to the festive look.

## Ham, Egg & Cheese Casserole

Turn a classic French grilled sandwich, croque-madame, into a saucy breakfast casserole no one will be able to resist.

—MELISSA MILLWOOD LYMAN, SC

**PREP:** 35 MIN. • **BAKE:** 40 MIN. + STANDING
**MAKES:** 12 SERVINGS

- 1 loaf (1 pound) frozen bread dough, thawed
- ¾ cup butter, cubed
- ⅓ cup all-purpose flour
- 2½ cups 2% milk
- 3 tablespoons Dijon mustard
- ¾ teaspoon pepper
- ½ teaspoon salt
- ½ teaspoon ground nutmeg
- ½ cup grated Parmesan cheese
- 1 pound sliced smoked deli ham
- 2 cups (8 ounces) shredded Swiss cheese
- 6 large eggs
- ¼ cup minced fresh parsley

**1.** Preheat oven to 350°. On a lightly floured surface, roll the dough into a 14x10-in. rectangle. Transfer dough to a greased 13x9-in. baking dish; build up edges slightly.

**2.** In a large saucepan, melt butter over medium heat. Stir in flour until smooth; gradually whisk in the milk. Bring to a boil, stirring constantly; cook and stir 3-4 minutes or until thickened. Stir in mustard, pepper, salt and nutmeg. Remove from heat; stir in Parmesan cheese.

**3.** Place a third of the ham over the dough; top with 1 cup sauce and ⅔ cup Swiss cheese. Repeat the layers twice. Bake, uncovered, 30 minutes or until bubbly and crust is golden brown.

**4.** Using back of a tablespoon, make six indentations in top of casserole to within 2 in. of the edges. Carefully break an egg into each indentation.

**5.** Bake 10-15 minutes longer or until the egg whites are completely set and the yolks begin to thicken but are not hard. (If desired, bake an additional 5 minutes for firmer eggs.) Sprinkle with parsley. Let stand for 10 minutes before cutting.

*Rise & Shine-iest*

### Holiday Helper

Follow these tips to make hosting your Christmas brunch stress-free:
- Measure the coffee the night before, then make it in the morning and transfer it to a thermal carafe for serving.
- Put condiments that are stored in the fridge (butter and jam) on the same shelf so you can quickly reach for them the next morning.
- Condiments stored at room temperature (syrup and honey) can be poured into serving pitchers and covered with plastic wrap.
- If children will be attending, consider offering them the old standby of cereal and milk. They may prefer it to the fancier foods.

# Gingerbread People

What cookie says "Christmas" more than decorated gingerbread cutouts?

—**JOAN TRUAX** PITTSBORO, IN

**PREP:** 45 MIN. + CHILLING
**BAKE:** 10 MIN./BATCH + COOLING
**MAKES:** 2½ DOZEN

- 6 **tablespoons butter, softened**
- ¾ **cup packed dark brown sugar**
- ½ **cup molasses**
- 1 **large egg**
- 2 **teaspoons vanilla extract**
- 1 **teaspoon grated lemon peel**
- 3 **cups all-purpose flour**
- 3 **teaspoons ground ginger**
- 1½ **teaspoons baking powder**
- 1¼ **teaspoons ground cinnamon**
- ¾ **teaspoon baking soda**
- ¼ **teaspoon salt**
- ¼ **teaspoon ground cloves**
  **Decorating icing and candies**

**1.** In a large bowl, cream the butter and brown sugar until light and fluffy. Beat in the molasses, egg, vanilla and peel. In another bowl, whisk flour, ginger, baking powder, cinnamon, baking soda, salt and cloves; gradually beat into creamed mixture. Divide the dough in half. Shape each into a disk; wrap in plastic wrap. Refrigerate 30 minutes or until easy to handle.

**2.** Preheat oven to 350°. On a lightly floured surface, roll each portion to ¼-in. thickness. Cut with a floured 4-in. gingerbread-man cookie cutter.

**3.** Place 2 in. apart on greased baking sheets. Bake 7-9 minutes or until the edges are firm. Remove from pans to wire racks to cool completely. Decorate as desired.

**ROYAL ICING** *In a bowl, combine 2 cups confectioners' sugar, 2 tablespoons plus 2 teaspoons water, 4½ teaspoons meringue powder and ¼ teaspoon cream of tartar; beat on low speed just until combined. Beat on high for 4-5 minutes or until stiff peaks form. If desired, tint with food coloring and pipe with a pastry bag and pastry tips. Keep unused icing covered at all times; beat again on high to restore texture as necessary. Yield: 1 cup icing.*

## Orange Fudge Sauce

Ice cream lovers will scream for this rich, citrusy fudge topping. It's wonderful served warm over pound cake, too.
—**ANNIE RUNDLE** MUSKEGO, WI

**START TO FINISH:** 15 MIN. • **MAKES:** 3 CUPS

- 24 **ounces bittersweet chocolate, chopped**
- 1 **cup heavy whipping cream**
- ¼ **cup butter**
- ¼ **cup thawed orange juice concentrate**
- 2 **teaspoons grated orange peel**
  **Vanilla ice cream, optional**

**1.** In a heavy saucepan, combine the chocolate, cream, butter and orange juice concentrate. Cook and stir over medium-low heat until smooth.
**2.** Stir in the orange peel. Serve warm with ice cream or transfer to covered jars and refrigerate.

## Caramel Snickerdoodle Bars

When I couldn't decide between two of the sweet treats I love most—snickerdoodles and blondies —I combined them into one yummy bar. Then I added caramel for good measure!
—**NIKI PLOURDE** GARDNER, MA

**PREP:** 30 MIN. • **BAKE:** 25 MIN. + CHILLING • **MAKES:** 4 DOZEN

- 1 **cup butter, softened**
- 2 **cups packed brown sugar**
- 2 **large eggs**
- 2 **teaspoons vanilla extract**

- 2½ **cups all-purpose flour**
- 2 **teaspoons baking powder**
- 1 **teaspoon salt**
- ¼ **cup sugar**
- 3 **teaspoons ground cinnamon**
- 2 **cans (13.4 ounces each) dulce de leche**
- 12 **ounces white baking chocolate, chopped**
- ⅓ **cup heavy whipping cream**
- 1 **tablespoon light corn syrup**

**1.** Preheat oven to 350°. Line a 13x9-in. baking pan with parchment paper, letting ends extend over sides by 1 inch.
**2.** In a large bowl, cream butter and brown sugar until light and fluffy. Beat in eggs and vanilla. In another bowl, whisk flour, baking powder and salt; gradually beat into creamed mixture. Spread onto bottom of prepared pan.
**3.** In a small bowl, mix the sugar and cinnamon; sprinkle 2 tablespoons mixture over the batter. Bake 25-30 minutes or until the edges are light brown. Cool completely in pan on a wire rack.
**4.** Spread dulce de leche over crust. In a small saucepan, combine white baking chocolate, cream and corn syrup; cook and stir over low heat until smooth. Cool slightly. Spread over dulce de leche. Sprinkle with the remaining cinnamon sugar. Refrigerate, covered, for at least 1 hour.
**5.** Lifting with the parchment paper, remove from pan. Cut into bars. Refrigerate leftovers.
**NOTE** *This recipe was tested with Nestle La Lechera dulce de leche; look for it in the international foods section. If using Eagle Brand dulce de leche (caramel flavored sauce), thicken according to package directions before using.*

Creamiest

## Creamy Hazelnut Pie

I've always been a big fan of peanut butter. Then I found chocolaty Nutella hazelnut spread and was hooked! I even changed one of my all-time favorite pie recipes by substituting that ingredient.

**—LISA VARNER** EL PASO, TX

**PREP:** 10 MIN. + CHILLING
**MAKES:** 8 SERVINGS

- **1 package (8 ounces) cream cheese, softened**
- **1 cup confectioners' sugar**
- **1¼ cups Nutella, divided**
- **1 carton (8 ounces) frozen whipped topping, thawed**
- **1 chocolate crumb crust (9 inches)**

**1.** In a large bowl, beat cream cheese, confectioners' sugar and 1 cup Nutella until smooth. Fold in whipped topping. Spread evenly into crust.

**2.** Warm the remaining Nutella in the microwave for 15-20 seconds; drizzle over pie. Refrigerate at least 4 hours or overnight.

### Holiday Helper

Made with both hazelnuts and cocoa, smooth Nutella is a sweet, chocolaty spread used in a variety of dessert recipes and often enjoyed as a topping on toast, muffins, bagels and other breads. Look for Nutella in the peanut butter aisle of your grocery store.

# Rustic Nut Bars

**PREP:** 20 MIN. • **BAKE:** 35 MIN. + COOLING
**MAKES:** ABOUT 3 DOZEN

- 1 tablespoon plus ¾ cup cold butter, divided
- 2⅓ cups all-purpose flour
- ½ cup sugar
- ½ teaspoon baking powder
- ½ teaspoon salt
- 1 large egg, lightly beaten

**TOPPING**

- ⅔ cup honey
- ½ cup packed brown sugar
- ¼ teaspoon salt
- 6 tablespoons butter, cubed
- 2 tablespoons heavy whipping cream
- 1 cup chopped hazelnuts, toasted
- 1 cup salted cashews
- 1 cup pistachios
- 1 cup salted roasted almonds

**1.** Preheat the oven to 375°. Line a 13x9-in. baking pan with foil, letting ends extend over sides by 1 inch. Grease foil with 1 tablespoon butter.
**2.** In a large bowl, whisk flour, sugar, baking powder and salt. Cut in the remaining butter until the mixture resembles coarse crumbs. Stir in the egg until blended (the mixture will be dry). Press firmly onto the bottom of prepared pan.
**3.** Bake 18-20 minutes or until edges are golden brown. Cool on a wire rack.
**4.** In a large heavy saucepan, combine the honey, brown sugar and salt; bring to a boil over medium heat, stirring frequently to dissolve the sugar. Boil 2 minutes, without stirring. Stir in the butter and whipping cream; return to a boil. Cook and stir 1 minute or until smooth. Remove from heat; stir in the nuts. Spread over crust.
**5.** Bake 15-20 minutes or until the topping is bubbly. Cool completely in the pan on a wire rack. Lifting with the foil, remove from pan. Discard foil; cut into bars.
**NOTE** *To toast nuts, bake in a shallow pan in a 350° oven for 5-10 minutes or cook in a skillet over low heat until lightly browned, stirring occasionally.*

*Nuttiest*

"*The caramel in the topping*
*adds ooey-gooey goodness to the crunchy*
*almonds, pistachios, hazelnuts and cashews*
*in Rustic Nut Bars. Everyone loves them.*"

—**BARBARA DRISCOLL** WEST ALLIS, WI

## Marinated Olive & Cheese Ring

When we host family and friends for an Italian feast, we kick things off with an antipasto plate that's almost too pretty to eat!
—**PATRICIA HARMON** BADEN, PA

**PREP:** 25 MIN. + CHILLING • **MAKES:** 16 SERVINGS

- 1 package (8 ounces) cream cheese, cold
- 1 package (10 ounces) sharp white cheddar cheese, cut into ¼-inch slices
- ⅓ cup pimiento-stuffed olives
- ⅓ cup pitted Greek olives
- ¼ cup balsamic vinegar
- ¼ cup olive oil
- 1 tablespoon minced fresh parsley
- 1 tablespoon minced fresh basil or 1 teaspoon dried basil
- 2 garlic cloves, minced
- 1 jar (2 ounces) pimiento strips, drained and chopped
  Toasted French bread baguette slices

**1.** Cut cream cheese lengthwise in half; cut each half into ¼-in. slices. On a serving plate, arrange cheeses upright in a ring, alternating the cheddar and cream cheese slices. Place olives in center.

**2.** In a small bowl, whisk the balsamic vinegar, oil, parsley, basil and garlic until blended; drizzle over the cheeses and olives. Sprinkle with the pimientos. Refrigerate, covered, at least 8 hours or overnight. Serve with baguette slices.

*Nibbliest*

*Bubbliest*

## Poinsettia

Mixing festive red cranberry juice, Triple Sec and champagne creates a fun cocktail for Christmas parties, a New Year's Eve bash or any get-together during the fall and winter seasons. Garnish with a few fresh berries and enjoy.
—*TASTE OF HOME* TEST KITCHEN

**START TO FINISH:** 5 MIN. • **MAKES:** 1 SERVING

- 1 ounce cranberry juice
- ½ ounce Triple Sec, optional
- 4 ounces chilled champagne or other sparkling wine

**GARNISH**

- 3 fresh cranberries

Pour the cranberry juice into a champagne flute or wine glass. Add Triple Sec if desired. Top with the champagne. Garnish with fresh cranberries.

Candy Cane-iest

## Peppermint Crunch Christmas Cookies

Using crushed candy, food coloring and chocolate, I turned basic shortbread into festive Christmas cookies. They're a must in our house during the holidays.

—**HEATHER CARTER** WASILLA, AK

**PREP:** 25 MIN. + CHILLING
**BAKE:** 10 MIN./BATCH + COOLING
**MAKES:** 3½ DOZEN

- **1 cup butter, softened**
- **½ cup sugar**
- **1 teaspoon peppermint extract**
- **1 teaspoon vanilla extract**
- **2¼ cups all-purpose flour**
  **Red and green paste food coloring**
- **8 ounces dark chocolate candy coating, melted**
- **¾ cup crushed peppermint candies**

**1.** In a large bowl, cream the butter and sugar until light and fluffy. Beat in extracts. Gradually beat in flour. Divide dough in half; tint one portion red and the other green. Wrap each in plastic wrap; refrigerate 2 hours or until easy to handle.

**2.** Preheat oven to 350°. On a lightly floured surface, roll each portion of dough to ¼-in. thickness. Cut with a floured 1½-in. round cookie cutter. Place 1 in. apart on ungreased baking sheets. Bake 8-10 minutes or until firm. Remove from the pans to wire racks to cool completely.

**3.** Dip half of each cookie into the melted dark chocolate candy coating; allow the excess to drip off. Sprinkle with crushed peppermint candies. Place the cookies on waxed paper; let stand until set.

# Yuletide Eggnog Cupcakes

Prefer the frosting on your cupcakes to be a little creamier? Just add another splash of eggnog. The nog lovers in your life won't complain a bit!

—**SALINA MOORE** WOODWARD, OK

**PREP:** 30 MIN. • **BAKE:** 20 MIN. + COOLING
**MAKES:** 2 DOZEN

- 4 large eggs, separated
- ⅔ cup butter, softened
- 1½ cups sugar, divided
- 2⅓ cups all-purpose flour
- 3 teaspoons baking powder
- ½ teaspoon ground nutmeg
- ¼ teaspoon salt
- 1 cup eggnog

**FROSTING**

- 1 package (8 ounces) cream cheese, softened
- ¼ cup butter, softened
- 3¾ cups confectioners' sugar
- 2 tablespoons eggnog
- Freshly grated or additional ground nutmeg

**1.** Place the egg whites in a large bowl; let stand at room temperature 30 minutes. Preheat oven to 350°. Line muffin cups with paper liners.

**2.** In a large bowl, cream butter and 1¼ cups sugar until light and fluffy. Add egg yolks, one at a time, beating well after each addition. In another bowl, whisk the flour, baking powder, nutmeg and salt; add to the creamed mixture alternately with the eggnog, beating well after each addition.

**3.** With clean beaters, beat the egg whites on medium speed until soft peaks form. Gradually add remaining sugar, 1 tablespoon at a time, beating on high after each addition until the sugar is dissolved. Continue beating until stiff glossy peaks form. Fold into cupcake batter.

**4.** Fill the prepared muffin cups three-fourths full. Bake 18-22 minutes or until a toothpick inserted in the center comes out clean. Cool in pans 10 minutes before removing to wire racks to cool completely.

**5.** For frosting, in a large bowl, beat cream cheese and butter until blended. Gradually beat in confectioners' sugar and the eggnog until smooth. Frost the cupcakes. Sprinkle tops with nutmeg. Refrigerate leftovers.

Noggiest

## Holiday Helper

To separate egg whites from the yolks when you don't have an egg separator, try using a small funnel. Simply break the egg over the wide end of the funnel—the egg white will run through the small bottom hole while the yolk stays inside.

—**ALICE N.** REED CITY, MI

# Cinnamon Crescents

We've been enjoying these crispy, cinnamon-sugar goodies for years. The crescents are easy to make, and my family considers them a real treat.

—**EMILY ENGEL** QUILL LAKE, SK

**PREP:** 30 MIN. • **BAKE:** 20 MIN.
**MAKES:** 3 DOZEN

- 2½ **cups all-purpose flour**
- 1 **teaspoon baking powder**
- 1 **cup cold butter**
- ½ **cup milk**
- 1 **large egg, beaten**
- 1 **cup sugar**
- 4 **teaspoons ground cinnamon**

**OPTIONAL GLAZE**
- 1 **cup confectioners' sugar**
- 1 **to 2 teaspoons ground cinnamon**
- 4 **teaspoons 2% milk**

**1.** Combine flour and baking powder in a large bowl; cut in the cold butter until crumbly. Stir in the milk and egg. Divide the dough into three portions; shape each portion into a ball.

**2.** Combine sugar and cinnamon; sprinkle a third over a pastry board or a surface. Roll one ball of dough into a 12-in. circle; cut into 12 wedges. Roll up wedges from the wide edge. Repeat with the remaining dough and cinnamon-sugar.

**3.** Place rolls with point side down on lightly greased baking sheets; form into crescent shapes. Bake at 350° for 16-18 minutes or until lightly browned (do not overbake).

**4.** For optional glaze, combine the confectioners' sugar, cinnamon and milk until smooth. Drizzle glaze over the cooled crescents.

Cinnamon-iest

# SOUTHERN CHRISTMAS

## Sweet Potato Praline Casserole

For a change from marshmallow-topped sweet potato casseroles, my mom served us this one. It became an instant favorite.

—**CAITLIN HOOKER** AUSTIN, TX

**PREP:** 15 MIN. • **BAKE:** 50 MIN.
**MAKES:** 8 SERVINGS

- 2 **large eggs, lightly beaten**
- 6 **cups mashed sweet potatoes (about 4 large)**
- ½ **cup sugar**
- ½ **cup butter, softened**
- ⅓ **cup 2% milk**
- 1 **teaspoon vanilla extract**

**TOPPING**
- ⅓ **cup butter, melted**
- 1 **cup packed brown sugar**
- 1 **cup chopped pecans**
- ½ **cup all-purpose flour**

**1.** Preheat oven to 350°. In a large bowl, combine the eggs, mashed sweet potatoes, sugar, butter, milk and vanilla. Transfer to a greased 11x7-in. baking dish.

**2.** In a small bowl, mix the butter, brown sugar, chopped pecans and flour; sprinkle over the top. Bake, uncovered, 50-60 minutes or until top is browned.

### Holiday Helper

Select sweet potatoes that are firm and have no cracks or bruises. Stored in a cool, dark, well-ventilated place, sweet potatoes will stay fresh for approximately two weeks. If the temperature is higher than 60°, they'll sprout sooner or become woody. Once sweet potatoes are cooked, they may be stored in the refrigerator for up to one week.

## Pimento Cheddar Spread

I was a theater major in college, and our director's mother always made sure we were well fed. I was particularly fond of her pimento cheese sandwiches and tried making a similar spread for crackers. It tastes just as good as I remember!

—**KATRINA JAMESON** BRANDON, MS

**PREP:** 15 MIN. + CHILLING
**MAKES:** 32 SERVINGS (2 TABLESPOONS EACH)

- 1 **package (8 ounces) cream cheese, softened**
- 2 **jars (4 ounces each) diced pimientos, drained**
- ¼ **cup mayonnaise**
- 2 **tablespoons finely chopped onion**
- 1 **pound sharp cheddar cheese, shredded (about 4 cups)**
  **Saltines**

In a large bowl, mix the cream cheese, diced pimientos, mayonnaise and onion until blended. Stir in the cheddar cheese. Refrigerate at least 2 hours before serving. Serve with saltine crackers.

## Black-Eyed Peas with Ham

Here's a regional favorite I grew to love after moving to the South. You'll never want black-eyed peas from a can again! Serve the dish as a side with grilled chicken...or make it your main course with greens and corn bread.

—**TAMMIE MERRILL** WAKE FOREST, NC

**PREP:** 10 MIN. + SOAKING • **COOK:** 8 HOURS • **MAKES:** 8 SERVINGS

- 1 **package (16 ounces) dried black-eyed peas**
- 1 **cup cubed fully cooked ham**
- 1 **medium onion, finely chopped**
- 3 **garlic cloves, minced**
- 2 **teaspoons seasoned salt**
- 1 **teaspoon pepper**
- 4 **cups water**

Rinse and sort the black-eyed peas; soak according to the package directions. Drain and rinse peas, discarding liquid. Transfer peas to a 4-qt. slow cooker. Stir in the remaining ingredients. Cook, covered, on low 8-10 hours or until peas are tender. Serve with a slotted spoon.

## Family-Favorite Sweet Potato Pie

My sweet potato pie recipe came from my great aunt. Both the taste and the aroma during baking are so enticing.

—**LAURA SPECK** NORTH LITTLE ROCK, AR

**PREP:** 30 MIN. • **BAKE:** 40 MIN. + COOLING
**MAKES:** 8 SERVINGS

- 2  **small sweet potatoes (8 ounces each)**
- ½  **cup butter, softened**
- 1½  **cups sugar**
- ¼  **cup packed brown sugar**
- 2  **teaspoons pumpkin pie spice**
- ½  **teaspoon salt**
- 3  **large eggs**
- ½  **cup buttermilk**
- 1  **teaspoon vanilla extract**
   **Pastry for single-crust deep-dish pie (9 inches)**
   **Sweetened whipped cream, optional**

**1.** Place the sweet potatoes in a small saucepan; add water to cover. Bring to a boil. Reduce heat; cook, uncovered, 30-40 minutes or until tender. Drain; cool potatoes slightly. Peel potatoes; return to pot. Mash until smooth.

**2.** Preheat the oven to 425°. In a large bowl, beat potatoes, butter, sugars, pie spice and salt. Beat in eggs, buttermilk and vanilla until smooth. Pour into the pastry shell. Bake on lowest oven rack 10 minutes.

**3.** Reduce oven setting to 375°. Bake 30-40 minutes longer or until edges are puffed and center is just set. Cool on a wire rack; serve within 2 hours or refrigerate and serve cold. If desired, serve with whipped cream.

**PASTRY FOR SINGLE-CRUST DEEP-DISH PIE (9 INCHES)**

*Combine 1½ cups all-purpose flour and ¼ teaspoon salt; cut in ⅔ cup cold butter until crumbly. Gradually add 3-6 tablespoons ice water, tossing with a fork until dough holds together when pressed. Wrap in plastic wrap and refrigerate 1 hour.*

## Oven-Baked Brisket

Texans like brisket cooked on the smoker, but this version offers convenient prep in the oven. Sometimes I make extra sauce to serve on the side. Round out the meal with potato salad and slaw.

—**KATIE FERRIER** HOUSTON, TX

**PREP:** 15 MIN. + MARINATING
**BAKE:** 1¼ HOURS
**MAKES:** 8 SERVINGS

- 1  **fresh beef brisket (4 to 5 pounds)**
- 2  **tablespoons Worcestershire sauce**
- 2  **tablespoons soy sauce**
- 1  **tablespoon onion salt**
- 1  **tablespoon liquid smoke**
- 2  **teaspoons salt**
- 2  **teaspoons pepper**
   **Dash hot pepper sauce**

**SAUCE**

- ½  **cup ketchup**
- 3  **tablespoons brown sugar**
- 1  **tablespoon lemon juice**
- 1  **tablespoon soy sauce**
- 1  **teaspoon ground mustard**
- 3  **drops hot pepper sauce**
   **Dash ground nutmeg**

**1.** Place the brisket, fat side down, in a 13x9-in. baking dish. In a small bowl, mix the Worcestershire sauce, soy sauce, onion salt, liquid smoke, salt, pepper and pepper sauce; pour over the brisket. Turn brisket fat side up; refrigerate, covered, overnight.

**2.** Remove brisket from refrigerator. Preheat oven to 300°. Bake brisket, covered, 4 hours.

**3.** In a small bowl, combine the sauce ingredients. Spread over the brisket. Bake, uncovered, for 15-30 minutes longer or until brisket is tender. Cut meat diagonally across the grain into thin slices.

**NOTE** *This is a fresh beef brisket, not corned beef.*

# Southern Pineapple Casserole

When I make pineapple casserole, I double the amount—because guests frequently request a second helping for dessert! Sweet-tangy fruit is even better combined with savory cheddar cheese and buttery cracker crumb topping.

**—CATHERINE GOZA** LELAND, NC

**PREP:** 15 MIN. • **BAKE:** 30 MIN. + STANDING
**MAKES:** 8 SERVINGS

- 1 **cup sugar**
- ⅓ **cup all-purpose flour**
- 2 **cups (8 ounces) shredded cheddar cheese**
- 1 **can (20 ounces) unsweetened crushed pineapple, drained**
- 1 **can (20 ounces) unsweetened pineapple chunks, drained**

**TOPPING**
- 2½ **cups crushed Ritz crackers (about 60 crackers)**
- ¼ **cup butter, melted**

**1.** Preheat oven to 350°. In a large bowl, mix the sugar and flour; stir in cheddar cheese. Stir in both cans of drained pineapple.

**2.** Transfer the mixture to a greased 1½-qt. baking dish. In a small bowl, mix crackers and butter. Sprinkle over top. Bake, uncovered, 30-40 minutes or until topping is brown and cheese is melted. Let stand 10 minutes.

## Holiday Helper

To make cracker crumbs easily, place crackers in a heavy-duty resealable plastic bag and seal the bag, pushing out as much air as possible. Then just press a rolling pin over it, crushing the crackers into fine crumbs. You can also make crumbs in a blender or food processor.

# Easy Memphis-Style BBQ Ribs

A friend of mine who loves barbecue gave me her recipe for ribs. Use just enough of the spice mixture to rub over them before baking, and sprinkle on the rest later.

—**JENNIFER ROSS** ARLINGTON, TN

**PREP:** 20 MIN. • **BAKE:** 3½ HOURS
**MAKES:** 6 SERVINGS

- ¼ **cup packed brown sugar**
- ¼ **cup paprika**
- 2 **tablespoons kosher salt**
- 2 **tablespoons onion powder**
- 2 **tablespoons garlic powder**
- 2 **tablespoons coarsely ground pepper**
- 3 **racks (1½-2 pounds each) pork baby back ribs**
  **Barbecue sauce, optional**

**1.** Preheat the oven to 350°. In a small bowl, mix the first six ingredients; rub ¾ cup over the ribs. Wrap the rib racks in large pieces of heavy-duty foil; seal tightly. Place on a 15x10x1-in. baking pan. Bake 1½ hours. Reduce the oven setting to 250°. Bake 1½ hours longer or until tender.

**2.** Carefully remove ribs from foil; return to baking pan. Sprinkle ribs with remaining spice mixture. Bake 30 minutes longer or until lightly browned, brushing with barbecue sauce if desired.

# Apple Stack Cake

My mom loved to bake this sky-high cake. Layer the apple goodness two days before serving. Later, a dusting of confectioners' sugar is the only topping you'll need.

—**LEVA CLEMENT** JACKSON, MO

**PREP:** 1 HOUR + CHILLING
**BAKE:** 10 MIN./BATCH + COOLING
**MAKES:** 16 SERVINGS

- 16 **ounces dried apples, chopped**
- 5 **cups water**
- 1 **cup packed brown sugar**
- 2 **teaspoons apple pie spice**
- 1 **cup butter, softened**
- 2 **cups granulated sugar**
- 2 **large eggs**
- 2 **teaspoons vanilla extract**

- 6 **cups all-purpose flour**
- 3 **teaspoons baking powder**
- 1 **teaspoon baking soda**
- ½ **cup buttermilk**
  **Confectioners' sugar, optional**

**1.** Place the dried apples and water in a 6-qt. stockpot;. Bring to a boil. Reduce the heat; simmer, uncovered, 40-45 minutes or until the apples are softened, stirring occasionally.

**2.** Mash the softened apples into a chunky sauce. Stir in brown sugar and apple pie spice; simmer, uncovered, 10-15 minutes longer or until liquid is absorbed and sauce is thickened. Cool completely.

**3.** Preheat oven to 400°. In a large bowl, cream the butter and sugar until light and fluffy. Add the eggs, one at a time, beating well after each addition. Beat in vanilla. In another bowl, whisk flour, baking powder and baking soda; add to creamed mixture alternately with buttermilk, beating well after each addition.

**4.** Divide dough into eight portions; shape each portion into a disk. Cut out eight 9-in circles of parchment paper. With a floured rolling pin, roll out a dough disk to fit each parchment circle. Transfer the disks to baking sheets. Bake 10-12 minutes or until golden brown. Remove from pans to wire racks to cool completely.

**5.** Place one cake layer on a serving plate; spread with ⅔ cup apple filling. Repeat layers. Top with the remaining cake layer. Wrap tightly in plastic wrap; refrigerate 1-2 days or until the layers soften. If desired, sprinkle cake with confectioner's sugar.

## Texas Pecan Rice

For a special holiday side dish, I dressed up an old recipe to give it a little more Texas character. Everyone loved the savory flavor and crunchy pecans.

**—JOAN HALLFORD**

NORTH RICHLAND HILLS, TX

**PREP:** 30 MIN. • **BAKE:** 1 HOUR
**MAKES:** 10 SERVINGS

- ½ cup unsalted butter, cubed
- 1½ cups sliced fresh mushrooms
- 3 green onions, sliced
- 2 cups uncooked long grain brown rice
- 1 garlic clove, minced
- 1½ cups chopped pecans, toasted
- ½ teaspoon salt
- ½ teaspoon dried thyme
- ½ teaspoon pepper
- ¼ teaspoon ground cumin
- 3 cans (10½ ounces each) condensed beef consomme, undiluted
- 2¼ cups water
- 5 bacon strips, cooked and crumbled
  Toasted pecan halves, optional

**1.** Preheat oven to 400°. In a Dutch oven, heat butter over medium-high heat. Add the mushrooms and green onions; cook and stir 3-5 minutes or until tender. Add the brown rice and garlic; cook and stir 3 minutes. Stir in the pecans, salt, thyme, pepper and cumin. Add the consomme and water; bring to a boil.
**2.** Bake, covered, for 1 to 1¼ hours or until liquid is absorbed and rice is tender. Transfer to a serving bowl. Top with the crumbled bacon and, if desired, pecan halves.

## Fried Dill Pickles

**START TO FINISH:** 20 MIN.
**MAKES:** 3½ CUPS

- 1 jar (32 ounces) whole dill pickles
- 1 cup buttermilk
- 2 tablespoons Louisiana-style hot sauce
- 1 cup all-purpose flour
- 1 cup cornmeal
- 2 tablespoons garlic salt
- 2 tablespoons paprika
- 1 tablespoon cayenne pepper
- 1 teaspoon pepper
  Oil for deep-fat frying
  Ranch salad dressing, optional

**1.** Drain pickles, discarding liquid. Cut pickles into ½-in.-thick slices. Drain on paper towels; blot with additional paper towels until dry.
**2.** In a shallow bowl, mix buttermilk and hot sauce. In another shallow bowl, mix flour, cornmeal, garlic salt, paprika, cayenne pepper and pepper. Dip pickles in the buttermilk mixture, then in the flour mixture. In a Dutch oven, heat 1 in. of oil to 375°. Working in batches, fry pickles 2-3 minutes on each side or until golden brown. Drain on paper towels. Serve immediately with ranch dressing if desired.

> *"You may be surprised when you see how easy it is to make a batch of Fried Dill Pickles. Don't be surprised if they get snatched up in a flash."*
>
> **—ELOISE MAYNOR** SCOTTSBORO, AL

## Real Southern Fried Chicken

As a Yankee originally from Vermont, I didn't know one fried chicken from another. They all seemed pretty much the same to me. Tasting the Southern version opened my eyes! A side of hot biscuits served with butter and honey is practically mandatory.

—LILY JULOW LAWRENCEVILLE, GA

**PREP:** 20 MIN. + MARINATING
**COOK:** 30 MIN. • **MAKES:** 4 SERVINGS

- 3 cups buttermilk, divided
- 3 teaspoons kosher salt, divided
- 1 teaspoon coarsely ground pepper, divided
- 1 broiler/fryer chicken (3 to 4 pounds), cut up
  Oil for deep-fat frying
- 2 cups all-purpose flour
- 1 teaspoon onion powder
- 1 teaspoon garlic powder
- 1 teaspoon paprika

**1.** In a shallow bowl, whisk 2 cups of buttermilk, 1 teaspoon salt and ⅛ teaspoon pepper. Add chicken pieces; turn to coat. Refrigerate, covered, overnight.

**2.** In an electric skillet or deep fryer, heat the oil to 375°. Meanwhile, place the remaining buttermilk in a shallow bowl. In another shallow bowl, whisk the flour, onion powder, garlic powder, paprika and remaining salt and pepper. Place half of flour mixture in another shallow bowl (for a second coat of breading).

**3.** Drain the chicken, discarding the marinade; pat chicken dry. Dip in the flour mixture to coat both sides; shake off excess. Dip in buttermilk, allowing excess to drain off. For the second coat of breading, dip chicken in remaining flour mixture, patting to help the coating adhere.

**4.** Fry chicken, a few pieces at a time, for 4-5 minutes on each side or until browned and the juices run clear. Drain on paper towels.

# South Carolina Chicken & Rice

Chicken Bog is the traditional name for this South Carolina Lowcountry dish. We always make a big batch the day after Thanksgiving, when we're working on our family's Christmas tree farm.

**—JEAN COCHRAN** LEXINGTON, SC

**PREP:** 10 MIN. • **COOK:** 50 MIN.
**MAKES:** 12 SERVINGS

- 2½ **pounds boneless skinless chicken thighs**
- 8 **cups chicken broth, divided**
- 2 **packages (13 to 14 ounces each) smoked sausage, sliced**
- 1 **large onion, finely chopped**
- 3 **cups uncooked long grain rice**
  **Salt and pepper to taste**

**1.** In a 6-quart stockpot, cook the chicken in 2 cups chicken broth over medium heat until a thermometer reads 170°, turning halfway through cooking. Remove the chicken and set aside to cool.

**2.** Add smoked sausage, onion and remaining chicken broth to stockpot; bring to a boil. Add rice. Reduce heat; simmer, uncovered, for 15-18 minutes or until the rice is almost tender (the mixture may be soupy).

**3.** Shred the chicken; add to the rice. Cook, covered, until rice is tender. Season with salt and pepper to taste.

## Holiday Helper

I often cook using chicken broth from a can. When I have more broth than I need for my recipe, I pour the excess into an ice cube tray and store it in the freezer for future use. Then I can pull out and thaw as many cubes as I need later.

**—MARALYN B.** SEBASTIAN, FL

# Southern-Style Biscuits

As a Southerner and our household cook, I experimented until I hit on just the right biscuit recipe. It practically screams to be smothered in gravy or stuffed with eggs and sausage.
—**SUSAN FLIPPIN** MOUNT AIRY, NC

**START TO FINISH:** 30 MIN. • **MAKES:** 8 BISCUITS

- 2½ cups self-rising flour, divided
- ¼ cup cold butter or shortening
- 1 to 1¼ cups 2% milk
  Melted butter

**1.** Preheat oven to 375°. Place 2 cups flour in a large bowl. Cut in the butter until butter is the size of peas. Stir in 1 cup milk. Dough should be wet and sticky; if needed, stir in some of the remaining milk.
**2.** Place remaining flour in a small bowl. Using a ¼-cup measuring cup dipped in flour, remove ¼ cup dough from the bowl and drop into flour; gently turn to coat. Place 2 in. apart on parchment paper-lined baking sheets. Repeat.
**3.** Bake 20-25 minutes or until golden brown. Brush with melted butter; serve warm.

# Quick & Easy Sausage Gravy

Breakfast doesn't get any heartier or more satisfying than this home-style classic. No one will leave the table hungry!
—**JOHN WILHELM** RICHMOND, VA

**START TO FINISH:** 25 MIN. • **MAKES:** 6 CUPS

- 2 pounds bulk pork sausage
- ⅓ cup all-purpose flour
- 3 teaspoons pepper
- 2 teaspoons sugar
- 1 teaspoon salt
- 2 cups 2% milk
- 2 cans (5 ounces each) evaporated milk

**1.** In a Dutch oven, cook the pork sausage over medium heat 8-10 minutes or until no longer pink, breaking into crumbles (do not drain).
**2.** Stir in the flour, pepper, sugar and salt; cook and stir 1-2 minutes. Stir in the milk and evaporated milk. Bring to a boil. Reduce heat; simmer, uncovered, 3-5 minutes or until thickened, stirring occasionally.

# Grandma's Collard Greens

My grandmother made the best collard greens in the world. Eating them with a slice of buttermilk corn bread is pure bliss.
—**SHERRI WILLIAMS** CRESTVIEW, FL

**PREP:** 30 MIN. • **COOK:** 2 HOURS • **MAKES:** 6 SERVINGS

- 3 tablespoons lard or shortening, divided
- 1 large onion, chopped
- 6 garlic cloves, minced

- 1½ pounds smoked ham hocks
- 6 cups water
- 2 teaspoons seasoned salt
- 1 to 3 teaspoons crushed red pepper flakes
- 1 large bunch collard greens (about 2 pounds), coarsely chopped
- 1½ cups white wine
- ¼ teaspoon sugar

**1.** In a 6-qt. stockpot, heat 1 tablespoon lard over medium heat. Add onion and garlic; cook and stir until tender. Add the ham hocks, water, seasoned salt and red pepper flakes. Bring to a boil. Reduce the heat; simmer, uncovered, for 55-60 minutes or until meat is tender.
**2.** Add the collard greens, wine, sugar and remaining lard. Return to a boil. Reduce the heat; simmer, uncovered, for 55-60 minutes or until the collard greens are very tender. Remove the meat from the bones; finely chop and return to pan. Discard bones. Serve with a slotted spoon.

## Southern Bourbon Pecan Pie

When I first made the original recipe for this bourbon-splashed pie, I added some vanilla extract and eliminated the flour. We loved the result.

—**PAUL FALDUTO** EFLAND, NC

**PREP:** 15 MIN. • **BAKE:** 55 MIN. + COOLING
**MAKES:** 8 SERVINGS

- ¼ **cup butter, cubed**
- 1 **cup sugar**
- 1 **cup dark corn syrup**
- 3 **large eggs**
- ¼ **cup bourbon**
- 1 **teaspoon vanilla extract**
- **Pinch salt**
- 1½ **cups pecan halves**
- 1 **frozen deep-dish pie shell**

**1.** Preheat the oven to 325°. In a large saucepan, combine butter, sugar and corn syrup. Cook over medium-low heat until the sugar is dissolved; cool slightly. In a large bowl, whisk the eggs, bourbon, vanilla and salt; slowly whisk in the sugar mixture. Stir in the pecans; pour into pastry shell.
**2.** Place the pie on a baking sheet. Bake 55-60 minutes or until knife inserted in center comes out clean. Cool on a wire rack.

## Holiday Helper

Tired of scraping? When measuring sticky liquids such as corn syrup, maple syrup, molasses or honey, spray the measuring cup with nonstick cooking spray before adding the liquid. This will make it easier to pour out the liquid and clean the cup later. Try the same technique when using a dry measuring cup to measure peanut butter.

## Mrs. Ina's Corn Relish

Mrs. Ina was an older lady who came to our church for many years. She made an amazing corn relish. I whip up my own batch to give to friends at Christmastime.

—BRENDA WOOTEN DAYTON, TN

**START TO FINISH:** 25 MIN.
**MAKES:** 1½ CUPS

- 1 **can (11 ounces) whole kernel corn**
- ⅓ **cup chopped onion**
- ⅓ **cup chopped celery**
- 3 **tablespoons chopped green pepper**
- 3 **tablespoons diced pimientos, drained**
- 1 **small garlic clove, minced, optional**
- ⅓ **cup sugar**
- 1 **teaspoon salt**
- 1 **teaspoon celery seed**
- 1 **teaspoon mustard seed**
- ¼ **teaspoon crushed red pepper flakes**
- ⅛ **teaspoon ground ginger**
- 1 **cup white vinegar, divided**
- 1 **tablespoon all-purpose flour**
- 1½ **teaspoons ground mustard**
- ¼ **teaspoon ground turmeric**

**1.** Drain corn, reserving 1 tablespoon liquid. In a small saucepan, combine onion, celery, green pepper, pimientos and, if desired, garlic. Stir in sugar, salt, celery seed, mustard seed, red pepper flakes, ginger and ¾ cup vinegar. Bring to a boil. Boil 5-7 minutes.

**2.** In a small bowl, mix flour, mustard and tumeric. Stir in the reserved corn liquid until smooth. Add to vegetable mixture; stir in the remaining vinegar. Cook, uncovered, 2-3 minutes or until slightly thickened. Add the corn; boil 1-2 minutes or until thickened.

## Four-Cheese Garlic Grits

My grandmother used to prepare grits for my grandfather, who was from the South. I adapted her recipe to make use of ingredients that are available in supermarkets today.

—ROBIN BASKETTE LEXINGTON, KY

**PREP:** 20 MIN. • **BAKE:** 30 MIN.
**MAKES:** 16 SERVINGS (½ CUP EACH)

- 6 **ounces cream cheese, softened**
- 4 **tablespoons butter, softened, divided**
- 3 **tablespoons grated Parmesan cheese**
- 1 **large garlic clove, minced**
- 2 **cups quick-cooking grits**
- 2 **large eggs, beaten**
- 1½ **cups (6 ounces) shredded cheddar cheese, divided**
- 1 **cup cubed process cheese (Velveeta)**
- ½ **teaspoon salt**
- ¼ **teaspoon garlic powder**
- ¼ **teaspoon pepper**

**1.** Preheat the oven to 350°. In a small bowl, beat the cream cheese, 2 tablespoons of butter, Parmesan cheese and garlic.

**2.** In a 6-qt. stockpot, prepare grits according to the package directions. Reduce the heat to low; add remaining butter. Fold in cream cheese mixture; stir in the eggs. Stir in ¾ cup cheddar cheese, Velveeta and seasonings until cheeses are melted.

**3.** Transfer the mixture to a greased 13x9-in. baking dish. Bake, uncovered, 25 minutes or until set. Sprinkle with the remaining cheese; bake 5 minutes longer or until cheese is melted.

## Down South Sweet Tea Cake

I think this recipe combines two of the best and most famous ingredients from the South: sweet tea and pecans! Using a cake mix simplifies prep and helps ease the holiday time-crunch.

**—MELISSA MILLWOOD** LYMAN, SC

**PREP:** 20 MIN. • **BAKE:** 45 MIN. + COOLING
**MAKES:** 12 SERVINGS

- 1 **package yellow cake mix (regular size)**
- 1 **package (3.4 ounces) instant vanilla pudding mix**
- 1 **cup strong brewed tea, cooled, divided**
- 4 **large eggs**
- ¾ **cup canola oil**
- 1 **teaspoon vanilla extract**
- ½ **teaspoon lemon extract**
- 1 **cup chopped pecans, toasted**
- 2 **cups confectioners' sugar**
- ⅓ **cup unsalted butter, melted**

**1.** Preheat oven to 350°. Grease and flour a 10-in. fluted tube pan. In a large bowl, combine yellow cake mix, vanilla pudding mix, ¾ cup brewed tea, eggs, oil, vanilla and lemon extract; beat on low speed 30 seconds. Beat on medium 2 minutes. Stir in pecans. Transfer to the prepared pan. Bake 45-50 minutes or until a toothpick inserted in center comes out clean.

**2.** Cool in pan 10 minutes before removing to a wire rack to cool completely. In a small bowl, mix the confectioners' sugar, butter and enough remaining tea to reach the desired consistency. Pour the glaze over the top of cake, allowing some to flow over the sides.

# SEASONAL GET-TOGETHERS

# BREAKFAST WITH SANTA

Ho ho ho! Round up the kiddies for a morning party that stars Santa Claus himself. After telling him what's on their wish lists, little guests will love digging into a yummy breakfast with their favorite jolly old elf.

# Peaches 'n' Cream Waffle Dippers

I've prepared these for many brunches—peaches are my favorite, but you can use strawberries or blueberries. People of all ages enjoy dunking crispy waffle strips into creamy dip.
—BONNIE GEAVARAS-BOOTZ SCOTTSDALE, AZ

**PREP:** 30 MIN. • **BAKE:** 5 MIN./BATCH
**MAKES:** 6 SERVINGS (2 CUPS SAUCE)

- 1 cup all-purpose flour
- 1 tablespoon sugar
- 1 teaspoon baking powder
- ¼ teaspoon salt
- 2 large eggs, separated
- 1 cup 2% milk
- 2 tablespoons butter, melted
- ¼ teaspoon vanilla extract
- 1¼ cups chopped frozen peaches, thawed, divided
- ¾ cup (6 ounces) peach yogurt
- 2 cups sweetened whipped cream or whipped topping
  Toasted pecans and ground cinnamon, optional

**1.** In a large bowl, whisk flour, sugar, baking powder and salt. In another bowl, whisk the egg yolks, milk, butter and vanilla until blended. Add to dry ingredients; stir just until moistened. Stir in 1 cup peaches.
**2.** In a small bowl, beat egg whites until stiff but not dry. Fold into batter. Bake in a preheated waffle iron according to manufacturer's directions until golden brown. Cut the waffles into 1-in. strips.
**3.** In a small bowl, fold the whipped cream into the yogurt. Sprinkle with remaining peaches and, if desired, pecans and cinnamon. Serve with waffles.

# Hot Cocoa with Almond Milk

Change up ordinary hot cocoa by stirring some dark baking cocoa into vanilla almond milk. Fluffy marshmallow creme and bright sprinkles make irresistible toppings.
—CINDY REAMS PHILIPSBURG, PA

**START TO FINISH:** 15 MIN. • **MAKES:** 8 SERVINGS (1 CUP EACH)

- ½ cup sugar
- ½ cup dark baking cocoa or baking cocoa
- 2 cartons (32 ounces each) vanilla almond milk
- 1 teaspoon vanilla extract
  Strawberry marshmallow creme
  Assorted sprinkles

**1.** In a large saucepan, combine the sugar and baking cocoa; gradually whisk in the vanilla almond milk. Heat until bubbles form around the sides of the pan, stirring cocoa occasionally.
**2.** Remove from the heat; stir in the vanilla extract. Pour into mugs; top with the strawberry marshmallow creme and sprinkles.

# North Pole Party Masks

Get the camera ready! Kids love playing with handheld party masks, and they're easy to make. Start by looking in books or online to find simple ideas for various hats, beards and glasses, and create the patterns.

Next, trace the patterns onto colorful craft foam and cut out the pieces. Glue them together as needed; glue a thin wood dowel to the side of each mask for a handle. Then let the fun begin!

**2.** Transfer the granola to a 15x10x1-in. baking pan coated with cooking spray. Bake 35-40 minutes or until golden brown, stirring occasionally. Cool completely on a wire rack. Stir in dried fruits; serve with yogurt. Store granola in an airtight container.

## Blueberry Cantaloupe Salad

The simple citrus and poppy seed dressing in this fruit medley really dresses up the refreshing mix of berries and melon.

**—R. JEAN RAND** EDINA, MN

**START TO FINISH:** 10 MIN. • **MAKES:** 4 SERVINGS

- ¾ cup (6 ounces) orange yogurt
- 1½ teaspoons lemon juice
- ¾ teaspoon poppy seeds
- ½ teaspoon grated orange peel
- 2 cups diced cantaloupe
- 1 cup fresh blueberries

In a small bowl, mix yogurt, lemon juice, poppy seeds and orange peel. To serve, divide cantaloupe and blueberries among four dishes; top with yogurt mixture.

## Maple Morning Granola

Salty and sweet ingredients combine for an easy, wholesome breakfast or snack. Hosting a kids' party? Pack the granola into treat bags and present them as take-home favors.

**—LIBBY WALP** CHICAGO, IL

**PREP:** 15 MIN. • **BAKE:** 35 MIN + COOLING • **MAKES:** 5 CUPS

- 3 cups old-fashioned oats
- ⅔ cup chopped pecans
- ⅓ cup salted pumpkin seeds or pepitas
- ½ cup maple syrup
- 4 teaspoons butter, melted
- 1½ teaspoons ground cinnamon
- ¼ teaspoon salt
- ¼ teaspoon ground nutmeg
- ½ cup dried apples, chopped
- ½ cup dried cranberries
  Plain yogurt

**1.** Preheat oven to 325°. In a large bowl, combine oats, pecans and pumpkin seeds. In a small bowl, mix maple syrup, butter, cinnamon, salt and nutmeg. Pour over the oat mixture and toss to coat.

## Cornflake-Coated Crispy Bacon

I've loved my aunt's crispy coated bacon ever since I was a child. Now I've shared the super-simple recipe with my own children. We still enjoy a big panful every Christmas morning—and on many other days throughout the year!

—BRENDA SEVERSON NORMAN, OK

**PREP:** 20 MIN. • **BAKE:** 25 MIN.
**MAKES:** 9 SERVINGS

- ½ cup evaporated milk
- 2 tablespoons ketchup
- 1 tablespoon Worcestershire sauce
  Dash pepper
- 18 bacon strips (1 pound)
- 3 cups crushed cornflakes

**1.** Preheat oven to 375°. In a large bowl, combine the evaporated milk, ketchup, Worcestershire sauce and pepper. Add the bacon strips, turning to coat. Dip the bacon strips in the crushed cornflakes, patting to help the coating adhere.
**2.** Place the bacon on two racks in ungreased 15x10x1-in. baking pans. Bake 25-30 minutes or until golden and crisp, rotating the pans halfway through baking.

### Holiday Helper

At a breakfast with Santa party, set out coloring books and plenty of crayons as an extra activity for young guests when they're not interacting with Santa or eating breakfast. Designate a roomy seating area where Santa can sit with the kids. And don't forget the cheery Christmas music!

# Double-Crusted Sausage Egg Casserole

This breakfast has become our Christmas tradition. I love being able to assemble and refrigerate the casserole the night before. Then I just pop it into the oven to bake while we open gifts in the morning.

**—LYNNE GERMAN** WOODLAND HILLS, CA

**PREP:** 25 MIN. + CHILLING • **BAKE:** 35 MIN.
**MAKES:** 12 SERVINGS

- 2 **pounds bulk pork sausage**
- 4 **cups (16 ounces) shredded Monterey Jack cheese**
- 2 **cans (8 ounces each) refrigerated crescent rolls**
- 7 **large eggs**
- ¼ **cup 2% milk**
- ¼ **teaspoon salt**
- ¼ **teaspoon pepper**
- ¼ **cup grated Parmesan cheese**

**1.** In a large skillet, cook sausage over medium heat 8-10 minutes or until no longer pink, breaking into crumbles; drain. Stir in Monterey Jack cheese.

**2.** Unroll one tube of dough into one long rectangle; press the perforations to seal. Press onto bottom of a greased 13x9-in. baking dish. Top with the sausage mixture.

**3.** Separate 1 egg; reserve egg white for brushing strips. In a small bowl, whisk egg yolk, milk, salt, pepper and remaining eggs until blended; pour over sausage mixture. Sprinkle with Parmesan cheese.

**4.** On a lightly floured surface, unroll the remaining dough and roll into a 13x9-in. rectangle; cut crosswise into 13 strips. Twist each strip and place over filling; brush with reserved egg white. Refrigerate, covered, overnight.

**5.** Remove from the refrigerator 30 minutes before baking. Preheat oven to 350°. Bake 35-40 minutes or until golden brown. Let stand 5-10 minutes before serving.

## Pumpkin-Chocolate Chip Pancakes

Who can resist a sky-high stack of golden, fluffy pancakes? Pumpkin and chocolate chips take them over the top!

—**LIBBY WALP** CHICAGO, IL

**START TO FINISH:** 30 MIN.
**MAKES:** 15 PANCAKES

- 2⅓ cups pancake mix
- ½ teaspoon ground cinnamon
- ¼ teaspoon ground nutmeg
- ¼ teaspoon ground cloves

- 2 large eggs
- 1¼ cups buttermilk
- ⅓ cup canned pumpkin
- ¼ cup butter, melted
- 1 tablespoon honey
- ½ cup miniature semisweet chocolate chips
  Additional miniature semisweet chocolate chips and honey

**1.** In a large bowl, combine pancake mix, cinnamon, nutmeg and cloves. In a small bowl, whisk the eggs, buttermilk, pumpkin, butter and honey; stir into the dry ingredients just until moistened. Fold in the miniature chocolate chips.

**2.** Lightly grease a griddle; heat over medium heat. Pour the pancake batter by ¼ cupfuls onto the griddle. Cook until the bubbles on top begin to pop and the bottoms are golden brown. Turn pancakes and cook until the second side is golden brown. Serve with additional miniature chocolate chips and honey.

# CHRISTMAS TOY DRIVE

It's all about sharing the spirit of the season! Throw a toy collection party and ask each guest to bring a toy you'll deliver later to a favorite charity. Then serve up a scrumptious lunch to spread the cheer even more.

# Italian-Style Beef Dip Sandwiches

I have fond memories of my mother in the kitchen preparing her amazing beef dip sandwiches. They always made our house smell like an Old World Italian restaurant. And as good as the aroma was, somehow the taste was even better! Set out a jar of giardiniera for spooning on top.
—**KIRA VOSK** MILWAUKEE, WI

**PREP:** 1 HOUR • **COOK:** 7 HOURS • **MAKES:** 12 SERVINGS

- 4 tablespoons olive oil, divided
- 1 boneless beef chuck roast (4 to 5 pounds)
- 2¼ teaspoons salt, divided
- 2¼ teaspoons pepper, divided
- 2 small onions, coarsely chopped
- 9 garlic cloves, chopped
- ¾ cup dry red wine
- 4 cups beef stock
- 3 fresh thyme sprigs
- 4 teaspoons Italian seasoning
- 1½ teaspoons crushed red pepper flakes
- 4 medium green peppers, cut into ½-inch strips
- 1 teaspoon garlic powder
- 12 crusty submarine buns or hoagie buns, split partway
- 12 slices provolone or part-skim mozzarella cheese
  Giardiniera, optional

**1.** In a 6-qt. stockpot, heat 3 tablespoons olive oil over medium-high heat; brown the roast on all sides. Sprinkle with 2 teaspoons each salt and pepper. Transfer roast to a 6-qt. slow cooker.

**2.** Add the onions to stockpot; cook and stir 2-3 minutes or until lightly browned. Add garlic; cook 30 seconds longer. Add wine; cook 3-5 minutes, stirring to loosen browned bits from pan. Stir in stock, thyme, Italian seasoning and pepper flakes; transfer to the slow cooker. Cook, covered, on low 7-9 hours or until beef is tender.

**3.** About ½ hour before serving, preheat oven to 350°. Place the peppers in a 15x10x1-in. baking pan. Drizzle with the remaining olive oil. Sprinkle with the garlic powder and remaining salt and pepper; toss to coat. Roast 15-20 minutes or until softened, stirring halfway.

**4.** Remove roast; cool slightly. Strain cooking juices into a small saucepan, reserving strained mixture and removing thyme stems. Skim fat from juices; heat through and keep warm. Coarsely shred beef with two forks; stir in reserved strained mixture. If desired, moisten beef with some of the cooking juices.

**5.** To serve, preheat broiler. Arrange the buns on baking sheets, cut side up. Broil 3-4 inches from heat until lightly toasted. Remove from oven; top each bun with ⅔ cup beef mixture and 1 slice cheese. Broil until the cheese is melted, about 30 seconds.

**6.** Top with the peppers and, if desired, giardiniera. Serve with cooking juices for dipping.

# Orange-Cinnamon Gelatin Mold

My family prefers this to traditional cranberry gelatin molds. The cinnamon zing really complements ham and turkey.
—**NANCY HEISHMAN** LAS VEGAS, NV

**PREP:** 15 MIN. + CHILLING • **MAKES:** 12 SERVINGS (½ CUP EACH)

- 2 packages (3 ounces each) cherry gelatin
- ½ cup Red Hots
- ⅓ cup sugar
- 1½ cups water
- 1¾ cups orange juice
- ⅓ cup sour cream
- 1½ cups orange sections, chopped
- 1 medium apple, peeled and finely chopped
- ½ cup chopped pecans

**1.** Place the gelatin in a large bowl. In a small saucepan, combine the Red Hots, sugar and water. Cook and stir until the candies are dissolved and the mixture comes to a boil. Stir into the gelatin. Stir in the orange juice and sour cream. Refrigerate 30-45 minutes or until thickened.

**2.** Stir in the oranges, apple and pecans. Pour into a 6-cup ring mold coated with cooking spray. Refrigerate 4 hours or until firm. Unmold onto a platter.

# Santa Deviled Eggs

I love creating special deviled eggs for parties. These little Santas are easier to make than they look, and everyone raves over them. (For helpful how-to photos, see page 107.)

—**CRYSTAL SCHLUETER** NORTHGLENN, CO

**PREP:** 40 MIN. • **MAKES:** 2 DOZEN

- 12 **hard-cooked large eggs**
  **Hot water**
- 2 **teaspoons red food coloring**
- ½ **cup mayonnaise**
- 4½ **teaspoons Dijon mustard**
- 1 **tablespoon sweet pickle relish**
- ¼ **teaspoon paprika**
- 1 **tablespoon horseradish sauce,
  optional**
- 1 **tablespoon capers, drained**
- 1 **to 2 ounces thick sliced deli ham,
  cut into 24 pieces**
- ½ **roasted sweet red pepper, cut into
  24 thin strips/pieces**
- ⅓ **cup cream cheese, softened**

**1.** Peel and cut the eggs lengthwise in half. Remove the yolks and place in a small bowl. Fill another small bowl ⅓ full with hot water. Stir in the red food coloring. Dip the narrow end of each egg into the red water; hold for 10-15 seconds. Drain the eggs on paper towels, cut side up.

**2.** In a small bowl, mash the yolks. Stir in mayonnaise, Dijon mustard, pickle relish, paprika and, if desired, horseradish sauce. Spoon or pipe into each egg white. Attach capers for eyes, a ham piece for a nose and a pepper piece for a mouth.

**3.** Cut a small hole in the tip of a pastry bag or in a corner of a food-safe plastic bag; insert #16 star pastry tip. Fill the bag with the softened cream cheese. Pipe eyebrows, mustache and beard on each face; pipe pom-pom and trim on each hat. Refrigerate, covered, until serving.

# Four-Layer Chocolate Dessert

With creamy layers in a big 13x9-in. pan, this simple dessert is tailor-made for a buffet table. I like to add a sprinkling of toasted slivered almonds on top for the finishing touch.

—**LINDA KNOLL** JACKSON, MI

**PREP:** 20 MIN. • **BAKE:** 15 MIN. + CHILLING • **MAKES:** 15 SERVINGS

- 2 cups all-purpose flour
- ¾ cup cold butter
- 1 cup finely chopped pecans
- 1 package (8 ounces) cream cheese, softened
- 1 cup confectioners' sugar
- 1 cup whipped topping
- 3 cups cold milk
- 2 packages (3.9 ounces each) instant chocolate pudding mix
- 2 cups heavy whipping cream, whipped
- ½ cup slivered almonds, toasted

**1.** Preheat oven to 350°. Place the flour in a bowl; cut in the butter until crumbly. Stir in pecans. Press onto the bottom of an ungreased 13x9-in. baking dish. Bake 15-20 minutes or until lightly browned. Cool on a wire rack.

**2.** In a small bowl, beat cream cheese and confectioners' sugar until smooth; fold in the whipped topping. Spread over the crust.

**3.** In a large bowl, whisk cold milk and chocolate pudding mixes 2 minutes. Let stand for 2 minutes or until soft-set. Gently spread over cream cheese layer. Top with whipped cream; sprinkle with almonds. Refrigerate until cold.

## Assembling Santa Deviled Eggs

Want to create these merry eggs (recipe on page 106)? Refer to the step-by-step photos here for easy assembly.

**1.** For the perfect-size hats, dip the narrow end of each egg into the tinted water just to the edge of the egg yolk cavity.

**2.** When spooning or piping the yolk filling into the eggs, keep them on the paper towel to prevent sliding.

**3.** After adding the eyes, nose and mouth to each egg, fill a pastry bag or food-safe plastic bag with the softened cream cheese and pipe on the white details—the hat brim, pom-pom, eyebrows, beard and mustache.

## Bacon & Broccoli Salad

You'll want to serve this family-friendly side dish year-round. The broccoli gets a big-time flavor boost from bacon, toasted pecans, dried berries and a mayo dressing.

—**CINDI READ** HENDERSONVILLE, TN

**START TO FINISH:** 30 MIN • **MAKES:** 16 SERVINGS (¾ CUP EACH)

- 3 bunches broccoli, cut into florets (about 10 cups)
- 1 pound bacon strips, cooked and crumbled
- 1 cup chopped pecans, toasted
- 1 cup dried blueberries
- 1 cup dried cherries
- ¼ cup finely chopped red onion

**DRESSING**
- 1 cup mayonnaise
- ¼ cup sugar
- ¼ cup cider vinegar

In a large bowl, combine the first six ingredients. For the dressing, in a small bowl, whisk the mayonnaise, sugar and cider vinegar. Pour over the broccoli mixture; toss to coat.

## Eggnog Fruit Salad

My grandmother prepared her creamy, eggnog-glorified fruit salad every year for Christmas, and now I do, too. The holiday season just wouldn't be the same without it!

—**MANDY NALL** MONTGOMERY, AL

**PREP:** 15 MIN. + CHILLING • **MAKES:** 12 SERVINGS (¾ CUP)

- 1½ cups cold eggnog
- 3 envelopes whipped topping mix (Dream Whip)
- ⅛ teaspoon ground nutmeg
- 1 can (20 ounces) pineapple chunks, drained
- 1 can (15¼ ounces) sliced peaches, drained
- 2 cups fresh blueberries
- 2 cups fresh sliced strawberries
- 2 medium apples, peeled and chopped
- 1 jar (6 ounces) maraschino cherries, drained and halved
- ½ cup chopped walnuts

**1.** In a small bowl, combine eggnog, whipped topping mix and nutmeg. Beat on high speed 2-4 minutes or until soft peaks form.

**2.** In a large bowl, combine fruits and nuts; fold in eggnog mixture. Refrigerate, covered, 2 hours before serving.

## Sweet & Savory Cheese Pie

Layer ruby-red preserves on a savory appetizer spread as the crowing touch

—**ANNETTE WHITMARSH** LINCOLN, NE

**PREP:** 15 MIN. + CHILLING
**MAKES:** 32 SERVINGS

- 1 cup chopped pecans
- 1 package (8 ounces) cream cheese, softened
- ½ cup mayonnaise
- 4 cups (16 ounces) shredded sharp cheddar cheese
- 6 green onions, chopped
- ½ pound bacon strips, cooked and crumbled
- 1 jar (10 ounces) seedless raspberry or strawberry preserves
  Sliced green onions, optional
  Assorted crackers or baguette slices

**1.** Spread pecans evenly over bottom of a greased 9-in. springform pan. In a large bowl, beat the cream cheese and mayonnaise until smooth. Stir in cheddar cheese, green onions and bacon. Carefully spread over pecans. Refrigerate, covered, overnight.

**2.** Loosen sides from the pan with a knife; remove rim. Spread preserves over top. If desired, top with onions. Serve with crackers or baguette slices.

# CHINESE NEW YEAR

Hosting a New Year's Eve party? Give it exotic flavor with a colorful, festive Chinese New Year theme. Guests will love nibbling Far East appetizers and making toasts at midnight with Asian champagne cocktails. Cheers!

# Exotic Five-Spice Chicken Wings

Savor the flavors you crave! These distinctive wings provide a sweet, salty and slightly spicy taste with every bite.
—**BARB MILLER** OAKDALE, MN

**PREP:** 15 MIN. + MARINATING • **BAKE:** 40 MIN. • **MAKES:** 2 DOZEN

- 12 chicken wings (about 3 pounds)
- 1 cup honey
- ½ cup canola oil
- 2 tablespoons reduced-sodium soy sauce
- 4 teaspoons Chinese five-spice powder
- 4 teaspoons minced fresh gingerroot
- 2 teaspoons salt
- 1 teaspoon garlic powder
- ½ teaspoon cayenne pepper
  Sesame seeds and sliced green onions, optional

**1.** Using a sharp knife, cut through the two wing joints; discard wing tips. In a small bowl, whisk honey, oil, soy sauce, five-spice powder, ginger, salt, garlic powder and cayenne until blended. Pour 1 cup into a large resealable plastic bag. Place the chicken wings in bag; seal bag and turn to coat. Refrigerate 4 hours. Cover and refrigerate remaining marinade.

**2.** Preheat oven to 400°. Drain the chicken, discarding the marinade. Place wings on a rack in a foil-lined 15x10x1-in. baking pan. Bake, uncovered, 25 minutes, turning once. Bake 15-20 minutes longer or until chicken juices run clear, turning and basting occasionally with reserved marinade. If desired, sprinkle with seeds and onions.

# Pork & Rice Meatballs

My appetizer meatballs combine two of my favorite Asian dishes—Chinese pork dumplings and steamed chicken balls.
—**ELIZABETH DUMONT** MADISON, MS

**PREP:** 45 MIN. • **COOK:** 15 MIN./BATCH
**MAKES:** ABOUT 4 DOZEN (1 CUP SAUCE)

- 1 pound ground pork
- 8 ounces fresh shiitake mushrooms, finely chopped
- 3 cups finely chopped Chinese or napa cabbage
- 1 can (8 ounces) bamboo shoots, drained and finely chopped
- 1 medium carrot, shredded
- 4 green onions, thinly sliced
- 3 tablespoons teriyaki sauce
- 2 tablespoons minced fresh gingerroot
- 1 tablespoon rice vinegar
- 1 tablespoon soy sauce
- 2 garlic cloves, minced
- ½ teaspoon salt
- ¼ teaspoon pepper
- 2½ cups sushi or small grain rice
  Cabbage leaves, optional

**DIPPING SAUCE**

- ¾ cup teriyaki sauce
- 1 tablespoon minced fresh gingerroot
- 2 teaspoons rice vinegar
- 1 teaspoon grated lemon peel
- 1 to 2 tablespoons Sriracha hot chili sauce, optional

**1.** In a large bowl, combine the first six ingredients. In a small bowl, mix teriyaki sauce, minced ginger, rice vinegar, soy sauce, garlic, salt and pepper. Pour over the meat mixture; mix lightly but thoroughly (mixture will be soft). With wet hands, shape into 1-in. balls; roll in the rice to coat evenly.

**2.** Line a steamer basket with cabbage leaves or parchment paper if desired. Arrange meatballs in batches 1 in. apart in steamer basket; place in a Dutch oven over 1 in. of water. Bring to a boil; steam, covered, 15-20 or until rice is tender, adding additional water as necessary. In a small bowl, mix dipping sauce ingredients. Serve with meatballs.

## Pear & Ginger Sparkler

I created this twist on a Bellini when a friend gave me some Asian pears she grew in her backyard. If you like ginger and want more of a kick, try substituting ginger liquor for the vodka.
—**JACYN SIEBERT** SAN FRANCISCO, CA

**PREP:** 10 MIN. • **COOK:** 20 MIN. + COOLING • **MAKES:** 18 SERVINGS

- 4 **cups pear nectar**
- 2 **medium Asian pears, cored and sliced**
- ½ **cup thinly sliced fresh gingerroot**
- ¼ **cup sugar**
- 1 **cup plain or pear vodka**
- 3 **bottles champagne (750 ml each), chilled**

**GARNISH**
    **Fresh pear slices**

**1.** In a large saucepan, combine pear nectar, pears, ginger and sugar. Bring to a boil. Reduce heat; simmer, uncovered, 15-20 minutes or until pears are softened. Cool.
**2.** Place the mixture in a blender; cover and process until smooth. Press the mixture through a fine-mesh strainer. Stir in the vodka. Pour 1½ ounces into each champagne flute or cocktail glass. Top with 4 ounces champagne. Garnish with pear slices.

## Homemade Fortune Cookies

Our home is frequently filled with guests, so I'm always cooking up something. I prepared my own fortune cookies when I was looking for a surprise treat for my husband. Have fun thinking of different fortunes to tuck inside!
—**SUSAN BETTINGER** BATTLE CREEK, MI

**PREP:** 45 MIN. • **BAKE:** 5 MIN./BATCH • **MAKES:** 10 COOKIES

- 3 **tablespoons butter, softened**
- 3 **tablespoons sugar**
- 1 **large egg white**
- ½ **teaspoon vanilla extract**
- ⅓ **cup all-purpose flour**

**1.** Preheat oven to 400°. Write fortunes on small strips of paper (3½ x ¼-in.); set aside. Line a baking sheet with parchment paper. Using a pencil, draw two 3½-in. circles on a sheet of parchment paper. Place paper, pencil mark down, on a baking sheet; set aside.
**2.** In a small bowl, beat butter, sugar, egg white and vanilla. Add flour; mix well. Spread 1 tablespoon batter over each circle. Bake 4-5 minutes or until lightly browned.
**3.** Slide parchment paper onto a work surface. Cover one cookie with a kitchen towel. Place a fortune in the center of the other cookie; loosen cookie from parchment paper with a thin spatula. Fold cookie in half over fortune strip so the edges meet; hold edges together for 3 seconds.
**4.** Place center of cookie over the rim of a glass; gently press ends down to bend cookie in middle. Cool 1 minute before removing to a wire rack. Repeat with second cookie. If cookies become too cool to fold, return to oven to soften for 1 minute. Repeat with remaining batter and fortunes.

## Pork & Shrimp Pinwheels

Here's my homemade version of the dim sum I enjoy in restaurants. The little pinwheels can be either fried or baked.

**—JULIE MERRIMAN** SEATTLE, WA

**PREP:** 20 MIN. + CHILLING
**COOK:** 5 MIN./BATCH • **MAKES:** 2 DOZEN

- ½ **pound ground pork**
- ½ **pound uncooked shrimp (31–40 per pound), peeled and deveined**
- 6 **green onions, thinly sliced**
- ½ **cup reduced-sodium soy sauce, divided**
- 2 **tablespoons oyster sauce**
- 3 **garlic cloves, minced**
- 3 **tablespoons sesame oil, divided**
- 1 **tablespoon grated fresh gingerroot**
- 2 **tubes (8 ounces each) refrigerated seamless crescent dough sheet**
  **Oil for frying**
- ¼ **cup sweet chili sauce**
- 1 **tablespoon sesame seeds**

**1.** Place pork, shrimp, green onions, ¼ cup soy sauce, oyster sauce, garlic, 2 tablespoons sesame oil and ginger in a food processor; pulse until finely chopped.

**2.** Unroll each sheet of crescent dough into a rectangle. Spread each with half of the pork mixture to within 1 in. of edges. Roll up jelly-roll style, starting with a long side; pinch seam to seal. Freeze 1 hour or until firm.

**3.** Using a serrated knife, cut each roll crosswise into 12 slices. In an electric skillet, heat ½ in. of oil to 350°. Fry the slices, a few at a time, 2-3 minutes on each side or until golden brown. Drain on paper towels. Or preheat oven to 375°. Place 1 in. apart on parchment paper-lined baking sheets. Bake 12-15 minutes or until golden brown. Remove from pans to wire racks to cool.

**4.** In a small bowl, mix chili sauce, remaining soy sauce and sesame oil. Arrange the slices on a serving platter; sprinkle with sesame seeds. Serve with sauce.

## Chinese Lantern Centerpiece

Give your Chinese New Year table even more Asian style with this decorative paper lantern.

**1.** On the back of a 12-in.-square sheet of paper, draw a horizontal line 2 in. above the bottom edge. Repeat 2 in. below the top edge. Between the lines, draw vertical lines to create 1-in.-wide bars all the way across the sheet. Using a craft knife, cut the vertical lines.

**2.** Fold the paper in half from top to bottom to make a crease. Unfold the paper, roll it vertically into a cylinder and glue to secure. From coordinating paper, cut two 2-in.-wide strips. Wrap one strip around each end of the lantern and glue in place. If desired, glue on a chenille stem for a handle.

**3.** Roll a 12-in.-square sheet of vellum into a cylinder that will fit inside the lantern. Glue cylinder to secure, then glue or stand it inside the lantern. When the lantern is completely dry, place a battery-operated candle inside.

## Baked Crab Rangoon

When I'm dining out, crab rangoon is one of my go-to dishes. I decided to create a better-for-you version at home.
—**EMILY HIGGINS** WINGDALE, NY

**PREP:** 30 MIN. • **BAKE:** 15 MIN. • **MAKES:** ABOUT 3 DOZEN

- 1 package (8 ounces) reduced-fat cream cheese
- ½ cup mayonnaise
- 2 green onions, sliced
- 1 tablespoon paprika
- 1 tablespoon lime juice
- 1 teaspoon garlic powder
- 1 teaspoon reduced-sodium soy sauce
- 8 ounces fresh crabmeat
- 40 wonton wrappers
  Chinese-style mustard

**1.** Preheat oven to 350°. In a small bowl, beat cream cheese and mayonnaise. Stir in green onions, paprika, lime juice, garlic powder and soy sauce. Fold in crab.

**2.** Spoon 2 teaspoons filling in the center of a wonton wrapper. (Cover remaining wrappers with a damp paper towel until ready to use.) Moisten wrapper edges with water. Fold opposite sides over filling, pressing centers together to seal. Repeat with remaining sides, making a four-pointed star. Repeat.

**3.** Transfer appetizers to an ungreased baking sheet. Bake 15-18 minutes or until golden brown. Serve with mustard.

## Asian Shrimp Pancakes

I keep these crisp, colorful appetizer pancakes on the small side so my guests can easily pick them up with chopsticks and eat them in a few bites. I think the little shrimp-topped cakes are as good as any I've tasted in Asian restaurants.
—**TONYA BURKHARD** DAVIS, IL

**PREP:** 25 MIN. • **COOK:** 5 MIN./BATCH • **MAKES:** ABOUT 2½ DOZEN

- 2 garlic cloves, minced
- ¾ teaspoon salt
- 2 large eggs
- ¾ cup water
- 2 teaspoons toasted sesame oil
- 1 cup all-purpose flour
- 6 green onions, thinly sliced
- ½ medium sweet red pepper, finely chopped
- ½ pound peeled and deveined cooked shrimp (31-40 per pound), halved lengthwise
  Optional toppings: wasabi mayonnaise, Sriracha hot chili sauce or fresh cilantro leaves

**1.** In a large bowl, mash garlic with salt. Beat in eggs, water and oil. Whisk in flour until blended. Stir in green onions and pepper.

**2.** Lightly grease a griddle; heat over medium heat. Pour batter by tablespoonfuls onto griddle. Cook until edges are dry and bottoms are light golden brown. Turn; cook until second side is golden brown. Arrange the pancakes on a serving platter; top each with a shrimp half. If desired, top with additional toppings.

# ENTERTAINING IN 30

## Caramel Fluff & Toffee Trifle

Talk about a stunning dessert! The best part? You need only five ingredients to put it together.
—**DANIEL ANDERSON** PLEASANT PRAIRIE, WI

**PREP:** 15 MIN. + CHILLING
**MAKES:** 12 SERVINGS

- 2 **cups heavy whipping cream**
- ¾ **cup packed brown sugar**
- 1 **teaspoon vanilla extract**
- 1 **prepared angel food cake (8 to 10 ounces), cut into 1-inch cubes**
- 1 **cup milk chocolate English toffee bits**

**1.** In a large bowl, beat cream, brown sugar and vanilla just until blended. Refrigerate, covered, 20 minutes. Beat until stiff peaks form.

**2.** In a 4-qt. glass bowl, layer one-third of each of the following: cake cubes, whipped cream and toffee bits. Repeat layers twice. Refrigerate until serving.

## Coconut Mashed Sweet Potatoes

Sweet potatoes and coconut milk are a match made in flavor heaven. The flecks of lemongrass are a nice surprise.
—**RACHEL DUEKER** GERVAIS, OR

**START TO FINISH:** 25 MIN.
**MAKES:** 10 SERVINGS

- 5 **large sweet potatoes (about 4 pounds), peeled and cubed**
- 1¼ **cups light coconut milk**
- ¾ **cup reduced-sodium chicken broth**
- ¼ **cup unsweetened apple juice**
- 2 **teaspoons butter**
- 2 **tablespoons brown sugar**
- 1 **teaspoon dried lemongrass**
- ½ **teaspoon salt**
- ½ **teaspoon pepper**

Place potatoes in a Dutch oven and cover with water. Bring to a boil. Reduce heat; cover and cook for 10-15 minutes or until tender. Drain. Mash with coconut milk, broth, juice and butter. Stir in the remaining ingredients.

### Holiday Helper

I add a 2-in. strip of orange peel to boiling sweet potatoes. When I mash it all up, the orange adds great flavor.

—**PAT W.** BLOOMFIELD, MO

## Parmesan Creamed Spinach

This rich and creamy spinach dish takes minutes to make. If I'm expecting guests, I'll double or triple the recipe.
—**LEANN ROSS** SANTAN VALLEY, AZ

**START TO FINISH:** 20 MIN. • **MAKES:** 4 SERVINGS

- ½ pound sliced fresh mushrooms
- 1 small onion, chopped
- 2 teaspoons butter
- 2 teaspoons olive oil
- 1 garlic clove, minced
- ¼ teaspoon salt
- ¼ teaspoon pepper
- 1 package (9 ounces) fresh spinach
- ½ cup cream cheese, cubed
- ½ cup shredded Parmesan cheese

**1.** In a large skillet, saute mushrooms and onion in butter and oil until tender. Add the garlic, salt and pepper; cook 1 minute longer.

**2.** Add spinach and cream cheese; cook and stir until cream cheese is smooth and spinach is wilted. Sprinkle with cheese.

## Lemon Mushroom Orzo

Sometimes I serve this side dish chilled; sometimes I serve it hot. It has a very lovely appearance and goes well with almost any entree.
—**SHELLY NELSON** AKELEY, MN

**START TO FINISH:** 25 MIN. • **MAKES:** 12 SERVINGS

- 1 package (16 ounces) orzo pasta
- 3 tablespoons olive oil, divided
- ¾ pound sliced fresh mushrooms
- ¾ cup chopped pecans, toasted
- ½ cup minced fresh parsley
- 1 teaspoon grated lemon peel
- 3 tablespoons lemon juice
- 1 teaspoon salt
- ½ teaspoon pepper

**1.** Cook orzo according to package directions. Meanwhile, in a large skillet, heat 2 tablespoons oil over medium-high heat. Add mushrooms; cook and stir until tender and lightly browned. Drain orzo.

**2.** In a large bowl, place orzo, mushrooms, pecans, parsley, lemon peel, lemon juice, salt, pepper and remaining oil; toss to combine.

## Chicken Cacciatore with Polenta

The microwave makes quick work of homemade polenta, and the rest is done in one skillet.

—YVONNE STARLIN WESTMORELAND, TN

**START TO FINISH:** 30 MIN.
**MAKES:** 4 SERVINGS

- 3 **cups water**
- ¾ **cup cornmeal**
- ½ **cup grated Parmesan cheese**
- ¾ **teaspoon salt**

**CACCIATORE**

- 1 **pound boneless skinless chicken thighs, cut into 1-inch pieces**
- ⅛ **teaspoon salt**
- ⅛ **teaspoon pepper**
- 1 **tablespoon olive oil**
- 1 **large onion, sliced**
- 1 **garlic clove, minced**
- 1 **can (14½ ounces) fire-roasted crushed tomatoes**
- ½ **cup pitted Greek olives**

**1.** In a microwave-safe bowl, whisk water and cornmeal; microwave, covered, on high for 6 minutes. Stir; cook, covered, 5-7 minutes longer or until the polenta is thickened, stirring every 2 minutes. Stir in cheese and salt.

**2.** Meanwhile, sprinkle chicken with salt and pepper. In a large skillet, heat oil over medium-high heat. Add chicken; cook and stir until browned. Remove with a slotted spoon.

**3.** Add onion to the same pan; cook and stir 2-4 minutes or until tender. Add garlic; cook 1 minute longer. Return the chicken to pan; stir in tomatoes and olives. Bring to a boil. Reduce heat; simmer, uncovered, 6-8 minutes or until chicken is no longer pink. Serve with polenta.

**FREEZE OPTION** *Do not prepare polenta until later. Freeze cooled chicken mixture in freezer containers. To use, partially thaw in refrigerator overnight. Prepare polenta as directed. Meanwhile, in a saucepan, reheat chicken, stirring occasionally and adding a little water if necessary. Serve with polenta.*

## Pork Medallions in Mustard Sauce

I like pork medallions with apricot preserves and wondered how else I could dress them up. I played around with different flavors until I found this combo. It wows my crowd every time.

—TAHNIA FOX TRENTON, MI

**START TO FINISH:** 30 MIN.
**MAKES:** 4 SERVINGS

- ½ **cup reduced-sodium chicken broth**
- 2 **tablespoons thawed apple juice concentrate**
- 4½ **teaspoons stone-ground mustard**
- 1 **pork tenderloin (1 pound), cut into ½-inch slices**
- ¼ **teaspoon salt**
- ¼ **teaspoon pepper**
- 1 **tablespoon olive oil**
- 2 **garlic cloves, minced**
- 1 **teaspoon cornstarch**
- 2 **tablespoons cold water**
- 1 **tablespoon minced fresh parsley**

**1.** In a small bowl, mix broth, apple juice concentrate and mustard. Sprinkle pork with salt and pepper. In a large nonstick skillet, heat oil over medium-high heat. Brown pork on both sides; remove from pan.

**2.** Add garlic to same pan; cook and stir 1 minute. Add broth mixture, stirring to loosen browned bits from pan. Bring to a boil. Reduce heat; simmer, uncovered, 6-8 minutes or until liquid is reduced to about ⅓ cup.

**3.** Return pork to pan; cook, covered, over low heat 3-4 minutes or until a thermometer inserted into pork reads 145°. Mix cornstarch and water until smooth; stir into pan. Bring to a boil; cook and stir 2 minutes or until thickened. Sprinkle with parsley.

# Hash Brown-Topped Steak

My husband and I enjoy cooking together. One night, we were craving grilled steak and cheese-stuffed baked potatoes, but didn't want to wait for the baking. Here's what we invented instead.

—JUDY ARMSTRONG PRAIRIEVILLE, LA

**START TO FINISH:** 30 MIN.
**MAKES:** 4 SERVINGS

- 2 tablespoons butter
- 1 small onion, chopped
- 3 garlic cloves, minced
- 2 cups frozen shredded hash brown potatoes, thawed
- ¾ teaspoon salt, divided
- 1 cup (4 ounces) shredded Jarlsberg cheese
- 1 beef top sirloin steak (1 inch thick and 1½ pounds), cut into 4 portions
- ½ teaspoon pepper
- 2 tablespoons minced fresh chives

**1.** In a large skillet, heat butter over medium-high heat. Add onion; cook and stir 2-3 minutes or until tender. Add garlic; cook 2 minutes longer.

**2.** Stir in the hash browns and ¼ teaspoon salt; spread in an even layer. Reduce heat to medium; cook 5 minutes. Turn hash browns over; cook, covered, 5-6 minutes longer or until heated through and bottom is lightly browned. Sprinkle with cheese; cover and remove from heat. Keep warm.

**3.** Sprinkle beef with pepper and remaining salt. Grill, covered, over medium heat 5-7 minutes on each side or until meat reaches desired doneness (for medium-rare, a thermometer should read 145°; medium, 160°; well-done, 170°).

**4.** Remove steaks from heat; top each with a fourth of the potato mixture. Sprinkle with chives.

## Cranberry Glazed Pork Chops

This main dish is simple enough for a weeknight, but the cranberries also make it a perfect choice for a Christmas dinner. It's colorful, juicy and easy. After all, it comes together in less than 30 minutes so you're out of the kitchen and with your family at the table in no time.

**—ROXANNE CHAN** ALBANY, CA

**START TO FINISH:** 25 MIN.
**MAKES:** 4 SERVINGS

- 4 **boneless pork loin chops (5 ounces each)**
- ¼ **teaspoon salt**
- ¼ **teaspoon pepper**
- 1 **cup fresh or frozen cranberries, thawed**
- ⅓ **cup water**
- ⅓ **cup sweet chili sauce**
- 1 **green onion, finely chopped**

**1.** Sprinkle pork chops with salt and pepper. Heat a large skillet over medium heat. Add pork chops; cook 4-6 minutes on each side or until a thermometer reads 145°. Remove from pan; keep warm.
**2.** In same skillet, add cranberries, water and chili sauce. Bring to a boil; cook, uncovered, 4-6 minutes or until berries pop, stirring occasionally. Serve with pork chops; sprinkle with the onion.

### Holiday Helper

Chili sauce is a staple in our house. I always have a bottle on hand to jazz up meat loaf, pour on sandwiches, spice up burgers and hot dogs, and even use to dress up eggs in the morning!

**—PAT WATTIE** STONEY CREEK, ON

## Honeyed Carrots with Basil Gremolata

I love the scent of fresh basil. It's even better when paired with fresh citrus peel! In this recipe, the carrots are sweetened with a touch of honey, then topped with a lively citrus-basil gremolata.

**—NAYLET LAROCHELLE** MIAMI, FL

**START TO FINISH:** 20 MIN.
**MAKES:** 4 SERVINGS

- ¼ **cup minced fresh parsley**
- 2 **tablespoons minced fresh basil**
- 1½ **teaspoons grated lemon peel**
- 1 **teaspoon grated orange peel**
- 1 **garlic clove, minced**
- ⅛ **teaspoon crushed red pepper flakes, optional**
- 1 **pound medium carrots, sliced**
- 2 **tablespoons honey**
- 1 **tablespoon olive oil**
- ¼ **teaspoon salt**
- ¼ **teaspoon coarsely ground pepper**

**1.** In a small bowl, combine the parsley, basil, lemon peel, orange peel, garlic and pepper flakes if desired; set aside.
**2.** In a 2-qt. microwave-safe dish, combine carrots and ¼ cup water. Cover and microwave on high for 3 minutes; stir. Cover and cook 3-4 minutes longer or until tender. Drain. Combine the honey, oil, salt and pepper; stir into carrots.
**3.** Transfer carrots to a serving plate and sprinkle with parsley mixture.
**NOTE** *This recipe was tested in a 1,100-watt microwave.*

## Tomato-Onion Green Beans

Fresh green beans are the star of this appealing side. Full of fresh-picked flavor, it's the perfect complement to chicken, pork tenderloin or seafood.

**—DAVID FEDER** BUFFALO GROVE, IL

**START TO FINISH:** 30 MIN.
**MAKES:** 6 SERVINGS

- 2 **tablespoons olive oil**
- 1 **large onion, finely chopped**
- 1 **pound fresh green beans, trimmed**
- 3 **tablespoons tomato paste**
- ½ **teaspoon salt**
- 2 **tablespoons minced fresh parsley**

**1.** In a large skillet, heat oil over medium-high heat. Add onion; cook until tender and lightly browned, stirring occasionally.

**2.** Meanwhile, place green beans in a large saucepan; add water to cover. Bring to a boil. Cook, covered, 5-7 minutes or until crisp-tender. Drain; add to onion. Stir in tomato paste and salt; heat through. Sprinkle with parsley.

### Holiday Helper

For bright-colored green beans, use only enough water to cover the beans, then cook until crisp-tender. If you like very tender, well-cooked beans, use more water and cook longer. You'll lose that vibrant green color, however.

# Ginger Salmon with Brown Rice

It's hard to believe this recipe has only a few ingredients, but it's true! The dressing does double duty as a glaze for the salmon and a flavor booster for the rice. Serve it with steamed veggies and dinner's done.

**—NAYLET LAROCHELLE** MIAMI, FL

**START TO FINISH:** 25 MIN.
**MAKES:** 4 SERVINGS

- 4 **salmon fillets (6 ounces each)**
- 5 **tablespoons reduced-fat sesame ginger salad dressing, divided**

**RICE**
- ⅓ **cup shredded carrot**
- 4 **green onions, chopped, divided**
- 1½ **cups instant brown rice**
- 1½ **cups water**
- ⅓ **cup reduced-fat sesame ginger salad dressing**

**1.** Preheat oven to 400°. Place fillets on a foil-lined baking sheet; brush with 3 tablespoons salad dressing. Bake, uncovered, 10-12 minutes or until fish just begins to flake easily with a fork. Brush with remaining salad dressing.

**2.** Meanwhile, place a large saucepan coated with cooking spray over medium heat. Add carrot and half of the green onions; cook and stir 2-3 minutes or until crisp-tender. Add rice and water; bring to a boil. Reduce heat; simmer, covered, 5 minutes.

**3.** Remove from heat; stir in salad dressing. Let stand, covered, for 5 minutes or until liquid is absorbed and rice is tender. Fluff with a fork; serve with salmon. Sprinkle with remaining green onions.

2. Drain mushrooms, discarding salad dressing. Place mushrooms in a foil-lined 15x10x1-in. baking pan. Broil 3-4 in. from heat 2-3 minutes on each side or until tender. Fill with spinach mixture; top with mozzarella cheese. Broil 2-4 minutes longer or until cheese is melted.

## Chicken Thighs with Tomato-Vodka Sauce

I originally invented this scrumptious dish to celebrate a friend's 21st birthday, and it has since become a quick and easy family favorite.

—**KAREN KUEBLER** DALLAS, TX

**START TO FINISH:** 30 MIN.
**MAKES:** 4 SERVINGS

- 4 boneless skinless chicken thighs (about 1 pound)
- ½ teaspoon salt
- ¼ teaspoon pepper
- 2 tablespoons butter
- 1 tablespoon olive oil
- 4 celery ribs, thinly sliced
- 1 can (14½ ounces) diced tomatoes, undrained
- ¼ cup vodka
- 1 teaspoon grated lime peel
- 2 tablespoons lime juice
- 1 teaspoon Worcestershire sauce
- 4 lime wedges
- 1 tablespoon chopped celery leaves
  Hot pepper sauce and celery salt, optional

1. Pound chicken thighs slightly with a meat mallet to uniform thickness; sprinkle with salt and pepper. In a large skillet, heat butter and oil over medium heat; brown chicken on both sides. Remove and keep warm.
2. In same pan, add the celery; cook and stir 3-4 minutes or until tender. Return chicken to pan. Add tomatoes, vodka, lime peel, lime juice and Worcestershire sauce; bring to a boil. Reduce heat; simmer, covered, 4-5 minutes or until a thermometer inserted into chicken reads 170°. Serve with lime wedges, celery leaves and, if desired, hot pepper sauce and celery salt.

## Broiled Cheese Stuffed Portobellos

My vegetarian friends do a happy dance when I serve my three-cheese portobellos. For a twist, use button mushrooms to create appetizers.

—**JENNIFER BENDER** BALDWIN, GA

**START TO FINISH:** 30 MIN.
**MAKES:** 6 SERVINGS

- 6 large portobello mushrooms (4 to 4½ inches), stems removed
- ⅔ cup Italian salad dressing
- 1 package (10 ounces) frozen chopped spinach, thawed and squeezed dry
- 1 package (8 ounces) cream cheese, softened
- ¼ cup grated Parmesan cheese
- 3 garlic cloves, minced
- ⅛ teaspoon salt
- ⅛ teaspoon pepper
- 6 slices part-skim mozzarella cheese

1. Preheat broiler. In a large resealable plastic bag, combine mushrooms and salad dressing. Seal bag and turn to coat. Let stand 15 minutes. Meanwhile, in a large bowl, combine spinach, cream cheese, Parmesan cheese, garlic, salt and pepper.

# Chocolate Lover's Pudding

I first made this dish when my husband asked me, "Why don't you ever make chocolate pudding?" It's not too rich, but it has an amazing chocolate flavor. I love preparing this homemade delight!

**—CHARIS O'CONNELL** MOHNTON, PA

**START TO FINISH:** 30 MIN.
**MAKES:** 6 SERVINGS

- ½ cup sugar, divided
- 3 cups 2% milk
- 3 tablespoons cornstarch
- ¼ teaspoon salt
- 2 large egg yolks, beaten
- ⅓ cup baking cocoa
- 2 ounces semisweet chocolate, chopped
- 1 tablespoon butter
- 2 teaspoons vanilla extract
  Fresh raspberries, optional

**1.** In a large heavy saucepan, combine ¼ cup sugar and milk. Bring just to a boil, stirring occasionally. Meanwhile, in a large bowl, combine cornstarch, salt and remaining sugar; whisk in egg yolks until smooth.

**2.** Slowly pour hot milk mixture in a thin stream into egg yolk mixture, whisking constantly. Whisk in cocoa. Return mixture to saucepan and bring to a boil, stirring constantly until thickened, about 1 minute. Remove from the heat immediately.

**3.** Stir in the chocolate, butter and vanilla until melted. Whisk until completely smooth. Cool pudding for 15 minutes, stirring occasionally. Transfer to dessert dishes. Serve warm or refrigerate, covered, 1 hour. Just before serving, top with raspberries if desired.

## Spinach, Apple & Pecan Salad

**START TO FINISH:** 15 MIN.
**MAKES:** 16 SERVINGS

- 2 packages (6 ounces each) fresh baby spinach
- 1 medium apple, chopped
- 1 cup (4 ounces) crumbled feta cheese
- 1 cup glazed pecans
- ½ cup chopped red onion
- ⅓ cup dried cranberries
- 5 bacon strips, cooked and crumbled, optional

**DRESSING**

- 2 tablespoons cider vinegar
- 1 tablespoon sugar
- ½ teaspoon Dijon mustard
- ⅛ teaspoon pepper
- ¼ cup canola oil

**1.** In a large bowl, combine the first six ingredients; stir in bacon if desired.
**2.** For dressing, in a small bowl, whisk vinegar, sugar, mustard and pepper until blended. Gradually whisk in oil. Pour over salad; toss to coat.

*"Company was on the way,*
*and I realized I'd forgotten to buy salad ingredients—epic fail! I scavenged the kitchen to come up with the right blend of ingredients and created an instant favorite. You can use any type of apple, but Galas are my favorite."*

**—KELLY WALSH** AVISTON, IL

## Lemon-Butter Tilapia with Almonds

Sometimes I want a special meal that doesn't require a ton of time or effort. Thankfully, I can always rely on this lemony, buttery entree.

**—RAMONA PARRIS** CANTON, GA

**START TO FINISH:** 10 MIN.
**MAKES:** 4 SERVINGS

- 4 tilapia fillets (4 ounces each)
- ½ teaspoon salt
- ¼ teaspoon pepper
- 1 tablespoon olive oil
- ¼ cup butter, cubed
- ¼ cup white wine or chicken broth
- 2 tablespoons lemon juice
- ¼ cup sliced almonds

**1.** Sprinkle the fillets with salt and pepper. In a large nonstick skillet, heat oil over medium heat. Add fillets; cook 2-3 minutes on each side or until fish just begins to flake easily with a fork. Remove and keep warm.
**2.** Add butter, wine and lemon juice to same pan; cook and stir until butter is melted. Serve with fish; sprinkle with almonds.

### Holiday Helper

If you're looking for fish that doesn't taste "fishy" for a special menu, I recommend tilapia. Because it has a very mild flavor, it satisfies most guests at your table. It also cooks quickly, is affordable and is widely available.

**—SANDY L.** LITITZ, PA

## West African Shrimp

My girls have always loved seafood, so I invented a shrimp dish with coconut milk and ginger. They raved; I was delighted. It's especially good with jasmine rice.
—**SHARON SCALETTA** JOHNSTOWN, PA

**START TO FINISH:** 30 MIN. • **MAKES:** 4 SERVINGS

- 3 **garlic cloves, minced**
- 1 **tablespoon grated fresh gingerroot**
- 1 **tablespoon olive oil**
- 1 **can (28 ounces) petite diced tomatoes, drained**
- 1 **can (13.66 ounces) coconut milk**
- 2 **tablespoons tomato paste**
- ½ **teaspoon salt**
- 2 **teaspoons cornstarch**
- 1 **tablespoon cold water**
- 1 **pound uncooked shrimp (31-40 per pound), peeled and deveined**
  **Hot cooked rice**
  **Minced fresh cilantro, optional**

**1.** Place garlic, ginger and oil in a large skillet. Cook and stir over medium-low heat 5-7 minutes or until fragrant. Add tomatoes, coconut milk, tomato paste and salt; bring to a boil.
**2.** In a small bowl, mix cornstarch and water until smooth; stir into the tomato mixture. Bring to a boil, stirring constantly; cook and stir 1-2 minutes or until thickened.
**3.** Add the shrimp. Reduce heat; simmer, uncovered, 4-6 minutes or until shrimp turn pink. Serve with rice and, if desired, cilantro.

## Creamy Sausage-Mushroom Rigatoni

When visiting Rome, we enjoyed an amazing dinner at a restaurant near the Pantheon. It lasted three hours! The restaurant is now gone, but its memory lives on in this tasty pasta dish.
—**BARBARA ROOZROKH** BROOKFIELD, WI

**START TO FINISH:** 30 MIN. • **MAKES:** 6 SERVINGS

- 1 **package (16 ounces) rigatoni**
- 1 **pound bulk Italian sausage**
- 2 **teaspoons butter**
- 1 **pound sliced fresh mushrooms**
- 2 **garlic cloves, minced**
- ½ **teaspoon salt**
- ¼ **teaspoon pepper**
- 2 **cups heavy whipping cream**
  **Minced fresh parsley, optional**

**1.** Cook rigatoni according to package directions.
**2.** Meanwhile, in a large skillet, cook sausage over medium heat 4-6 minutes or until no longer pink, breaking into crumbles; drain and remove sausage from pan.
**3.** In same skillet, heat butter over medium heat. Add mushrooms, garlic, salt and pepper; cook, covered, 4 minutes, stirring occasionally. Uncover; cook and stir 2-3 minutes or until mushrooms are tender and liquid is evaporated.
**4.** Stir in cream; bring to a boil. Reduce heat; cook, uncovered, 8-10 minutes or until slightly thickened. Return sausage to skillet; heat through. Drain pasta; serve with sauce. If desired, sprinkle with parsley.

# Steak Diane

When I want to make a memorable dinner without spending hours in the kitchen, I rely on this recipe.

**—PHOEBE CARRE** MULLICA HILL, NJ

**START TO FINISH:** 20 MIN.
**MAKES:** 4 SERVINGS

- 4 **beef ribeye steaks (½ inch thick and 8 ounces each)**
- ¼ **teaspoon pepper**
- ⅛ **teaspoon salt**

- 4 **tablespoons butter, divided**
- 1 **green onion, finely chopped**
- ½ **teaspoon ground mustard**
- 1 **tablespoon lemon juice**
- 1½ **teaspoons Worcestershire sauce**
- 1 **tablespoon minced fresh parsley**
- 1 **tablespoon minced chives**

**1.** Sprinkle the steaks with pepper and salt. In a large skillet, heat 2 tablespoons butter over medium heat. Add green onion and mustard; cook 1 minute. Add steaks; cook 2-5 minutes on each side or until meat reaches desired doneness (for medium-rare, a thermometer should read 145°; medium, 160°; well-done, 170°).

**2.** Remove steaks to a serving platter and keep warm. In same skillet, add lemon juice, Worcestershire sauce and remaining butter; cook and stir 2 minutes or until thickened. Add parsley and chives. Serve with steaks.

# Quick Apple Crisp

This dessert can be assembled in a snap and cooks up in minutes, giving me more time to work on other things. You'll love it served with a scoop of vanilla ice cream or whipped topping.

—**SUZIE SALLE** RENTON, WA

**START TO FINISH:** 30 MIN.
**MAKES:** 8 SERVINGS

- 1 **cup graham cracker crumbs (about 16 squares)**
- ½ **cup all-purpose flour**
- ½ **cup packed brown sugar**
- 1 **teaspoon ground cinnamon**
- ½ **teaspoon ground nutmeg**
- ½ **cup butter, melted**
- 8 **medium tart apples, peeled and sliced**
  **Whipped topping or ice cream**

**1.** In a large bowl, combine the cracker crumbs, flour, brown sugar, cinnamon, nutmeg and butter. Place apples in a greased microwave-safe 2½-qt. dish. Top with crumb mixture.

**2.** Microwave, uncovered, on high for 8-9 minutes or until apples are tender. Serve warm with whipped topping or ice cream.

**NOTE** *This recipe was tested in a 1,100-watt microwave.*

## Holiday Helper

Because it comes together so quickly, remember Quick Apple Crisp for other holiday meals and cool-weather treats. It makes a great dessert for Thanksgiving or even New Year's brunch, and is a heartwarming bite after raking leaves or shoveling snow.

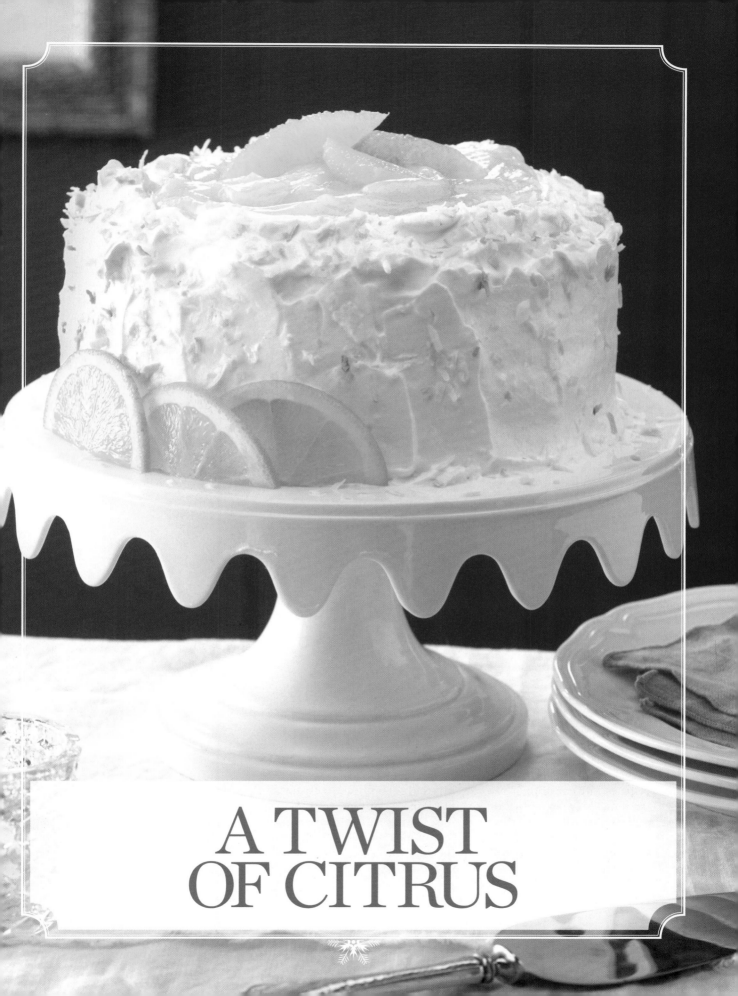

# A TWIST OF CITRUS

# Mushroom-Stuffed Flank Steak Roll

My daughter and her family, who live in Hong Kong, love to make my flank steak because it reminds them of home.

—**ETHEL KLYASHEFF** GRANITE CITY, IL

**PREP:** 25 MIN. + MARINATING
**BAKE:** 1¼ HOURS + STANDING
**MAKES:** 6 SERVINGS

- 1 beef flank steak (about 1½ pounds)
- ½ cup lemon juice
- ½ cup soy sauce
- ½ cup honey
- 2 teaspoons ground mustard
- 1 teaspoon pepper
- ½ teaspoon grated lemon peel, optional

**MUSHROOM FILLING**

- 1 pound sliced fresh mushrooms
- 1 medium onion, finely chopped
- ¼ cup butter, cubed
- ½ cup minced fresh parsley
- 2 cups beef broth
- 2 tablespoons cornstarch

**1.** Cut steak horizontally from a long side to within ½ in. of opposite side. Open steak so it lies flat; cover with plastic wrap. Flatten to ¼-in. thickness.
**2.** In a small bowl, combine lemon juice, soy sauce, honey, mustard, pepper and, if desired, peel. Pour half of the marinade into a large resealable plastic bag; add beef. Seal bag and turn to coat; refrigerate overnight. Cover and refrigerate remaining marinade.
**3.** In a large skillet, saute mushrooms and onion in the butter until tender. Remove from the heat; stir in parsley. Drain and discard the marinade. Open the steak; spoon the filling over steak to within ½ in. of the edges. Roll up tightly jelly-roll style, starting with a long side. Tie with kitchen string. Place in a greased shallow roasting pan. Pour reserved marinade over steak.
**4.** Cover; bake at 350° for 45 minutes. Uncover; baste with pan drippings. Bake 30 minutes longer or until the meat reaches desired doneness (for medium-rare, a thermometer should read 145°, medium, 160°, well-done, 170°). Remove and keep warm.
**5.** Meanwhile, transfer the cooking juices to a saucepan; skim the fat. Bring the cooking juices to a boil. Mix the beef broth and cornstarch until smooth. Stir into the cooking juices. Bring to a boil; cook and stir 1-2 minutes or until thickened. Cut the steak roll into slices and serve with the sauce.

## Holiday Helper

I grate the peel from oranges, lemons and limes before I use them. Then I either freeze or dry it so I always have zest on hand.

—**REBECCA B.** SALT LAKE CITY, UT

## Brussels Sprouts and Mandarin Oranges

This bright, wholesome side dish goes on the dinner table in just 30 minutes. What's more, it requires only a handful of simple ingredients. Holiday cooking doesn't get much easier than that!

—MONIQUE HOOKER DESOTO, WI

**START TO FINISH:** 30 MIN. • **MAKES:** 4 SERVINGS

- 1 **pound fresh Brussels sprouts, halved**
- 1 **cup shredded celery root**
- ⅓ **cup finely chopped onion**
- 4 **teaspoons olive oil**
- 1½ **teaspoons grated tangerine peel**
- 2 **tangerines, peeled and sectioned**

**1.** In a large saucepan, bring ½ in. of water to a boil. Add Brussels sprouts; cover and cook for 8-10 minutes or until crisp-tender. Drain.

**2.** In a large nonstick skillet, saute celery root and onion in oil until tender. Add tangerine peel and Brussels sprouts. Cover and cook for 5-6 minutes or until vegetables are tender. Gently stir in tangerines; serve immediately.

## Luscious Lime Slush

Guests really go for this frosty, sweet-tart refresher. If you prefer, swap in lemonade concentrate for the limeade.

—BONNIE JOST MANITOWOC, WI

**PREP:** 20 MIN. + FREEZING • **MAKES:** 28 SERVINGS (¾ CUP EACH)

- 9 **cups water**
- 4 **individual green tea bags**
- 2 **cans (12 ounces each) frozen limeade concentrate, thawed**
- 2 **cups sugar**
- 2 **cups lemon rum or rum**
- 7 **cups lemon-lime soda, chilled**

**1.** In a Dutch oven, bring the water to a boil. Remove from the heat; add the tea bags. Cover and steep for 3-5 minutes. Discard the tea bags. Stir in the limeade concentrate, sugar and rum.

**2.** Transfer to a 4-qt. freezer container; cool. Cover and freeze for 6 hours or overnight.

**TO USE FROZEN LIMEADE MIXTURE** *Combine limeade mixture and lemon-lime soda in a 4-qt. pitcher. Or for one serving, combine ½ cup limeade mixture and ¼ cup soda in a glass. Serve immediately.*

## Roasted Herb & Lemon Cauliflower

A standout cauliflower side is easy to prepare with just a few ingredients. Crushed red pepper flakes add a touch of heat.

—**SUSAN HEIN** BURLINGTON, WI

**PREP:** 15 MIN. • **BAKE:** 25 MIN. • **MAKES:** 4 SERVINGS

- 1 medium head cauliflower, cut into florets (about 6 cups)
- 4 tablespoons olive oil, divided
- ¼ cup minced fresh parsley
- 1 tablespoon minced fresh rosemary
- 1 tablespoon minced fresh thyme
- 1 teaspoon grated lemon peel
- 2 tablespoons lemon juice
- ½ teaspoon salt
- ¼ teaspoon crushed red pepper flakes

**1.** Preheat oven to 425°. Place cauliflower in an ungreased 15x10x1-in. baking pan. Drizzle with 2 tablespoons oil and toss to coat. Roast 20-25 minutes or until golden brown and tender, stirring occasionally.

**2.** In a small bowl, combine remaining ingredients; stir in remaining oil. Transfer cauliflower to a large bowl; drizzle with herb mixture and toss to combine.

## Gingered Lemon Cheese Balls

Roll your cheese balls in the gingersnap crumbs just before serving to keep the cookie bits crisp and crunchy—a nice contrast to the smooth, creamy spread underneath.

—**LIBBY WALP** CHICAGO, IL

**PREP:** 15 MIN. + CHILLING
**MAKES:** 2 CHEESE BALLS (1½ CUPS EACH)

- 2 packages (8 ounces each) cream cheese, softened
- ½ cup butter, softened
- ⅓ cup sugar
- 3 tablespoons light brown sugar
- 3 tablespoons grated lemon peel
- 2 tablespoons lemon juice
- 1 teaspoon vanilla extract
- 10 gingersnap cookies, crushed
  Assorted sliced fresh fruit and graham crackers

**1.** In a large bowl, beat the cream cheese, butter and sugars until smooth. Stir in the grated lemon peel, lemon juice and vanilla. Shape the mixture into two balls. Cover; refrigerate for at least 4 hours.

**2.** Just before serving, place cookie crumbs in a shallow bowl. Roll balls in crumbs. Serve with fruit and crackers.

4. Stir in the flour until blended. Cook 30-45 seconds, stirring to loosen browned bits from pan. Gradually stir in broth and reserved marinade. Bring to a boil, stirring constantly; cook and stir 1-2 minutes or until thickened.

5. Stir in the green onions, roasted garlic, orange peel and remaining minced thyme. Return the chicken to pan; reduce heat to medium-low. Cook, covered, 4-5 minutes or until a thermometer inserted in the meat reads 165°. If desired, serve chicken with orange slices and thyme sprigs.

## Citrus Candle

Freshen up your holiday table! Cut an orange or other citrus fruit in half and remove the fruit from the shell. Then wash and dry the shell and rub the outside with olive oil. Melt candle wax using a double boiler, and add a few drops of essential oil if you like. Place a candle wick in the center of the shell and pour the melted wax around the wick.

## Orange-Thyme Chicken in Garlic Sauce

The roasted garlic sauce in this recipe makes ordinary chicken breasts amazing. To switch things up, replace the orange juice and zest with lime.

—**CHARLENE CHAMBERS** ORMOND BEACH, FL

**START TO FINISH:** 30 MIN.
**MAKES:** 4 SERVINGS

- 2 cups orange juice
- 3 tablespoons minced fresh thyme or 3 teaspoons dried thyme, divided
- 4 boneless skinless chicken breast halves (6 ounces each)
- 3 tablespoons butter
- ½ teaspoon salt
- ¼ teaspoon freshly ground pepper
- 1 tablespoon all-purpose flour
- ⅔ cup chicken broth
- 4 green onions, chopped
- 1 tablespoon jarred roasted minced garlic
- 1 teaspoon grated orange peel
  Orange slices, optional
  Fresh thyme sprigs, optional

1. Place the juice and 2 tablespoons thyme in an 8-in.-square baking dish; add the chicken. Refrigerate, covered, 30 minutes.

2. Remove the chicken from the juice mixture; pat the chicken dry. Reserve ⅓ cup of the marinade; discard the remaining marinade.

3. In a large skillet, heat the butter over medium-high heat. Add chicken; sprinkle with salt and pepper. Cook chicken 2-3 minutes on each side or until lightly browned. Using tongs, remove chicken from pan, reserving the butter in pan.

# Coconut Citrus Layer Cake

Make a showstopper holiday treat: tender white cake layered with tangy grapefruit curd and topped with fluffy cream cheese frosting. To make it more spectacular add a little toasted coconut and some citrus garnishes. Your guests will never guess you started with a convenient boxed mix.

**—CARMELL CHILDS** FERRON, UT

**PREP:** 40 MIN. + CHILLING
**BAKE:** 30 MIN. + COOLING
**MAKES:** 12 SERVINGS

- 1 **package white cake mix (regular size)**
- ⅔ **cup orange juice**
- ⅓ **cup canola oil**
- ¼ **cup water**
- 2 **tablespoons lemon juice**
- 1 **teaspoon grated lemon peel**
- 1 **teaspoon grated orange peel**
- 3 **large eggs**

**GRAPEFRUIT CURD FILLING**
- ¾ **cup sugar**
- 3 **tablespoons cornstarch**
- ¼ **teaspoon salt**
- ¾ **cup water**
- ⅔ **cup ruby red grapefruit juice**
- 1 **tablespoon butter**

**FROSTING**
- ¾ **cup whipped cream cheese**
- ¼ **cup sugar**
- 3 **tablespoons orange juice**
- 1 **tablespoon ruby red grapefruit juice**
- 2 **teaspoons grated orange peel**
- 1 **cup heavy whipping cream, whipped**
- ¾ **cup flaked coconut**
  **Toasted flaked coconut, optional**
  **Orange and grapefruit slices**

**1.** In a large bowl, combine cake mix, orange juice, oil, water, lemon juice, peels and eggs; beat on low speed for 30 seconds. Beat on medium for 2 minutes. Pour into two greased and floured 8-in. baking pans. Bake at 350° for 28-32 minutes or until a toothpick inserted near center comes out clean. Cool for 10 minutes before removing from pans to wire racks to cool completely.

**2.** Combine sugar, cornstarch and salt in a saucepan. Stir in water and grapefruit juice until smooth. Cook and stir over medium-high heat until thickened and bubbly. Reduce heat; cook and stir for 2 minutes longer. Remove from heat; gently stir in the butter. Cool to room temperature without stirring. Cover the pan and refrigerate filling until chilled.

**3.** Place one cake layer on a serving plate; top with half the filling. Repeat.

**4.** In a large bowl, beat cream cheese, sugar, juices and peel until blended. Gently fold in the whipped cream and coconut. Spread over the sides of the cake. If desired lightly frost the top. Refrigerate until cold, 3-4 hours. Sprinkle top with toasted coconut if desired; top with fruit slices.

## Christmas Coleslaw

In our family, this is a must-have side dish for Christmas dinner. The colorful slaw combines sweet, crunchy and nutty ingredients with tongue-tingling results. It's such a refreshing counterpoint to our meaty main course.

—**LYNDSAY WELLS** LADYSMITH, BC

**PREP:** 15 MIN. + CHILLING
**MAKES:** 8 SERVINGS

- 1 **package (14 ounces) coleslaw mix**
- 1 **medium Granny Smith apple, chopped**
- 1 **cup slivered almonds, toasted**
- ½ **cup maraschino cherries, halved**
- 1 **cup reduced-fat mayonnaise**
- ¼ **cup 1% milk**
- 2 **tablespoons unsweetened applesauce**
- ¾ **teaspoon salt**
- ¼ **teaspoon paprika**
- ¼ **teaspoon pepper**
- 1 **can (11 ounces) mandarin oranges, drained**

**1.** In a large bowl, combine coleslaw mix, apple, almonds and cherries; toss to combine.

**2.** In a small bowl, whisk mayonnaise, milk, applesauce, salt, paprika and pepper until blended. Pour over the coleslaw mixture; toss to coat. Gently stir in mandarin oranges. Refrigerate until serving.

**NOTE** *To toast nuts, bake in a shallow pan in a 350° oven for 5-10 minutes or cook in a skillet over low heat until lightly browned, stirring occasionally.*

### Holiday Helper

Don't have all of the ingredients for Christmas Coleslaw? Feel free to experiment with other fruits or vegetables. For example, try using seedless grapes, raisins, pineapple tidbits, celery or green pepper. You could also replace the almonds with different nuts or sunflower seeds.

## Honey-Orange Glazed Pork Loin

After discovering this idea in a magazine, I changed it up to make it my own. I like to keep a pork loin in the freezer so we can have this special dish anytime.

**—MARLYS PETERSON** CENTERVILLE, SD

**PREP:** 10 MIN.
**BAKE:** 1¼ HOURS + STANDING
**MAKES:** 12 SERVINGS

- 1 cup orange juice
- ½ cup cider vinegar
- ½ cup packed brown sugar
- ¼ cup honey
- 2 tablespoons chili powder
- 1 tablespoon ground coriander
- 1 tablespoon ground cumin
- 1½ teaspoons ground cinnamon
- 1 boneless whole pork loin roast (4 pounds)
- 1 teaspoon salt
- ¼ teaspoon pepper
  Orange slices, optional

**1.** In a small saucepan, combine the first eight ingredients. Bring to a boil. Reduce the heat; simmer, uncovered, for 45 minutes or until the glaze is reduced to 1 cup.

**2.** Sprinkle the pork roast with the salt and pepper. Place the roast on a rack in a shallow roasting pan lined with heavy-duty foil. Bake roast at 350° for 1¼-1¾ hours or until a thermometer reads 160°, brushing occasionally with glaze. Let stand for 10 minutes before slicing. If desired, serve with orange slices.

### Holiday Helper

I keep cans of frozen orange juice concentrate in the freezer so I can easily make small amounts when needed. The ratio to reconstitute the juice is 3 parts water to 1 part concentrate. After opening the can, I keep the whole container in a resealable plastic bag.

**—PEGGY S.** HOT SPRINGS VILLAGE, AR

## Candied Lemon Christmas Bread

Make your baking pay off in a big way: with four large, moist, slightly sweet loaves, you'll have extras for gifts.

**—MICHAELA ROSENTHAL** INDIO, CA

**PREP:** 30 MIN. + RISING
**BAKE:** 35 MIN. + COOLING
**MAKES:** 4 LOAVES (12 SLICES EACH)

- 9¾ to 10¼ cups bread flour
- ¾ cup sugar
- 3 packages (¼ ounce each) active dry yeast
- 2 cans (12 ounces each) reduced-fat evaporated milk
- 1 cup (8 ounces) reduced-fat plain yogurt
- 1 cup butter, cubed
- ½ cup water
- 1 teaspoon vanilla extract
- 1 cup chopped candied lemon peel
- 6 large egg yolks
- 2 large eggs

**1.** In a large small bowl, combine 9¼ cups flour, sugar and yeast. In a large saucepan, heat the milk, yogurt, butter and water to 120°-130°; stir in the vanilla and peel. Add to the dry ingredients. Beat on medium speed for 2 minutes. Add egg yolks, eggs and ½ cup flour; beat 2 minutes longer. Stir in enough remaining flour to form a firm dough.

**2.** Turn the dough onto a lightly floured surface; knead until smooth and elastic, about 6-8 minutes. Place in a bowl coated with cooking spray, turning once to coat the top. Cover; let rise in a warm place until doubled, about 1 hour.

**3.** Punch the dough down. Shape into loaves. Place on baking sheets coated with cooking spray. Cover and let rise until doubled, about 30 minutes.

**4.** Bake at 350° for 35-40 minutes or until golden brown. Remove from pans to cool on wire racks.

# Lemony Walnut-Raisin Galette

This flaky, buttery pastry dessert has a filling of fruit, walnuts, coconut and cinnamon. There's a lot to love! For even more appeal, dollop sweetened whipped cream on top of each serving.

**—ELLEN KOZAK** MILWAUKEE, WI

**PREP:** 30 MIN. • **BAKE:** 30 MIN. + COOLING
**MAKES:** 10 SERVINGS

- 1 **medium lemon**
- 1 **cup finely chopped walnuts**
- 1 **cup raisins**
- 1 **cup apricot spreadable fruit**
- ⅔ **cup finely shredded unsweetened coconut**
- 2 **teaspoons ground cinnamon**
- 8 **sheets phyllo dough (14x9-inch size)**
- ⅓ **cup butter, melted**
  **Sweetened whipped cream, optional**

**1.** Preheat oven to 350°. Cut unpeeled lemon into eight wedges; remove the seeds. Place the lemon wedges in a food processor; process until finely chopped. Transfer to a large bowl; stir in walnuts, raisins, spreadable fruit, coconut and cinnamon.

**2.** Place one sheet of phyllo dough on a parchment paper-lined baking sheet; brush with butter. Layer with remaining phyllo sheets, brushing each layer. (Keep remaining phyllo covered with plastic wrap and a damp towel to prevent it from drying out.)

**3.** Spoon filling onto center of phyllo, leaving a 2 in. border on all sides. Fold the edges of phyllo over filling, leaving center uncovered. Brush folded edges with butter. Bake 30-35 minutes or until golden brown. Using parchment paper, carefully slide the galette onto a wire rack to cool. If desired, serve with whipped cream.

**NOTE** *Look for unsweetened coconut in the baking or health food section.*

## Pink Grapefruit Cheesecake

Cheesecake from a slow cooker? Yes. My mini version never goes in the oven.

**—KRISTA LANPHIER** MILWAUKEE, WI

**PREP:** 20 MIN. • **COOK:** 2 HOURS + CHILLING
**MAKES:** 6 SERVINGS

- ¾ **cup graham cracker crumbs**
- 1 **tablespoon plus ⅔ cup sugar, divided**
- 1 **teaspoon grated grapefruit peel**
- ¼ **teaspoon ground ginger**
- 2½ **tablespoons butter, melted**
- 2 **packages (8 ounces each) cream cheese, softened**
- ½ **cup sour cream**
- 2 **tablespoons pink grapefruit juice**
- 2 **large eggs, lightly beaten**

**1.** Place a greased 6-in. springform pan on a double thickness of heavy-duty foil (about 12-in. square). Wrap foil securely around pan. Pour 1 in. water into a 6-qt. slow cooker. Layer two 24-in. pieces of aluminum foil. Starting with a long side, fold up foil to create a 1-in.-wide strip; roll into a coil. Place in slow cooker to form a rack for the cheesecake.

**2.** In a small bowl, mix the crumbs, 1 tablespoon sugar, peel and ginger; stir in butter. Press onto bottom and about 1 in. up sides of prepared pan.

**3.** In a large bowl, beat cream cheese and the remaining sugar until smooth. Beat in the sour cream and grapefruit juice. Add the eggs and beat on low speed just until combined.

**4.** Pour into the graham cracker crust. Place the springform pan on top of the coil. Cover slow cooker with a double layer of paper towels; place the lid securely over the paper towels. Cook, covered, on high for 2 hours. Do not remove the lid; turn off slow cooker and let the cheesecake stand, covered, in the slow cooker 1 hour. The center of the cheesecake will be just set and the top will appear dull.

**5.** Remove the springform pan from the slow cooker; remove the foil from the pan. Cool the cheesecake on a wire rack 1 hour.

**6.** Loosen the sides from pan with a knife but do not remove. Refrigerate overnight, covering when completely cooled. Remove the rim from pan.

## Mediterranean Rack of Lamb

When guests see this impressive rack of lamb, they'll think you went all out. No one will guess how simple it really is.

—**SUSAN NILSSON** STERLING, VA

**PREP:** 10 MIN. • **BAKE:** 30 MIN.
**MAKES:** 4 SERVINGS

- 2 **racks of lamb (1½ pounds each)**
- ¼ **cup grated lemon peel**
- ¼ **cup minced fresh oregano or 4 teaspoons dried oregano**
- 6 **garlic cloves, minced**
- 1 **tablespoon olive oil**
- ¼ **teaspoon salt**
- ¼ **teaspoon pepper**
  **Fresh oregano and lemon slices, optional**

**1.** Preheat oven to 375°. Place lamb in a shallow roasting pan. In small bowl, combine grated lemon peel, oregano, garlic, oil, salt and pepper. Rub over meat.

**2.** Bake the lamb 30-40 minutes or until the meat reaches desired doneness (for medium-rare, a thermometer should read 145°; medium, 160°; well-done, 170°). Let stand 5 minutes before cutting. If desired, serve with fresh oregano and lemon slices.

## No-Knead Citrus Rolls

Treat 'em to homemade breakfast rolls without getting up at the break of dawn. This dough goes together the night before and doesn't require kneading.

—**MARGARET OTLEY** WAVERLY, NE

**PREP:** 20 MIN. + CHILLING • **BAKE:** 20 MIN.
**MAKES:** 2½ DOZEN

- 2 packages (¼ ounce each) active dry yeast
- 7 tablespoons sugar, divided
- ¼ cup warm water (110° to 115°)
- 3½ to 4 cups all-purpose flour
- 1 teaspoon salt
- ¾ cup cold butter, divided
- 1 cup warm heavy whipping cream (110° to 115°)
- 3 large egg yolks, lightly beaten

**FILLING**
- ½ cup sugar
- 2 tablespoons grated lemon peel
- 2 tablespoons grated orange peel

**GLAZE**
- 1⅓ cups confectioners' sugar
- 2 tablespoons 2% milk
- 1 tablespoon lemon juice
- 1 tablespoon orange juice

**1.** Dissolve yeast and 1 tablespoon sugar in the warm water in a small bowl. Let stand 5 minutes. In a large bowl, combine 3½ cups of flour, the remaining sugar and salt. Cut in ½ cup butter until crumbly. Add the yeast mixture, cream and egg yolks. Add enough remaining flour to form a soft dough. Place in a greased bowl, turning once to grease top. Refrigerate for 6-8 hours or overnight.

**2.** Punch dough down. Turn onto a lightly floured surface. Divide in half; roll each into a 15x12-in. rectangle. Melt remaining butter; brush over dough. Combine filling ingredients; sprinkle over dough.

**3.** Roll up, jelly-roll style, beginning with a long side; pinch seam to seal. Cut each roll into 15 slices; place the slices cut side down in two greased 9-in. pie plates. Cover; let rise until doubled, about 45 minutes.

**4.** Bake at 375° for 20-25 minutes or until golden brown. Combine the glaze ingredients until smooth; drizzle over the warm rolls. Cool in the pans on wire racks.

## Zesty Lemon Cream Turkey Pasta

Here's a main dish recipe you'll want to keep handy year-round. It's elegant enough for Christmas get-togethers but easy enough for any weeknight.

—**STEPHANIE DECKER** HAPPY VALLEY, OR

**PREP:** 20 MIN. • **COOK:** 15 MIN.
**MAKES:** 4 SERVINGS

- 2 tablespoons olive oil
- 1 pound ground turkey
- 1 medium onion, chopped
- ½ medium sweet red pepper, chopped
- 1 cup fresh baby spinach
- 1 garlic clove, minced
- 3 teaspoons curry powder
- 3 teaspoons ground coriander
- ½ teaspoon salt
- ½ teaspoon pepper
- ¼ teaspoon crushed red pepper flakes
- 1 cup chicken broth
- 1½ teaspoons grated lemon peel
- 3 tablespoons lemon juice
- 1 tablespoon sugar
- 1 tablespoon reduced-sodium soy sauce, optional
- ½ cup sour cream
  Hot cooked wide egg noodles

**1.** In a large skillet, heat the oil over medium heat. Add turkey, onion and red pepper; cook and stir 6-8 minutes or until turkey is no longer pink and vegetables are tender, breaking up turkey into crumbles; drain.

**2.** Stir in the spinach, garlic and seasonings; cook 1-2 minutes longer. In a small bowl, combine broth, lemon peel, lemon juice, sugar and, if desired, soy sauce; pour over turkey mixture. Bring to a boil. Reduce heat; simmer, uncovered, 6-8 minutes or until liquid is reduced by half.

**3.** Remove from the heat; stir in the sour cream. Serve with egg noodles.

## Halibut with Citrus-Olive Sauce

Transform mild halibut fillets into an elegant, flavorful entree you'll want not only during the holiday season, but year round. The chunky topping features two kinds of olives.

**—GLORIA BRADLEY** NAPERVILLE, IL

**PREP:** 30 MIN. • **COOK:** 15 MIN.
**MAKES:** 4 SERVINGS

- 2½ cups orange juice, divided
- ⅓ cup white wine
- 2 tablespoons lime juice
- 2 tablespoons chopped shallot
- ¼ cup butter, cut into four pieces
- 2 tablespoons chopped sweet red pepper
- 1 tablespoon chopped pitted green olives
- 1 tablespoon chopped Greek olives
- 3 garlic cloves, minced
- 1 teaspoon dried oregano
- 4 halibut fillets (6 ounces each)

**1.** In a small saucepan, bring 1½ cups orange juice, white wine, lime juice and shallot to a boil; cook until liquid is reduced to ½ cup, about 15 minutes. Reduce heat to low; gradually whisk in the butter until butter is melted. Remove from heat; stir in red pepper and olives. Keep warm.

**2.** In a large skillet, bring the garlic, oregano and remaining orange juice to a boil. Reduce the heat; add the halibut fillets and steam, uncovered, for 8-10 minutes or until fish flakes easily with a fork. Serve with sauce.

---

### Holiday Helper

When I need canned pineapple but not the drained juice, I save it to make an easy marinade for chicken breasts. I just add a little oil, soy sauce and garlic, then refrigerate the chicken overnight in the marinade. The next day, the chicken is ready to bake.

**—LENORA C.** TALLAHASSEE, FL

---

## Christmas Morning French Toast

I dress up French toast for Christmastime by stuffing thick bread slices with a nutty, fruity cream-cheese filling. You can skip the maple syrup—the recipe includes a simple but delectable orange sauce.

**—JANET CAICO** FLEMING ISLAND, FL

**PREP:** 25 MIN. • **BAKE:** 5 MIN./BATCH
**MAKES:** 12 SERVINGS

- 1 package (8 ounces) cream cheese, softened
- ½ cup crushed pineapple, drained
- 1 jar (12 ounces) orange marmalade, divided
- ½ cup chopped pecans, toasted
- 12 slices French bread (1½ inches thick)
- 5 large eggs
- 2 teaspoons brown sugar
- 1 teaspoon ground cinnamon
- ½ teaspoon vanilla extract
- ⅛ teaspoon ground nutmeg
- 1½ cups heavy whipping cream, divided
- ¼ cup orange juice
  Confectioners' sugar

**1.** In a small bowl, beat cream cheese, pineapple and ¼ cup of marmalade until light and fluffy. Stir in pecans. Cut a pocket in the side of each bread slice; fill with cream cheese mixture.

**2.** In a shallow bowl, whisk eggs, brown sugar, cinnamon, vanilla, nutmeg and 1 cup cream. Dip both sides of bread into the egg mixture.

**3.** Cook on a greased hot griddle for 2-3 minutes on each side or until golden brown.

**4.** Meanwhile, in a small saucepan, combine the orange juice and remaining marmalade. Cook and stir over medium heat until smooth. Add remaining cream; heat through. Dust French toast with confectioners' sugar and serve with sauce.

# MAKE-AHEAD
# COOKIES

# Apricot Pinwheels

I decorate my little spirals with vanilla icing, but they're yummy without it, too. Dried apricots and lots of spice give the cookies Old World flavor.

**—BEVERLY SADERGASKI** ST. CLOUD, MN

**PREP:** 45 MIN. + CHILLING
**BAKE:** 10 MIN./BATCH + COOLING
**MAKES:** 8 DOZEN

- 1 **cup chopped dried apricots**
- ¾ **cup water**
- ½ **cup sugar**
- 1 **cup finely chopped pecans**
- 1 **cup butter, softened**
- 2 **cups packed brown sugar**
- 2 **large eggs**
- 3½ **cups all-purpose flour**
- ½ **teaspoon baking soda**
- ½ **teaspoon salt**
- ¼ **teaspoon ground nutmeg**
- ⅛ **teaspoon ground cardamom**
- ⅛ **teaspoon ground cloves**

**ICING**
- 1½ **cups confectioners' sugar**
- 6 **tablespoons butter, softened**
- ¾ **teaspoon vanilla extract**
- 1 **to 2 tablespoons 2% milk**

**1.** In a small saucepan, combine apricots, water and sugar. Bring to a boil. Reduce heat; simmer, uncovered, 10 minutes. Cool slightly. Transfer to a blender; cover and process until pureed. Stir in pecans; set aside.

**2.** In a large bowl, cream butter and brown sugar until light and fluffy. Beat in eggs. In a large bowl, whisk flour, baking soda, salt, nutmeg, cardamom and cloves; gradually add to creamed mixture and mix well. Refrigerate, covered, at least 2 hours or overnight.

**3.** Divide dough into two portions. On a baking sheet, roll out each portion between two sheets of waxed paper into a 15x9-in. rectangle. Refrigerate 30 minutes.

**4.** Remove waxed paper. Spread half of the apricot mixture over one portion of dough. Roll up tightly jelly-roll style, starting with a long side; wrap in plastic wrap. Repeat with remaining dough. Refrigerate 2 hours or until firm.

**5.** Unwrap and cut into ¼-in. slices. Place 2 in. apart on lightly greased baking sheets. Bake at 350° for 10-12 minutes or until lightly browned. Remove to wire racks.

**6.** In a small bowl, mix confectioners' sugar, butter, vanilla and enough milk to achieve desired consistency. Pipe onto cool cookies. Let stand until set.

**TO MAKE AHEAD** *Dough can be made 2 days in advance. Wrap logs in plastic wrap and place in a resealable bag. Store in the refrigerator.*

**FREEZE OPTION** *Place wrapped logs in resealable plastic freezer bags and freeze. To use, unwrap frozen logs and cut into slices. Bake as directed.*

## White Chocolate Maple Bacon Fudge

Bored with the same old fudge? Prepare it with white chips, add maple flavoring and load it up with bacon. Then be prepared to share the recipe!

—**MINDIE HILTON** SUSANVILLE, CA

**PREP:** 10 MIN. + CHILLING
**MAKES:** ABOUT 2½ POUNDS

- 1 **teaspoon plus ¼ cup butter, cubed, divided**
- 10 **slices ready-to-serve fully cooked bacon**
- 2 **packages (10 to 12 ounces each) white baking chips**
- 1 **can (14 ounces) sweetened condensed milk**
- ¾ **teaspoon maple flavoring**

**1.** Line a 9-in. square pan with foil; grease foil with 1 teaspoon of butter. Heat bacon according to package directions. Crumble bacon and set aside.

**2.** In a large microwave-safe bowl, combine baking chips, condensed milk, flavoring and remaining butter. Microwave on high 1 minute; stir until smooth. (If baking chips aren't completely melted, microwave for 10- to 20-second intervals until melted; stir until smooth.) Stir in the bacon; pour into prepared pan. Refrigerate, covered, 2 hours or until firm.

**3.** Using foil, lift fudge out of pan. Remove the foil; cut fudge into 1-in. squares.

**TO MAKE AHEAD** *Store fudge, layered between waxed paper, in an airtight container in the refrigerator. Serve at room temperature.*

**FREEZE OPTION** *Wrap fudge in waxed paper, then in foil. Place in freezer containers and freeze. To thaw, bring wrapped fudge to room temperature.*

## Easy Microwave Mint Fudge

I make these creamy, smooth squares not only for Christmas, but also for Valentine's Day. This easy microwave fudge is just as good as any you'd buy in a confectionery.

**—DONNA ROBERTS** MANHATTAN, KS

**PREP:** 15 MIN. + CHILLING
**MAKES:** ABOUT 3 POUNDS (117 PIECES)

- 2 teaspoons butter
- 7½ cups confectioners' sugar
- 1 cup baking cocoa
- 15 tablespoons butter, softened
- 7 tablespoons 2% milk
- 2 teaspoons vanilla extract
- 1 cup Andes creme de menthe baking chips

**1.** Line a 13x9-in. pan with foil; grease foil with 2 teaspoons butter.

**2.** In a large microwave-safe bowl, sift together confectioners' sugar and cocoa. Add butter and milk (do not stir). Microwave on high 2-2½ minutes. Remove from microwave; stir until blended. Stir in vanilla. Spread into prepared pan. Sprinkle with baking chips, pressing chips lightly into fudge. Refrigerate 1 hour or until firm.

**3.** Using foil, lift fudge out of pan. Remove foil; cut fudge into 1-in. squares. Store in an airtight container in the refrigerator.

**TO MAKE AHEAD** *Store fudge, layered between waxed paper, in an airtight container in the refrigerator. Serve at room temperature.*

**FREEZE OPTION** *Wrap fudge in waxed paper, then in foil. Place in freezer containers and freeze. To thaw, bring wrapped fudge to room temperature.*

## Gingerbread Caramels

I created this recipe for two simple reasons: I love caramel, and I love molasses! Combining those ingredients resulted in my new favorite candy.

—**WENDY RUSCH** TREGO, WI

**PREP:** 10 MIN. • **COOK:** 30 MIN. + STANDING
**MAKES:** ABOUT 2 POUNDS

- 2 **teaspoons butter**
- ½ **cup butter, cubed**
- 2 **cups packed brown sugar**
- 1 **can (14 ounces) sweetened condensed milk**
- ⅔ **cup dark molasses**
- ⅓ **cup dark corn syrup**
- ¾ **teaspoon ground ginger**
- ¾ **teaspoon ground allspice**
- ½ **teaspoon salt**
- ¼ **teaspoon pepper**
- 1 **teaspoon vanilla extract**

**1.** Line a 9-in. square baking pan with foil; grease foil with 2 teaspoons butter.
**2.** In a large heavy saucepan, combine cubed butter, brown sugar, milk, molasses, corn syrup, ginger, allspice, salt and pepper. Cook and stir over medium heat until a candy thermometer reads 238° (soft-ball stage).
**3.** Using a pastry brush dipped in water, wash down the sides of the pan to eliminate sugar crystals. Cook and stir until thermometer reads 245° (firm-ball stage).
**4.** Remove from heat; stir in vanilla. Immediately pour into prepared pan (do not scrape saucepan). Let stand until firm, about 4 hours or overnight. Refrigerate 1 hour.
**5.** Using foil, lift candy out of pan; remove foil. Using a buttered knife, cut caramel into 1-in. squares. Wrap individually in waxed paper; twist ends.
**TO MAKE AHEAD** *Store wrapped caramels in an airtight container at room temperature.*
**FREEZE OPTION** *Place wrapped caramels in a freezer container and freeze. Thaw at room temperature.*

## Mexican Chocolate Sugar Crisps

My grandma loved these so much, she would hide them from my grandpa! I think of her every time I make a batch. Like Mexican spice? Try stirring in a little chili powder.

—**MICHELE LOVIO** THOUSAND OAKS, CA

**PREP:** 30 MIN. • **BAKE:** 10 MIN./BATCH • **MAKES:** 4½ DOZEN

- ¾ **cup shortening**
- 1¼ **cups sugar, divided**
- 1 **large egg**
- ¼ **cup light corn syrup**
- 2 **ounces unsweetened chocolate, melted and cooled**
- 1¾ **cups all-purpose flour**
- 1½ **teaspoons ground cinnamon**
- 1 **teaspoon baking soda**
- ¼ **teaspoon salt**
- 1 **cup (6 ounces) semisweet chocolate chips**

**1.** Preheat oven to 350°. In a large bowl, cream shortening and 1 cup sugar until fluffy. Beat in egg, corn syrup and melted chocolate. In another bowl, whisk flour, cinnamon, baking soda and salt; gradually beat into creamed mixture. Stir in chocolate chips.
**2.** Shape dough into 1-in. balls; roll in remaining sugar. Place cookies 2 in. apart on ungreased baking sheets (do not flatten). Bake 8-10 minutes or until tops are puffed and cracked. Cool on pans 2 minutes. Remove to wire racks to cool.
**TO MAKE AHEAD** *Dough can be made 2 days in advance. Wrap in plastic wrap and place in a resealable bag. Store in the refrigerator.*
**FREEZE OPTION** *Freeze shaped balls of dough on baking sheets until firm. Transfer to resealable plastic freezer bags; return to freezer. To use, bake cookies as directed.*

# Hungarian Walnut Cookies

As a child, I always looked forward to eating these goodies at Christmastime. Now I make them for my own family.

—**SHARON KURTZ** EMMAUS, PA

**PREP:** 50 MIN. + CHILLING
**BAKE:** 10 MIN./BATCH + COOLING
**MAKES:** 4 DOZEN

- 1 **cup butter, softened**
- 1 **package (8 ounces) cream cheese, softened**
- 2½ **cups all-purpose flour**

**FILLING**
- 3 **large egg whites**
- ¾ **teaspoon vanilla extract**
- ⅓ **cup sugar**
- 3½ **cups ground walnuts**
  **Confectioners' sugar**

**1.** In a large bowl, cream butter and cream cheese until blended. Gradually beat flour into creamed mixture. Divide dough into three portions. Shape each into a disk; wrap in plastic wrap. Refrigerate 1 hour or until firm enough to roll.

**2.** Preheat oven to 375°. For filling, in a small bowl, beat egg whites and vanilla on medium speed until foamy. Gradually add sugar, 1 tablespoon at a time, beating on medium after each addition until well blended. Stir in walnuts.

**3.** Generously coat a work surface with confectioners' sugar. Roll one portion of dough into a 12-in. square, about ⅛-in. thick, sprinkling with additional confectioners' sugar as necessary to coat well. Cut into sixteen 3-in. squares.

**4.** Shape 2 teaspoons filling into a small log, about 2 in. long. Place diagonally onto a square. Overlap opposite corners of dough over filling; pinch tightly to seal. Place 2 in. apart on greased baking sheets. Repeat with remaining dough and filling.

**5.** Bake 9-11 minutes or until bottoms are golden brown. Remove from pans to wire racks to cool completely. Dust with confectioners' sugar.

**TO MAKE AHEAD** *Dough can be made 2 days in advance. Wrap in plastic wrap and place in a resealable bag. Store in the refrigerator.*

**FREEZE OPTION** *Freeze cookies in freezer containers. To use, thaw before serving. If desired, dust with additional confectioners' sugar.*

# Pumpkin Pie Marshmallows

Love pumpkin spice lattes? Let these pale orange, fall-flavored marshmallows slowly melt in your favorite hot coffee or cocoa. Pure bliss!

—**JENNIFER RODRIGUEZ** WEST JORDAN, UT

**PREP:** 30 MIN. • **COOK:** 25 MIN. + STANDING
**MAKES:** ABOUT 9½ DOZEN

- ½ cup plus ¾ cup water, divided
- ½ cup pumpkin pie filling
- 4 envelopes unflavored gelatin
- 3 cups sugar
- 1¼ cups light corn syrup
- ¼ teaspoon salt
- ½ cup confectioners' sugar
- 1½ teaspoons pumpkin pie spice, optional

1. Line a 13x9-in. pan with foil; coat with cooking spray.
2. In a heatproof bowl of a stand mixer, combine ½ cup water and pie filling. Sprinkle gelatin over top to soften.
3. In a large heavy saucepan, combine sugar, corn syrup, salt and the remaining water. Bring to a boil, stirring occasionally. Cook, without stirring, over medium heat until a candy thermometer reads 240° (soft-ball stage).
4. Remove from heat; slowly drizzle into gelatin mixture, beating on high speed. Continue beating until very stiff and doubled in volume, about 10 minutes. Spread into the prepared pan. Cover and let cool at room temperature 6 hours or overnight.
5. In a small bowl, combine confectioners' sugar and, if desired, pumpkin pie spice. Using foil, lift candy out of pan. Using a lightly buttered knife or kitchen scissors, cut into 1-in. pieces. Roll in confectioners' sugar mixture. Store in an airtight container in a cool, dry place.

**TO MAKE AHEAD** *Store marshmallows, layered between waxed paper, in airtight containers in the refrigerator for up to 1 week.*

**FREEZE OPTION** *Freeze marshmallows in freezer containers for up to 1 month.*

**NOTE** *We recommend that you test your candy thermometer before each use by bringing water to a boil; the thermometer should read 212°. Adjust your recipe temperature up or down based on your test.*

# Lemon Slice Sugar Cookies

Here's a refreshing variation of my grandmother's sugar cookie recipe. Lemon pudding mix and icing add a subtle tartness that tingles your taste buds.

—**MELISSA TURKINGTON** CAMANO ISLAND, WA

**PREP:** 15 MIN. + CHILLING • **BAKE:** 10 MIN. + COOLING
**MAKES:** 2 DOZEN

- ½ cup unsalted butter, softened
- 1 package (3.4 ounces) instant lemon pudding mix

- ½ cup sugar
- 1 large egg
- 2 tablespoons 2% milk
- 1½ cups all-purpose flour
- 1 teaspoon baking powder
- ¼ teaspoon salt

**ICING**
- ⅔ cup confectioners' sugar
- 2 to 4 teaspoons lemon juice

1. In a large bowl, cream butter, pudding mix and sugar until light and fluffy. Beat in egg and milk. In another bowl, whisk flour, baking powder and salt; gradually beat into creamed mixture.
2. Divide dough in half. On a lightly floured surface, shape each into a 6-in.-long roll. Wrap in plastic wrap; refrigerate 3 hours or until firm.
3. Preheat oven to 375°. Unwrap and cut dough crosswise into ½-in. slices. Place 1 in. apart on ungreased baking sheets. Bake 8-10 minutes or until edges are light brown. Cool on pans 2 minutes. Remove to wire racks to cool completely.
4. In a small bowl, mix confectioners' sugar and enough lemon juice to reach a drizzling consistency. Drizzle over cookies. Let stand until set.

**TO MAKE AHEAD** *Dough can be made 2 days in advance. Wrap in plastic wrap and place in a resealable bag. Store in the refrigerator.*

**FREEZE OPTION** *Place wrapped logs in a resealable plastic freezer bag and freeze. To use, unwrap frozen logs and cut into slices. Bake as directed, increasing time by 1-2 minutes.*

## Chocolate-Filled Cookies with Peppermint Frosting

Baking is one of the things I enjoy most about Christmas. These special cookies draw you in with candy-topped frosting and seal the deal with a chocolate center.
—**DEBORAH PUETTE** LILBURN, GA

**PREP:** 35 MIN. + CHILLING • **BAKE:** 10 MIN.
**MAKES:** 2 DOZEN

- ⅔ cup shortening
- 1 cup sugar
- 1 large egg
- 1¾ cups all-purpose flour
- ½ teaspoon baking powder
- ½ teaspoon baking soda
- ½ teaspoon salt
- 2 milk chocolate candy bars (1.55 ounces each)

**FROSTING**

- 2 cups confectioners' sugar
- 2 tablespoons unsalted butter, melted
- ¼ teaspoon peppermint extract
- 3 to 4 tablespoons evaporated milk
- 24 miniature candy canes, crushed

**1.** In a large bowl, cream shortening and sugar until light and fluffy. Beat in the egg. In another bowl, whisk flour, baking powder, baking soda and salt; gradually beat into creamed mixture.
**2.** Divide dough in half. Shape each into a disk; wrap in plastic wrap. Refrigerate 30 minutes or until firm enough to roll.
**3.** Preheat oven to 350°. Break each candy bar into 12 pieces. On a lightly floured surface, roll each portion of dough to ⅛-in. thickness. Cut with a floured 2-in. square cookie cutter. Place half of squares 2 in. apart on ungreased baking sheets. Place a chocolate piece in the center of each square; cover with remaining squares, pressing edges to seal.
**4.** Bake 9-11 minutes or until edges are golden brown. Remove from pans to wire racks to cool completely.
**5.** In a small bowl, combine the confectioners' sugar, butter, extract and enough milk to reach a spreading consistency. Spread over cookies;

sprinkle with crushed candies.
**TO MAKE AHEAD** *Dough can be made 2 days in advance. Wrap in plastic wrap and place in a resealable bag. Store in the refrigerator.*
**FREEZE OPTION** *Place wrapped dough in a resealable plastic freezer bag and freeze. If necessary, let dough stand 15 minutes at room temperature before cutting. Prepare and bake cookies as directed. Iced cookies can be frozen for up to 1 month.*

## No-Fuss Filling

When it comes to creating a chocolate filling for these change-of-pace cookies, the answer is simple! Section off a candy bar, set the pieces on a 2-inch square piece of cookie dough and top with a second square of dough. Press the edges to seal and bake as directed. Guests are sure to delight in the sweet surprise that awaits in every bite!

# Christmas Lights Cookies

What better way to brighten chilly winter days than with light-shaped cookies? My classic dough recipe has been a holiday tradition in our family for years.

—CAROLYN MOSELEY DAYTON, OH

**PREP:** 45 MIN. + CHILLING
**BAKE:** 10 MIN./BATCH + COOLING
**MAKES:** 1½ DOZEN

- ½ cup butter, softened
- ½ cup sugar
- 1 large egg
- ¾ teaspoon vanilla extract
- ¼ teaspoon almond extract
- 1¾ cups all-purpose flour
- ½ teaspoon ground cinnamon
- ¼ teaspoon salt
- ¼ teaspoon baking powder

**FROSTING**

- 5 cups confectioners' sugar
- 1 tablespoon light corn syrup
- ¾ teaspoon vanilla extract
- 5 to 6 tablespoons water
  Red, blue, green and yellow paste food coloring
  Silver pearl dust

**1.** In a large bowl, cream butter and sugar until light and fluffy. Beat in egg and extracts. In another bowl, whisk the flour, cinnamon, salt and baking powder; gradually beat into creamed mixture. Shape into a disk; wrap in plastic wrap. Refrigerate 1 hour or until firm enough to roll.

**2.** Preheat oven to 350°. On a lightly floured surface, roll dough to ⅛-in. thickness. Cut with a floured 4-in. Christmas light-shaped cookie cutter. Place 1 in. apart on ungreased baking sheets. Bake 9-11 minutes or until light brown. Remove from pans to wire racks to cool completely.

**3.** In a small bowl, beat confectioners' sugar, corn syrup, vanilla and enough water to reach desired consistency. Reserve ⅔ cup frosting for bottom of cookies and reflections. Divide the remaining frosting between four bowls. Tint one red, one blue, one green and one yellow. Frost tops of cookies. Frost bottom of cookies with about half of the reserved frosting; sprinkle with pearl dust. With remaining white frosting and a #5 round tip, pipe on reflections. Let stand until completely set.

**TO MAKE AHEAD** *Dough can be made 2 days in advance. Wrap in plastic wrap and place in a resealable bag. Store in the refrigerator.*

**FREEZE OPTION** *Freeze undecorated cookies in freezer containers. To use, thaw in covered containers and decorate as desired.*

## Crescent Chip Cookies

With their cute curved shape, crescents always make charming additions to a Christmas platter. I dip the cooled cookies in chocolate and sprinkle on walnuts.

**—ANN EASTMAN** SACRAMENTO, CA

**PREP:** 30 MIN. + CHILLING
**BAKE:** 10 MIN./BATCH + COOLING
**MAKES:** 10 DOZEN

- 1 cup butter, softened
- 1 package (8 ounces) cream cheese, softened
- 2 cups sugar
- 1 large egg
- 1 teaspoon vanilla extract
- ¼ teaspoon almond extract
- 3½ cups all-purpose flour
- 1 teaspoon baking powder
- 1½ cups miniature chocolate chips

**GLAZE**
- 3 cups semisweet chocolate chips
- ¼ cup shortening
- 1¼ cups ground walnuts

**1.** In a large bowl, cream the butter, cream cheese and sugar until light and fluffy. Beat in egg and extracts. In another bowl, whisk flour and baking powder; gradually beat into creamed mixture. Stir in chocolate chips.

**2.** Divide dough into 10 portions. Shape each into a disk; wrap in plastic wrap. Refrigerate 2 hours or until easy to roll.

**3.** Preheat oven to 375°. On a lightly floured surface, roll each portion into a 24-in. rope; cut into 2-in. lengths.

Place 1 in. apart on ungreased baking sheets; curve each piece to form a crescent. Bake 6-8 minutes or until edges are light brown. Remove to wire racks to cool completely.

**4.** In a small bowl, melt chocolate chips and shortening; stir until smooth. Dip each cookie halfway into chocolate mixture; allow excess to drip off. Sprinkle with walnuts. Place on waxed paper; let stand until set.

**TO MAKE AHEAD** *Dough can be made 2 days in advance. Wrap in plastic wrap and place in a resealable bag. Store in the refrigerator.*

**FREEZE OPTION** *Freeze cookies, layered between waxed paper, in freezer containers. To use, thaw before serving.*

# Banana Cream Sandwich Cookies

**PREP:** 40 MIN. + CHILLING
**BAKE:** 10 MIN./BATCH + COOLING
**MAKES:** ABOUT 2½ DOZEN

- 1 **cup butter, softened**
- 1 **cup sugar**
- 1 **medium banana, cut into ¼-inch slices**
- 1 **teaspoon vanilla extract**
- 2⅓ **cups all-purpose flour**
- ¼ **teaspoon salt**
- ½ **cup chopped salted peanuts**

**FROSTING**

- 3 **cups confectioners' sugar**
- 3 **tablespoons creamy peanut butter**
- 2 **tablespoons butter, softened**
- 1 **teaspoon vanilla extract**
- 3 **to 4 tablespoons 2% milk**

**1.** In a large bowl, cream the butter and sugar until light and fluffy. Beat in the banana and vanilla. In another bowl, whisk flour and salt; gradually beat into creamed mixture. Stir in peanuts. Divide dough in half. Shape each into a disk; wrap in plastic wrap. Refrigerate 30 minutes or until firm enough to roll.

**2.** Preheat oven to 350°. On a lightly floured surface, roll each portion of dough to ¼-in. thickness. Cut with a floured 2-in. round cookie cutter. Place 1 in. apart on ungreased baking sheets. Bake 10-12 minutes or until edges are light brown. Remove from pans to wire racks to cool completely.

**3.** In a small bowl, beat confectioners' sugar, peanut butter, butter, vanilla and enough milk to reach spreading consistency. Drop a heaping teaspoon in the center of half of the cookies; press remaining cookies on top to spread frosting.

**TO MAKE AHEAD** *Dough can be made 2 days in advance. Wrap in plastic wrap and place in a resealable bag. Store in the refrigerator.*

**FREEZE OPTION** *Freeze plain cookies in freezer containers. To use, thaw in the covered containers, then prepare as directed.*

*"People go bananas for these!*
*These rich little sandwiches are a nice change of pace on a Christmas platter, and they ship well, too."*

**—ELAINE OWENS** DUBUQUE, IA

## Anise Gumdrops

With their bright color and frosty sugared look, these homemade gumdrops are irresistible. They're softer than the store-bought kind and have tongue-tingling anise flavor.

—**RICHARD BUNT** PAINTED POST, NY

**PREP:** 25 MIN. + STANDING • **MAKES:** 1 POUND

- 4 envelopes unflavored gelatin
- 1¼ cups water, divided
- 2 cups sugar
- ½ teaspoon anise extract
- 4 drops each pink and red food coloring
  Additional sugar

**1.** In a small bowl, sprinkle gelatin over ½ cup water; let stand 5 minutes. In a small saucepan, bring sugar and remaining water to a boil over medium heat, stirring constantly. Reduce heat; simmer, uncovered, 5 minutes. Remove from heat. Stir in gelatin mixture until gelatin is dissolved. Stir in extract.

**2.** Divide mixture between two bowls; tint one pink and the other red with food coloring. Transfer to two greased 8x4-in. loaf pans. Refrigerate 30 minutes or until firm.

**3.** Loosen sides from pan with a knife; turn onto a sugared board. Cut into ½-in. cubes; roll in additional sugar. Let stand, uncovered, at room temperature 3-4 hours or until all sides are dry, turning every hour.

**TO MAKE AHEAD** *Store candy in a covered container. Refrigerate for up to two weeks.*

**FREEZE OPTION** *Freeze candy in an airtight freezer container.*

## Martha Washington Candy

Passed down by my grandmother and mother, this recipe is a cherished family tradition. We've even had each grandchild and great-grandchild take a turn stirring the candy mixture!

—**CINDI BOGER** ARDMORE, AL

**PREP:** 45 MIN. + CHILLING • **MAKES:** ABOUT 8½ DOZEN

- 1 cup butter, softened
- 4 cups confectioners' sugar
- 1 can (14 ounces) sweetened condensed milk
- 1 teaspoon vanilla extract
- 3 cups flaked coconut
- 2 cups chopped pecans, toasted
- 6 cups (36 ounces) semisweet chocolate chips
- ¼ cup shortening

**1.** In a large bowl, beat butter, confectioners' sugar, milk and vanilla until blended. Stir in coconut and pecans. Divide dough in half; refrigerate, covered, 1 hour.

**2.** Working with half the dough at a time, shape mixture into 1-in. balls; place on waxed paper-lined baking sheets. Refrigerate 30 minutes longer.

**3.** In top of a double boiler or a metal bowl over barely simmering water, melt chocolate chips and shortening; stir until smooth. Dip balls in melted chocolate; allow excess to drip off. Return to waxed paper. Refrigerate until set.

**TO MAKE AHEAD** *Store in an airtight container in the refrigerator.*

**FREEZE OPTION** *Freeze candy, layered between waxed paper, in freezer containers. To use, thaw in refrigerator 2 hours before serving.*

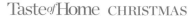

## Christmas Crunch Candy

Treat family and friends to a yummy brittle for the holidays. Made with cashews and Rice Krispies cereal, it's loaded with crunchy goodness.
—**AMANDA MCLEMORE** MARYVILLE, TN

**PREP:** 10 MIN. • **COOK:** 25 MIN. + COOLING
**MAKES:** ABOUT 1½ POUNDS

- 1 teaspoon butter, softened
- 2 cups sugar
- ⅔ cup light corn syrup
- ½ cup water
- 3 tablespoons butter, cubed
- 2 cups Rice Krispies
- 1 cup salted cashews
- 1½ teaspoons baking soda
- 1 teaspoon vanilla extract

**1.** Line a 15x10x1-in. baking pan with foil. Grease foil with 1 teaspoon butter.
**2.** In a large heavy saucepan, combine sugar, corn syrup and water; bring to a boil over medium heat, stirring constantly. Cook and stir over medium heat until a candy thermometer reads 240° (soft-ball stage). Stir in butter; cook without stirring until mixture reaches 300° (hard-crack stage), brushing down sides of pan with a pastry brush dipped in water as needed.
**3.** Remove from heat. Stir in cereal, cashews, baking soda and vanilla. Quickly pour into prepared pan. Using a buttered metal spatula, spread mixture to ¼-in. thickness. Cool completely; break into pieces.
**TO MAKE AHEAD** *Store candy in an airtight container up to 1 month.*

## Cherry Pistachio Cookies

Dried cherries, crunchy nuts, bits of orange, white chocolate—there's a lot to love in this cookie! It's very different from any I've had before.
—**KATHY HARDING** RICHMOND, MO

**PREP:** 25 MIN. + CHILLING • **BAKE:** 10 MIN./BATCH + COOLING
**MAKES:** ABOUT 3½ DOZEN

- 1 cup unsalted butter, softened
- 1½ cups confectioners' sugar
- 1 large egg
- 4 teaspoons grated orange peel
- 2¼ cups all-purpose flour
- 1 teaspoon baking soda
- 1 teaspoon cream of tartar
- 1½ cups chopped dried cherries or cranberries
- ½ cup chopped pistachios
- 8 ounces white baking chocolate, melted

**1.** In a large bowl, cream butter and confectioners' sugar until blended. Beat in egg and orange peel. In another bowl, whisk flour, baking soda and cream of tartar; gradually beat into creamed mixture. Stir in cherries and pistachios.
**2.** Divide dough in half; shape each into an 11-in.-long roll. Wrap in plastic wrap; refrigerate at least 2 hours or until firm.
**3.** Preheat oven to 375°. Unwrap and cut dough crosswise into ½-in. slices. Place 2 in. apart on ungreased baking sheets. Bake 8-10 minutes or until edges are light golden brown. Remove from pans to wire racks to cool completely. Frost cookies with melted white chocolate; let stand until set.
**TO MAKE AHEAD** *Dough can be made 2 days in advance. Wrap in plastic wrap and place in a resealable bag. Store in the refrigerator.*

**FREEZE OPTION** *Place wrapped rolls in a resealable plastic freezer bag and freeze. To use, unwrap frozen logs and cut into slices. If necessary, let dough stand 15 minutes at room temperature before cutting. Bake as directed, increasing time by 1-2 minutes. Decorate as directed.*

## Citrus Gingerbread Cookies

Orange and lemon zest give gingerbread cutouts a refreshing twist. Brushing a honey glaze over the top adds a subtle shine and an extra touch of sweetness.
—**MONIQUE HOOKER** DESOTO, WI

**PREP:** 40 MIN. + CHILLING
**BAKE:** 10 MIN./BATCH + COOLING
**MAKES:** 6 DOZEN

- ¾ cup sugar
- ½ cup honey
- ½ cup molasses
- ½ cup unsalted butter, cubed
- 1 large egg
- 3½ cups all-purpose flour
- ¼ cup ground almonds
- 2 teaspoons baking powder
- 2 teaspoons grated lemon peel
- 2 teaspoons grated orange peel
- 1 teaspoon each ground cardamom, ginger, nutmeg, cinnamon and cloves

**GLAZE**
- ½ cup honey
- 2 tablespoons water

**1.** In a large saucepan, combine the sugar, honey and molasses. Bring to a boil; remove from heat. Let stand 20 minutes. Stir in butter; let stand 20 minutes longer.

**2.** Beat in egg. In another bowl, whisk flour, almonds, baking powder, lemon peel, orange peel and spices; gradually beat into sugar mixture. Refrigerate, covered, 8 hours or overnight.

**3.** Preheat oven to 375°. On a lightly floured surface, divide dough into three portions. Roll each portion to ¼-in. thickness. Cut with a floured 2-in. tree-shaped cookie cutter. Place 2 in. apart on baking sheets coated with cooking spray.

**4.** Bake 7-8 minutes or until lightly browned. Cool on pans 1 minute. Remove cookies to wire racks to cool completely. In a small bowl, mix glaze ingredients; brush over cookies. Let stand until set.

**TO MAKE AHEAD** *Dough can be made 2 days in advance. Wrap in plastic wrap and place in a resealable bag. Store in the refrigerator.*

**FREEZE OPTION** *Freeze undecorated cookies in freezer containers. To use, thaw in covered containers and decorate as directed.*

## Big & Soft Molasses Cookies

Some of the best molasses cookies I ever had came from a Mennonite store, and I finally found a recipe that compares to them. A sprinkling of coarse sugar adds a pretty look for special occasions.
—**NANCY FOUST** STONEBORO, PA

**PREP:** 45 MIN. + CHILLING
**BAKE:** 15 MIN./BATCH
**MAKES:** ABOUT 2½ DOZEN

- 1 cup butter-flavored shortening
- 1 cup sugar
- 2 large eggs
- 2 cups molasses
- 1 cup (8 ounces) sour cream
- ½ teaspoon vanilla extract
- 8 cups all-purpose flour
- 3 teaspoons baking soda
- 1½ teaspoons ground cinnamon
- 1 teaspoon ground ginger
- ½ teaspoon salt
- ½ teaspoon ground cloves
- ½ teaspoon ground nutmeg
- ½ cup coarse sugar

**1.** In a large bowl, cream shortening and sugar until light and fluffy. Beat in eggs, molasses, sour cream and vanilla. In another bowl, whisk flour, baking soda, cinnamon, ginger, salt, cloves and nutmeg; gradually beat into the creamed mixture.

**2.** Divide dough in half. Shape each into a disk; wrap in plastic wrap. Refrigerate 2 hours or until firm enough to roll.

**3.** Preheat oven to 350°. On a floured surface, roll each portion of dough to ½-in. thickness. Cut with a floured 3-in. round cookie cutter. Place 2 in. apart on parchment paper-lined baking sheets. Sprinkle with sugar. Bake for 15-18 minutes or until set. Remove from pans to wire racks to cool.

**TO MAKE AHEAD** *Dough can be made 2 days in advance. Wrap in plastic wrap and place in a resealable bag. Store in the refrigerator.*

**FREEZE OPTION** *Freeze cookies, layered between waxed paper, in freezer containers. To use, thaw before serving.*

## Glazed Candied Fruit Cookies

Even if your family doesn't care for fruitcake, they'll love these festive cookies studded with candied fruit and pecans. A caramel glaze adds a delectable touch on top.

—**SUSAN HEIN** BURLINGTON, WI

**PREP:** 30 MIN. + CHILLING
**BAKE:** 10 MIN./BATCH + COOLING
**MAKES:** 6 DOZEN

- 1 cup butter, softened
- 1 cup confectioners' sugar
- ½ cup sugar
- 1 large egg
- 2 teaspoons vanilla extract
- 2¼ cups all-purpose flour
- ½ teaspoon baking soda
- ⅔ cup chopped candied pineapple
- ½ cup chopped pecans
- ⅓ cup red candied cherries, chopped

**CARAMEL GLAZE**
- ½ cup packed brown sugar
- ¼ cup butter, cubed
- ⅔ cup confectioners' sugar
- 2 tablespoons 2% milk

**1.** In a large bowl, cream butter and sugars until light and fluffy. Beat in egg and vanilla. In another bowl, whisk flour and baking soda; gradually beat into creamed mixture. Stir in pineapple, pecans and cherries. Divide dough in half; shape each into a 9-in.-long roll; wrap each in plastic wrap. Refrigerate 2 hours or until firm.

**2.** Preheat oven to 350°. Unwrap and cut crosswise into ¼-in. slices. Place 2 in. apart on ungreased baking sheets. Bake 7-9 minutes or until lightly browned. Remove to wire racks to cool completely.

**3.** In a small saucepan, combine brown sugar and butter. Bring to a boil over medium heat. Cook and stir 30 seconds. Remove from heat; cool 5 minutes. Beat in confectioners' sugar and milk. Immediately drizzle over cookies. Let stand until set.

**TO MAKE AHEAD** *Dough can be made 2 days in advance. Wrap in plastic wrap and place in a resealable plastic bag. Store in the refrigerator.*
**FREEZE OPTION** *Place wrapped rolls in a resealable plastic freezer bag. To use, unwrap frozen rolls and cut into slices. If necessary, let dough stand a few minutes at room temperature before cutting. Bake and decorate as directed, increasing time by 1-2 minutes.*

# SWEET SENSATIONS

## Candy Cane Pie

When my college roommate first made this pie, I couldn't get enough! Using a store-bought crust helps save time when you're in the midst of the holidays.
—**CHARLOTTE STEWART** MESA, AZ

**PREP:** 15 MIN. + CHILLING
**MAKES:** 8 SERVINGS

- 24 **large marshmallows**
- ½ **cup milk**
- 1 **teaspoon vanilla extract**
- ⅛ **teaspoon salt**

- 6 **drops peppermint extract**
- 6 **drops red food coloring**
- 2 **tablespoons plus 1 teaspoon crushed peppermint candy, divided**
- 1 **cup heavy whipping cream, whipped**
- 1 **chocolate crumb crust (8 inches)**

**1.** In a heavy saucepan, combine the large marshmallows and milk over low heat. Cook and stir until the marshmallows are melted and the mixture is smooth. Remove from heat.
**2.** Stir in the vanilla, salt, peppermint extract and red food coloring. Cool for 30 minutes, stirring several times. Stir in 2 tablespoons crushed candies; fold in whipped cream.
**3.** Spoon into the chocolate crumb crust. Refrigerate, covered, 8 hours or overnight. Just before serving, sprinkle with remaining candy.

# Michigan Cherry Pie

This tart Michigan cherry pie is delicious with the crisp streusel topping but even better with a scoop of vanilla ice cream on top.

—**DIANE SELICH** VASSAR, MI

**PREP:** 20 MIN. + CHILLING • **BAKE:** 45 MIN. + COOLING
**MAKES:** 8 SERVINGS

Pastry for single-crust pie (9 inches)
5 cups frozen pitted tart cherries, thawed and drained or fresh tart cherries, pitted
1¼ cups dried cherries
1 tablespoon lemon juice
½ teaspoon grated lemon peel
½ teaspoon almond extract
1 cup sugar
¼ cup cornstarch

**TOPPING**
¾ cup old-fashioned oats
½ cup all-purpose flour
½ cup packed brown sugar
⅓ cup butter, melted
¼ teaspoon salt
Vanilla ice cream, optional

**1.** On a lightly floured surface, roll pastry dough to a ⅛-in.-thick circle; transfer to a 9-in. pie plate. Trim pastry to ½ in. beyond rim of plate; flute edge. Refrigerate 30 minutes.
**2.** Meanwhile, preheat oven to 375°. In a large bowl, toss tart and dried cherries with lemon juice, lemon peel and almond extract. In a small bowl, mix sugar and cornstarch; add to cherry mixture and toss to coat. For topping, in a small bowl, mix ingredients until crumbly. Transfer cherry filling to pastry-lined pie plate; sprinkle topping over filling.
**3.** Bake on a lower oven rack 45-55 minutes or until crust is golden brown and filling is bubbly. Cool on a wire rack. If desired, serve with ice cream.
**PASTRY FOR SINGLE-CRUST PIE (9 INCHES)** *Combine 1¼ cups all-purpose flour and ¼ tsp. salt; cut in ½ cup cold butter until crumbly. Gradually add 3-5 Tbsp. ice water, tossing with a fork until dough holds together when pressed. Wrap in plastic and refrigerate 1 hour.*

# Spiced Sherry Cake

My mother received this recipe from a friend years ago when fluted tube pans first became popular. The cake lasts a few days in the refrigerator, but I personally love to serve it warm with a scoop of vanilla ice cream.

—**DEBBIE PELLETIER** JUPITER, FL

**PREP:** 15 MIN. • **BAKE:** 35 MIN. + COOLING • **MAKES:** 12 SERVINGS

1 package yellow cake mix (regular size)
1 package (3.4 ounces) instant vanilla pudding mix
1 tablespoon grated orange peel
1 teaspoon ground cinnamon
½ teaspoon ground allspice
½ teaspoon ground nutmeg
4 large eggs
¾ cup canola oil
¾ cup sherry
Confectioners' sugar

**1.** Preheat oven to 350°. Grease and flour a 10-in. fluted tube pan.
**2.** In a large bowl, whisk the first six ingredients; add eggs, oil and sherry. Beat on low speed 30 seconds. Beat on medium 2 minutes. Transfer to prepared pan. Bake 35-40 minutes or until a toothpick inserted in center comes out clean.
**3.** Cool in pan 10 minutes before removing to a wire rack to cool completely. Dust with confectioners' sugar.
**NOTE** *To remove cakes easily, use solid shortening to grease plain and fluted tube pans.*

# Mile-High Cranberry Meringue Pie

Your holiday crowd will be blown away when they see this pie with towering meringue on top. Let it sit in your refrigerator for at least four hours for best results.

**—MARCIA WHITNEY** GAINESVILLE, FL

**PREP:** 1 HOUR • **BAKE:** 25 MIN. + CHILLING
**MAKES:** 8 SERVINGS

> Pastry for single-crust pie
>   (9 inches)
> 4 large eggs, separated
> 4 cups fresh or frozen cranberries
> 2¼ cups sugar, divided
> ¾ cup water
> 2 tablespoons all-purpose flour
> ¼ teaspoon salt
> 2 tablespoons butter
> 2 teaspoons vanilla extract, divided
> ½ teaspoon cream of tartar

**1.** Preheat oven to 425°. On a floured surface, roll the pastry dough to fit a 9-in. pie plate. Trim and flute edge. Refrigerate 30 minutes. Place egg whites in a large bowl; let stand for 30 minutes at room temperature.

**2.** Line pastry with a double thickness of foil. Fill with pie weights. Bake on a lower oven rack for 20-25 minutes or until golden brown. Remove foil and weights; bake 3-6 minutes or until bottom is golden brown. Cool on a wire rack.

**3.** Lower oven to 325°. In a saucepan, combine cranberries, 1½ cups sugar and water. Bring to a boil, stirring to dissolve the sugar. Reduce heat to medium; cook, uncovered, for 4-6 minutes or until berries stop popping, stirring occasionally. Remove from heat. In a small bowl, whisk the egg yolks, ¼ cup sugar, flour and salt until blended. Gradually whisk in ½ cup of the hot cranberry liquid; return all to saucepan, stirring constantly. Bring to a gentle boil; cook and stir 2 minutes. Remove from heat; stir in butter and 1 teaspoon vanilla.

**4.** For meringue, add cream of tartar and the remaining vanilla extract to egg whites; beat on medium speed until foamy. Gradually add remaining 8 tablespoons sugar, 1 tablespoon at a time, beating on high after each addition until sugar is dissolved. Continue beating until stiff glossy peaks form.

**5.** Transfer hot filling to crust. Spread meringue evenly over filling, sealing to edge of crust. Bake 25-30 minutes or until meringue is golden brown.

Cool 1 hour on a wire rack. Refrigerate at least 4 hours before serving.

**PASTRY FOR SINGLE-CRUST PIE (9 INCHES)** *Combine 1¼ cups all-purpose flour and ¼ tsp. salt; cut in ½ cup cold butter until crumbly. Gradually add 3-5 Tbsp. ice water, tossing with a fork until dough holds together when pressed. Wrap in plastic and refrigerate 1 hour.*

# Pumpkin Gingersnap Parfaits

Enjoy these lovely, light parfaits as an unforgettable seasonal finale to your holiday feast. If you include the spiced rum, it adds a fun new flavor to the mix.

—**LORRI HAZEN** TWIN FALLS, ID

**PREP:** 20 MIN. + CHILLING
**MAKES:** 6 SERVINGS

- 1⅓ cups canned pumpkin
- 1 package (8 ounces) mascarpone cheese
- ⅓ cup packed brown sugar
- 1 teaspoon ground cinnamon
- 1 teaspoon grated orange peel
- ½ teaspoon ground cloves
- ¼ teaspoon ground ginger
- ⅓ cup spiced rum or amaretto, optional
- 1 cup heavy whipping cream
- ¼ cup confectioners' sugar
- 1 teaspoon vanilla extract
- 1 cup crumbled gingersnap cookies (about 20 cookies)

**1.** In a large bowl, combine the first seven ingredients; stir in the rum if desired. Refrigerate, covered, for at least 2 hours.

**2.** In a small bowl, beat cream until it begins to thicken. Add confectioners' sugar and vanilla extract; beat until soft peaks form.

**3.** Just before serving, spoon half of the pumpkin mixture into six parfait glasses. Top with half the whipped cream and half the crumbled cookies. Repeat layers.

## Holiday Helper

Use up any leftover canned pumpkin from this recipe by dressing up a few staples in your home. Stir some of the pumpkin in to the batter for cakes, cupcakes, pancakes or waffles. Add a tablespoon or two to whipped topping for an extra burst of flavor.

# Danish Pastry

It's worth the extra effort to make this delightful candy-cane-shaped dessert. Best of all, the recipe makes two pastries, so it's perfect for gift-giving.

—**SUSAN GAROUTTE** GEORGETOWN, TX

**PREP:** 45 MIN. • **BAKE:** 1 HOUR + COOLING
**MAKES:** 2 PASTRIES (8 SERVINGS EACH)

- 1 cup all-purpose flour
- ½ cup cold butter, cubed
- 2 to 3 tablespoons cold water

**TOPPING**

- 1 cup water
- ½ cup butter, cubed
- ¼ teaspoon salt
- 1 cup all-purpose flour
- 3 large eggs
- ½ teaspoon almond extract

**FROSTING**

- 1½ cups confectioners' sugar
- 2 tablespoons butter, softened
- 2 tablespoons water
- 1½ teaspoons vanilla extract
- ½ cup sliced almonds, toasted

**1.** Place flour in a small bowl; cut in butter until crumbly. Gradually add water, tossing with a fork until dough holds together when pressed. Divide dough in half. On a lightly floured surface, roll each into a 14x2½-in. rectangle. Transfer to an ungreased baking sheet; curve one end of each pastry to form the tops of the canes. Refrigerate while preparing topping.
**2.** Preheat oven to 350°. In a large saucepan, combine water, butter and salt; bring to a rolling boil. Add flour all at once and beat until blended. Cook over medium heat, stirring vigorously until mixture pulls away from sides of pan and forms a ball. Remove from heat; let stand 5 minutes.
**3.** Add eggs, one at a time, beating well after each addition until smooth. Add extract; continue beating until mixture is smooth and shiny. Spread over pastry dough.
**4.** Bake for 60-70 minutes or until puffed and golden brown. Cool on pans 10 minutes before removing to a wire rack; cool completely.

**5.** In a small bowl, beat confectioners' sugar, butter, water and extract until smooth. Spread over pastries; sprinkle with almonds. Refrigerate leftovers.

## The Perfect Topping

**1.** After shaping the dough into a 14x2½-in. rectangle, slightly curve the top to form a candy cane shape; set in the refrigerator.

**2.** Once you have prepared the almond-flavored topping on the stovetop, carefully spread the topping over the pastry. An offset spatula works great!

**3.** Bake and decorate pastry as directed.

**NOTE** *To toast nuts, bake in a shallow pan in a 350° oven for 5-10 minutes or cook in a skillet over low heat until lightly browned, stirring occasionally.*

# Cheesecake Layered Red Velvet Cake

**PREP:** 35 MIN. • **BAKE:** 70 MIN. + CHILLING
**MAKES:** 16 SERVINGS

- 2 packages (8 ounces each) cream cheese, softened
- ½ cup sugar
- ½ cup sour cream
- 4 teaspoons all-purpose flour
- 1½ teaspoons vanilla extract
- 2 large eggs, lightly beaten

**CAKE**

- 1½ cups sugar
- 1½ cups canola oil
- 1 cup buttermilk
- 2 large eggs
- 1 bottle (1 ounce) red food coloring
- 2 teaspoons cider vinegar
- 1 teaspoon vanilla extract
- 2½ cups cake flour
- 2 tablespoons baking cocoa
- 1½ teaspoons baking soda
- 1 teaspoon salt

**FROSTING**

- 3 packages (8 ounces each) cream cheese, softened
- 1½ cups butter, softened
- 1 tablespoon vanilla extract
- 3 to 3½ cups confectioners' sugar

**1.** Preheat oven to 325°. Line the bottom of a 9-in. springform pan with parchment paper; grease paper.
**2.** In a large bowl, beat cream cheese and sugar until smooth. Beat in sour cream, flour and vanilla. Add eggs; beat on low speed just until blended. Pour into prepared pan. Place on a baking sheet.
**3.** Bake 40-50 minutes or until center is set. Cool on a wire rack 10 minutes. Loosen sides from pan with a knife. Cool 1 hour longer. Refrigerate until ready to assemble, covering when completely cooled.
**4.** For red velvet cake, increase oven setting to 350°. Line bottoms of two greased 9-in. round baking pans with parchment paper; grease paper.
**5.** In a large bowl, beat the sugar, oil, buttermilk, eggs, red food coloring, vinegar and vanilla until well blended. In another bowl, whisk flour, cocoa,

baking soda and salt; gradually beat into sugar mixture.
**6.** Transfer to prepared pans. Bake 30-35 minutes or until a toothpick inserted in center comes out clean. Cool in pans for 10 minutes before removing to wire racks; remove the paper. Cool completely.
**7.** For frosting, in a large bowl, beat cream cheese, butter and vanilla until smooth. Gradually beat in enough

confectioners' sugar to reach desired consistency. Place one cake layer on a serving plate. Spread with 1 cup frosting. Carefully place cheesecake over frosting.
**8.** Spread cheesecake with another 1 cup frosting. Top with remaining cake layer. Frost top and sides of cake with remaining frosting. Refrigerate overnight before serving.

*"I love both red velvet cake and cheesecake. So why not combine them into one stunning dessert? It's best when served ice cold from the refrigerator."*

**—MELISSA GAINES** KNOXVILLE, TN

## Meringue Snowballs in Custard

My family has passed down this elegant dessert generation by generation. It started with my Russian great-grandmother, who traveled to America more than 100 years ago. I love continuing the tradition with her recipe.

—TONYA BURKHARD PALM COAST, FL

**PREP:** 5 MIN. • **COOK:** 20 MIN. + CHILLING • **MAKES:** 12 SERVINGS

- 4 large egg whites
- 4 large egg yolks plus 2 large eggs
- 1½ cups sugar, divided
- 1 tablespoon cornstarch
- 6¼ cups whole milk, divided
- 2 teaspoons vanilla extract, divided
- ½ teaspoon cream of tartar
  Chopped glazed pecans, optional

**1.** Place the egg whites in a large bowl; let stand at room temperature 30 minutes. In a heavy saucepan, whisk egg yolks, eggs, 1 cup sugar and cornstarch until blended; stir in 4 cups milk. Cook over medium-low heat 10-15 minutes or until mixture is just thick enough to coat a metal spoon and a thermometer reads at least 160°, stirring constantly. Do not allow to boil. Remove from heat immediately. Strain through a fine-mesh strainer into a large bowl.
**2.** Place bowl in an ice-water bath. Stir occasionally for 5 minutes. Stir in 1½ teaspoons vanilla. Press plastic wrap onto surface of custard. Refrigerate until cold, about 1 hour.
**3.** For snowballs, add cream of tartar to egg whites; beat on medium speed until foamy. Gradually add remaining sugar, 1 tablespoon at a time, beating on high after each addition until sugar is dissolved. Stir in remaining vanilla. Continue beating until stiff glossy peaks form.
**4.** In a large heavy skillet, bring the remaining milk barely to a simmer over medium-low heat. Working in batches and using two soup spoons, drop meringue by ⅓ cupfuls into milk; poach meringues for 4-6 minutes or until firm to the touch, turning once. Using a slotted spoon, remove the meringues to paper towels to drain. Repeat with remaining meringue, making a total of 12 snowballs. (Discard remaining milk.) If desired, serve with pecans.

## German Chocolate Tres Leches Cake

I first tried tres leches cake several years ago while in Ecuador. Since then, I've changed it up by adding some of my favorite ingredients, namely chocolate and coconut. This version also has a bit of rum for an adults-only treat.

—LISA VARNER EL PASO, TX

**PREP:** 20 MIN. + STANDING • **BAKE:** 25 MIN. + CHILLING
**MAKES:** 15 SERVINGS

- 1 package chocolate cake mix
- 1 can (14 ounces) sweetened condensed milk
- 1 can (12 ounces) evaporated milk
- 1½ cups heavy whipping cream, divided
- ¼ cup rum
- 3 tablespoons confectioners' sugar
- ½ cup flaked coconut, toasted
- ½ cup chopped pecans, toasted
  Chocolate syrup, optional

**1.** Preheat oven to 350°. Prepare and bake the cake mix according to package directions, using a 13x9-in. baking pan. Cool on a wire rack.
**2.** Meanwhile, in a large bowl, whisk milks, ½ cup cream and rum. With a wooden skewer, poke holes in cake about ½ in. apart. Slowly pour milk mixture over cake, allowing mixture to absorb into the cake. Let stand for 30 minutes. Refrigerate, covered, 8 hours or overnight.
**3.** In a small bowl, beat remaining cream until it begins to thicken. Add confectioners' sugar; beat until stiff peaks form. Spread over top of cake. Sprinkle with coconut and pecans. If desired, drizzle servings with chocolate syrup.

## Rum Raisin Creme Brulee

Inspired by a favorite ice cream flavor, I created this make-ahead recipe to free up some time in the kitchen. You can also serve this as a custard if you choose to not caramelize the top.

**—ELEANOR FROEHLICH** ROCHESTER, MI

**PREP:** 20 MIN. • **BAKE:** 30 MIN. + CHILLING
**MAKES:** 6 SERVINGS

- ⅓ **cup raisins**
- ¼ **cup dark rum**
- 2½ **cups heavy whipping cream**
- 7 **large egg yolks**
- ½ **cup plus 6 teaspoons superfine sugar, divided**

**1.** Preheat oven to 325°. In a small bowl, toss the raisins with dark rum; microwave for 30 seconds. Let stand 10 minutes.

**2.** Meanwhile, in a small saucepan, heat cream until bubbles form around sides of pan; remove from heat. In a bowl, whisk egg yolks and ½ cup sugar until blended but not foamy. Slowly stir in hot cream. Strain raisin mixture into cream mixture, stirring in rum to combine; reserve raisins.

**3.** Put six 6-oz. broiler-safe ramekins or custard cups in a baking pan that's large enough to hold them without touching. Divide the reserved raisins among ramekins; pour egg mixture over top. Place pan on oven rack; add very hot water to pan within ¾ in. of top of ramekins.

**4.** Bake for 30-35 minutes or until the center is just set and the top appears dull. Immediately remove ramekins from water bath to a wire rack; cool for 10 minutes. Refrigerate until cold, about 4 hours.

**5.** To caramelize the topping with a kitchen torch, sprinkle the custards evenly with remaining sugar. Hold torch flame about 2 in. above custard surface and rotate it slowly until the sugar is evenly caramelized. Serve immediately or refrigerate for up to 1 hour.

# Brownie Torte

My mother-in-law first shared this recipe, and now it's often requested for birthdays and other special occasions. I like to serve it at Christmastime on an antique platter surrounded by ornaments for decoration.

—CANDACE MCCLURE BROOKVILLE, IN

**PREP:** 30 MIN. • **BAKE:** 15 MIN. + COOLING
**MAKES:** 12 SERVINGS

- 1 cup miniature semisweet chocolate chips
- ⅔ cup butter, cubed
- 4 large eggs
- 1½ cups sugar
- 1½ cups all-purpose flour
- 1 teaspoon baking powder
- ½ teaspoon salt
- ½ cup coarsely chopped walnuts

**FROSTING**

- 2 cups heavy whipping cream
- ¼ cup confectioners' sugar
- 1 teaspoon vanilla extract
- 1 cup miniature semisweet chocolate chips
  Additional miniature semisweet chocolate chips, optional

**1.** Preheat oven to 350°. Line a 15x10x1-in. baking pan with parchment paper. In a microwave, melt chocolate chips and butter; stir until smooth. Cool slightly. In a large bowl, beat eggs and sugar. Stir in the chocolate mixture. In another bowl, mix flour, baking powder and salt; gradually add to chocolate mixture, mixing well. Fold in walnuts.

**2.** Transfer to the prepared pan. Bake for 15-20 minutes or until a toothpick inserted in the center comes out clean (do not overbake). Cool 10 minutes. Invert onto a flat surface dusted with confectioners' sugar. Gently peel off paper. Cool completely.

**3.** Beat cream, confectioners' sugar and vanilla until stiff peaks form. Fold in chocolate chips. Trim cake edges; cut crosswise into fourths. Place one layer on a serving plate; top with ¾ cup frosting. Repeat twice. Top with remaining layer. Frost top, sides and ends of cake. If desired, sprinkle with additional chocolate chips. Store in the refrigerator until ready to serve.

# Raspberry Chocolate Mousse

If you're looking for a rich, chocolaty dessert, look no further. Quick and easy to make, the only hard part is waiting for it to chill!

—STEFFANY LOHN BRENTWOOD, CA

**PREP:** 20 MIN. • **COOK:** 10 MIN. + CHILLING
**MAKES:** 8 SERVINGS

- 2½ cups heavy whipping cream, divided
- ½ cup sugar
- 4 large egg yolks
- 12 ounces bittersweet chocolate, chopped
- ¼ cup raspberry liqueur or seedless raspberry jam
- 2 teaspoons vanilla extract
- 2 cups fresh raspberries
  Sweetened whipped cream
  Chocolate curls

**1.** In a saucepan, combine 1½ cups cream and sugar; cook over medium heat until bubbles form around sides of pan. In a small bowl, whisk a small amount of hot mixture into egg yolks; return all to pan, whisking constantly. Cook over low heat until mixture is just thick enough to coat a metal spoon and a thermometer reads at least 160°, stirring constantly. Do not allow to boil.

**2.** Immediately remove from heat. Stir in chocolate, liqueur and vanilla until chocolate is melted. Transfer to a large bowl; cool slightly. Refrigerate, covered, until cold, at least 2 hours.

**3.** In a large bowl, beat remaining cream until soft peaks form; fold into chocolate mixture. Serve with raspberries. Top with whipped cream and chocolate curls.

melt shortening and the remaining chocolate chips. Dip the bottoms of cookies into chocolate, allowing excess to drip off. Stack cookies on prepared platter into a ring to form a wreath. Drizzle remaining melted chocolate over wreath; sprinkle with remaining candies. Let stand until set, about 30 minutes. Store in an airtight container at room temperature.

## Coconut Dream Cupcakes

My daughter, Elizabeth, came up with this incredible recipe. The cream cheese in the middle is a fun surprise when someone takes their first bite.

**—JULIE FLOURNOY** LAURELVILLE, OH

**PREP:** 40 MIN. • **BAKE:** 20 MIN. + COOLING • **MAKES:** 1½ DOZEN

- 6 ounces cream cheese, softened
- 1⅓ cups sugar, divided
- ¼ teaspoon coconut extract
- 6 tablespoons butter, softened
- 2 large eggs
- 1 teaspoon clear vanilla extract
- 2 cups all-purpose flour
- ½ teaspoon baking powder
- ¼ teaspoon baking soda
- ⅛ teaspoon salt
- 1 cup 2% milk

**FROSTING**

- 12 ounces cream cheese, softened
- 6 tablespoons butter, softened
- 1 tablespoon water
- 2 teaspoons clear vanilla extract
- 1½ cups confectioners' sugar
- 1 cup flaked coconut

**1.** Preheat oven to 350°. Line 18 muffin cups with paper liners. In a small bowl, beat cream cheese, ⅓ cup sugar and coconut extract until smooth.
**2.** In a large bowl, cream butter and remaining sugar until light and fluffy. Add eggs, one at a time, beating well after each addition. Beat in the vanilla extract. In another bowl, whisk flour, baking powder, baking soda and salt; add to creamed mixture alternately with milk, beating well after each addition.
**3.** Spoon 1 rounded tablespoon batter into each prepared cup. Drop cream cheese mixture by scant tablespoonfuls into center of each cupcake. Cover with remaining batter, about 1 scant tablespoon each.
**4.** Bake for 16-20 minutes or until a toothpick inserted in the cake portion comes out clean. Cool in pans 10 minutes before removing to wire racks to cool completely.
**5.** For frosting, in a small bowl, beat cream cheese, butter, water and vanilla extract until blended. Gradually beat in the confectioners' sugar until smooth. Frost the cupcakes; sprinkle with coconut. Refrigerate leftovers.

## Chocolate-Candy Cane Meringue Wreath

These stunning meringues have a minty taste and melt in your mouth. Set the finished masterpiece in the center of the table to accent your spread, then enjoy it for dessert later.

**—NICOLE TRAN** SASKATOON, SK

**PREP:** 40 MIN. + STANDING • **BAKE:** 35 MIN. + COOLING
**MAKES:** 7 DOZEN

- 4 large egg whites
- ½ teaspoon cream of tartar
- 1 cup sugar
- 2¾ cups miniature semisweet chocolate chips, divided
- ¾ cup finely crushed candy canes or peppermint candies, divided

**12-inch round doily or parchment circle**

- 3 teaspoons shortening

**1.** Place egg whites in a large bowl; let stand at room temperature 30 minutes.
**2.** Preheat oven to 250°. Add cream of tartar to egg whites; beat on medium speed until soft peaks form. Gradually add the sugar, 1 tablespoon at a time, beating on high after each addition until the sugar is dissolved. Continue beating until stiff glossy peaks form. Fold in 1 cup chocolate chips and ½ cup crushed candies.
**3.** Drop rounded teaspoonfuls 1 in. apart onto parchment paper-lined baking sheets. Bake 35-40 minutes or until firm to the touch. Remove to wire racks to cool completely.
**4.** Line the serving platter with a doily. In a microwave,

## Cranberry-Pumpkin Praline Pie

It just wouldn't be Christmas at our house without pie. We have traditional pies that appear every year, but I decided to put my own spin on praline pie. It has a nice crunch from the pecans, brightness from the orange zest, pop from the cranberries and creaminess from the cream cheese.

—**BARB MILLER** OAKDALE, MN

**PREP:** 25 MIN. • **BAKE:** 50 MIN. + CHILLING
**MAKES:** 8 SERVINGS

- 12 ounces cream cheese, softened
- ⅓ cup sugar
- 1 large egg
- 1½ teaspoons grated orange peel
  Pastry for single-crust pie (9 inches)

**PUMPKIN LAYER**
- 1 can (15 ounces) solid-pack pumpkin
- ¾ cup sugar
- 2 teaspoons pumpkin pie spice
- 3 large eggs
- ¾ cup half-and-half cream

**CRANBERRY TOPPING**
- ¾ cup dried cranberries
- ¾ cup chopped pecans
- ¼ cup packed brown sugar
- 1½ teaspoons grated orange peel
  Whipped cream and ground nutmeg, optional

**1.** In small bowl, combine cream cheese and sugar; beat on medium speed until smooth. Beat in egg and orange peel. Refrigerate, covered, 30 minutes.

**2.** Meanwhile, preheat oven to 375°. On a lightly floured surface, roll dough to a ⅛-in.-thick circle; transfer to a 9-in. deep-dish pie plate. Trim the pastry to ½ in. beyond rim of plate; flute edge. In a large bowl, combine pumpkin, sugar and pumpkin pie spice. Add eggs and cream; mix well.

**3.** Spread cream cheese mixture into pastry. Pour pumpkin mixture over cream cheese layer. Bake 25 minutes.

**4.** In a bowl, combine cranberries, pecans, brown sugar and orange peel. Sprinkle over pumpkin. Cover edges with foil to prevent overbrowning. Bake 25-30 minutes longer or until a knife inserted near the center comes out clean. Cool on a wire rack.

**5.** Refrigerate at least 2 hours. If desired, serve with whipped cream and nutmeg. Refrigerate leftovers.

# Holiday White Fruitcake

A friend gifted me this recipe when I attended her missionary church in Hawaii years ago. Now I bake up more than 60 loaves for the holidays.

**—EILEEN ORTH-SOKOLOWSKI** CHANDLER, AZ

**PREP:** 20 MIN. • **BAKE:** 50 MIN. + COOLING
**MAKES:** 4 LOAVES (16 SLICES EACH)

- 1 package (8 ounces) chopped mixed candied fruit
- 1¼ cups golden raisins
- 1 cup chopped walnuts, toasted
- 3 cups all-purpose flour, divided
- 2 cups butter, softened
- 2 cups sugar
- 6 large eggs

**1.** Preheat oven to 275°. Line bottoms of four greased 9x5-in. loaf pans with parchment paper; grease paper.
**2.** In a small bowl, toss candied fruit, raisins and walnuts with ½ cup flour. In a large bowl, cream the butter and sugar until light and fluffy. Add eggs, one at a time, beating well after each addition. Gradually beat in remaining flour. Fold in fruit mixture.
**3.** Transfer to prepared pans. Bake 50-60 minutes or until a toothpick inserted in center comes out clean. Cool in pans for 10 minutes before removing to wire racks to cool.

**NOTE** *To toast nuts, bake in a shallow pan in a 350° oven for 5-10 minutes or cook in a skillet over low heat until lightly browned, stirring occasionally.*

# Homemade Pear Pie

I entered this pie in a local baking contest and ended up winning! Bartlett pears hold up well when baked, adding a nice layer of texture.

**—DARLENE JACOBSON** WATERFORD, WI

**PREP:** 40 MIN. + CHILLING
**BAKE:** 45 MIN. + COOLING
**MAKES:** 8 SERVINGS

- 2 cups all-purpose flour
- 1 teaspoon salt
- ¾ cup shortening
- 6 tablespoons cold water

**FILLING**
- 5 cups sliced peeled fresh pears
- 1 tablespoon lemon juice
- ⅓ cup all-purpose flour
- ½ cup plus 1 tablespoon sugar, divided
- 1 teaspoon ground cinnamon
- 2 tablespoons butter

**1.** In a bowl, mix flour and salt; cut in shortening until crumbly. Gradually add water, tossing with a fork until dough holds together when pressed. Shape into a disk; wrap in plastic. Refrigerate 1 hour or overnight.
**2.** Preheat oven to 425°. In a large bowl, toss pears with lemon juice. In a small bowl, mix flour, ½ cup sugar and cinnamon; add to pear mixture and toss to coat.
**3.** On a lightly floured surface, roll one half of dough to a ⅛-in.-thick circle; transfer to a 9-in. pie plate. Trim pastry even with the rim. Add filling; dot with butter.
**4.** Roll the remaining dough into a ⅛-in.-thick circle. Place over filling. Trim, seal and flute edge. Cut slits in top. Sprinkle with remaining sugar. Bake 45-50 minutes or until crust is golden brown and filling is bubbly. Cover edge loosely with foil during the last 20 minutes if needed to prevent overbrowning. Remove foil. Cool on a wire rack.

# Peanut Butter-Chocolate Cake Rolls

Who knew something this impressive could start with a cake mix! The mini chocolate chips add a tasty crunch to each slice.

**—TAMMY REX** NEW TRIPOLI, PA

**PREP:** 20 MIN. + CHILLING
**BAKE:** 15 MIN. + CHILLING
**MAKES:** 2 CAKE ROLLS (12 SLICES EACH)

1 package chocolate cake mix (regular size)
6 large eggs
⅔ cup water
¼ cup canola oil

**FILLING**

1¾ cups half-and-half cream
1 package (3.4 ounces) instant vanilla pudding mix
¾ cup chunky peanut butter
1 carton (8 ounces) frozen whipped topping, thawed
½ cup miniature semisweet chocolate chips
Baking cocoa, optional

**1.** Preheat oven to 350°. Line two greased 15x10x1-in. baking pans with parchment paper.

**2.** In a large bowl, combine the cake mix, eggs, water and oil; beat on low speed 30 seconds. Beat on medium 2 minutes. Transfer to prepared pans.

**3.** Bake 12-14 minutes or until cakes spring back when lightly touched. Cool for 5 minutes. Invert each cake onto a kitchen towel dusted with confectioners' sugar. Gently peel off parchment paper. Roll up each cake in the towel jelly-roll style, starting with a short side. Cool completely on wire racks.

**4.** In a small bowl, whisk cream and pudding mix until thickened; whisk in peanut butter. Fold in the whipped topping and chocolate chips. Unroll the cakes; spread half of filling over each to within ½ in. of edges. Roll up again, without towels. Place on serving platters, seam sides down. Refrigerate, covered, at least 3 hours before serving. If desired, sprinkle with cocoa.

## Turtle Tart with Caramel Sauce

Between the creamy filling, crispy crust and gooey caramel sauce, there's a lot to love about this tart. Plus, you can make it two to three days in advance. One of my daughters even asks for this instead of cake on her birthday.

**—LEAH DAVIS** MORROW, OH

**PREP:** 15 MIN. • **BAKE:** 15 MIN. + CHILLING
**MAKES:** 12 SERVINGS

- 2 **cups pecan halves, toasted**
- ½ **cup sugar**
- 2 **tablespoons butter, melted**

**FILLING**

- 2 **cups (12 ounces) semisweet chocolate chips**
- 1½ **cups heavy whipping cream**
- ½ **cup finely chopped pecans, toasted**

**CARAMEL SAUCE**

- ½ **cup butter, cubed**
- 1 **cup sugar**
- 1 **cup heavy whipping cream**

**1.** Preheat oven to 350°. Place pecans and sugar in a food processor; pulse until pecans are finely ground. Add melted butter; pulse until combined. Press onto bottom and up sides of a 9-in. fluted tart pan with removable bottom. Bake 12-15 minutes or until golden brown. Cool completely on a wire rack.

**2.** For filling, place chocolate chips in a small bowl. In a small saucepan, bring the cream just to a boil. Pour over chocolate; stir with a whisk until smooth. Pour into cooled crust; cool slightly. Refrigerate until slightly set, about 30 minutes.

**3.** Sprinkle the pecans over filling. Refrigerate, covered, until set, about 3 hours.

**4.** For caramel sauce, in a large heavy saucepan, melt butter over medium heat; stir in the sugar until dissolved. Bring to a boil; cook for 10-12 minutes or until deep golden brown, stirring occasionally. Slowly whisk in cream until blended. Remove from heat; cool slightly. Serve with tart.

**NOTE** *To toast nuts, bake in a shallow pan in a 350° oven for 5-10 minutes or cook in a skillet over low heat until lightly browned, stirring occasionally.*

# Mocha Baked Alaskas

Make these baked alaskas ahead of time—you can torch the completed desserts and freeze them up to 24 hours before serving.

**—KERRY DINGWALL** PONTE VEDRA, FL

**PREP:** 30 MIN. + FREEZING • **BROIL:** 5 MIN.
**MAKES:** 6 SERVINGS

- **8** ounces semisweet chocolate, chopped
- **1** cup heavy whipping cream
- **1** loaf (10¾ ounces) frozen pound cake, thawed
- **¼** cup strong brewed coffee
- **3** cups coffee ice cream
- **6** large egg whites
- **1** cup sugar
- **½** teaspoon cream of tartar
- **1** teaspoon vanilla extract
- **⅛** teaspoon salt

**1.** Place chocolate in a small bowl. In a small saucepan, bring cream just to a boil. Pour over chocolate; whisk until smooth. Refrigerate, stirring occasionally, until completely cooled, about 1 hour.

**2.** Meanwhile, slice the pound cake horizontally into three layers. Cut cake into six 3-in. circles; brush tops with coffee (save remaining cake for another use).

**3.** Line six jumbo muffin cups with foil liners. Spoon ice cream into each. Top with ganache, spreading evenly. Place cake, coffee side down, over ganache, pressing gently. Cover and freeze until firm, about 3 hours.

**4.** In a large heavy saucepan, combine egg whites, sugar and cream of tartar. With a hand mixer, beat on low speed 1 minute. Continue beating over low heat until egg white mixture reaches 160°, about 10 minutes. Transfer to a bowl. Add vanilla extract and salt; beat until stiff glossy peaks form and sugar is dissolved.

**5.** Invert layered cakes onto an ungreased foil-lined baking sheet; remove foil liners. Immediately spread meringue over cakes, sealing to cover completely.

**6.** Heat with a kitchen torch or broil 8 in. from the heat for 3-4 minutes or until meringue is lightly browned. Serve immediately.

## Spiked Eggnog Bread Pudding

With a little imagination and creativity, I transformed my family's favorite holiday drink into a delightful dessert. If I have leftover eggnog, I'll use it up in here.

**—MARIE BRUNO** GREENSBORO, GA

**PREP:** 10 MIN. + STANDING • **BAKE:** 40 MIN.
**MAKES:** 8 SERVINGS

- **2** tablespoons butter, softened
- **8** large eggs, lightly beaten
- **2** cups prepared eggnog
- **¼** cup sugar
- **¼** cup rum or ½ teaspoon rum extract plus 2 tablespoons eggnog
- **3** tablespoons butter, melted
- **1½** teaspoons baking powder
- **½** teaspoon ground nutmeg, divided
- **10** cups cubed day-old egg bread or challah (about 12 ounces)
  Sweetened whipped cream, optional

**1.** Generously grease the bottom and sides of an 11x7-in. baking dish with softened butter. In a large bowl, whisk the eggs, eggnog, sugar, rum, melted butter, baking powder and ¼ teaspoon nutmeg until blended. Stir in bread; let stand 30 minutes. Preheat oven to 350°.

**2.** Transfer the bread mixture to the prepared dish; sprinkle with the remaining nutmeg. Bake for 40-45 minutes or until puffed, golden brown and a knife inserted near the center comes out clean. Serve warm; if desired, top with whipped cream.

## Hot Chocolate Tiramisu

Instead of using coffee and rum, I let cinnamon shine in this tiramisu. Don't store this dessert for more than two days—if it even lasts that long!

—**CATHY GENITI** SARATOGA SPRINGS, NY

**PREP:** 25 MIN. • **COOK:** 10 MIN. + CHILLING
**MAKES:** 12 SERVINGS

- 3 **tablespoons baking cocoa**
- 3 **tablespoons sugar**
- 2 **tablespoons water**
- 2 **cups whole milk**

**TIRAMISU**

- 3 **large egg yolks**
- 1 **cup sugar, divided**
- 2 **cups (16 ounces) mascarpone cheese**
- 1 **cup heavy whipping cream**
- 45 **crisp ladyfinger cookies (about 13 ounces)**
- ¼ **cup miniature semisweet chocolate chips**
- 2 **teaspoons ground cinnamon**

**1.** For hot cocoa, in a small saucepan, mix the cocoa, sugar and water until smooth. Bring to a boil; cook, stirring constantly, 2 minutes. Stir in milk until blended; transfer to a shallow bowl. Cool completely.

**2.** For tiramisu, in a heatproof bowl of a stand mixer, whisk egg yolks and ½ cup sugar until blended. Place over simmering water in a saucepan over medium heat. Whisking constantly, heat mixture until a thermometer reads 160°, about 2-3 minutes.

**3.** Remove from heat. With the whisk attachment of a stand mixer, beat on high speed until thick and pale yellow, about 5 minutes. Add mascarpone, beat on medium speed until smooth, scraping down the sides of the bowl as needed.

**4.** In another bowl, beat the cream until it begins to thicken. Add the remaining sugar; beat until soft peaks form. Fold the whipped cream into the mascarpone mixture.

**5.** To assemble, spread one-third of the cream mixture into a 13x9-in. baking dish. Quickly dip half of the ladyfingers halfway into cooled hot cocoa; arrange over cream. Repeat layers. Spread with remaining cream mixture. Sprinkle with chocolate chips and cinnamon. Refrigerate, covered, at least 8 hours or overnight.

**NOTE** *This recipe was prepared with Alessi brand ladyfinger cookies.*

### Holiday Helper

Save time by using a mix to prepare the hot cocoa in this recipe. You can also create an adult version by adding a little brandy or Frangelico liqueur to the cocoa.

# GIFTS FROM THE KITCHEN

# Texas Pecan Pralines

My praline recipe is special to me because it came from my mother. I use pecans from a grower in South Texas.
**—CAROL JONES** BLUE RIDGE, TX

**PREP:** 30 MIN. • **COOK:** 30 MIN. + CHILLING
**MAKES:** ABOUT 2¼ POUNDS

- 3 **teaspoons butter**
- ½ **cup butter, cubed**
- 2 **cups sugar**
- 1 **cup packed brown sugar**
- 1 **cup half-and-half cream**
- ½ **cup sweetened condensed milk**
- 1 **tablespoon light corn syrup**
  **Dash salt**
- 3 **cups pecan halves**
- ½ **teaspoon vanilla extract**

**1.** Line three baking sheets with foil and grease the foil with 1 teaspoon butter each; set aside.

**2.** In a large heavy saucepan over medium heat, melt cubed butter. Stir in sugars, cream, milk, corn syrup and salt; cook and stir until mixture comes to a boil. Cook, stirring occasionally, until a candy thermometer reads 236° (soft-ball stage), about 20 minutes.

**3.** Remove from heat; stir in pecans and vanilla. Cool, without stirring, to 170°, about 20 minutes. Stir with a wooden spoon until mixture just begins to thicken but is still glossy, about 2 minutes.

**4.** Quickly drop by rounded tablespoonfuls onto prepared baking sheets. Let stand until pralines are set and no longer glossy. Refrigerate for 1 hour or until completely set. Store in an airtight container in the refrigerator.

# Cherry-Almond Tea Mix

Our family enjoys giving homemade gifts for Christmas, and hot beverage mixes are especially popular. This flavored tea mix is a favorite.

**—ANDREA HORTON** KELSO, WA

**START TO FINISH:** 10 MIN.
**MAKES:** 40 SERVINGS (2½ CUPS TEA MIX)

- 2¼ cups iced tea mix with lemon and sugar
- 2 envelopes (0.13 ounces each) unsweetened cherry Kool-Aid mix
- 2 teaspoons almond extract

**EACH SERVING**

- 1 cup boiling or cold water

Place tea mix, Kool-Aid mix and extract in a food processor; pulse until blended. Store in an airtight container in a cool, dry place for up to 6 months.
**TO PREPARE TEA** *Place 1 tablespoon tea mix in a mug. Stir in 1 cup boiling or cold water until blended.*

# Date Nut Balls

A friend gave me this recipe more than 30 years ago. It is my husband's favorite treat. I like these with pecans or walnuts. If you do not like nuts, omit them and use 3 cups Rice Krispies.

**—MELINDA LORD** WASHINGTON, IA

**PREP:** 30 MIN. • **COOK:** 10 MIN. • **MAKES:** ABOUT 3½ DOZEN

- 2 cups Rice Krispies
- 1 cup chopped pistachios or almonds
- ⅓ cup butter, cubed
- 1 package (8 ounces) pitted dates, finely chopped
- 1 cup sugar
- 1 teaspoon vanilla extract
  Confectioners' sugar, optional

**1.** In a large bowl, combine Rice Krispies and pistachios. In a large saucepan, combine butter, dates and sugar. Cook and stir over medium heat until mixture is combined.
**2.** Remove from heat. Stir in vanilla. Pour over Rice Krispies mixture; stir to coat. When cool enough to handle, press into 1¼-in. balls. Cool. If desired, roll in confectioners' sugar. Store in an airtight container at room temperature.

## Pomegranate Pepper Jelly

Stirring pomegranate juice into my jalapeno jelly creates a beautiful red version for the holidays. Spread it on crackers, fish or poultry. My husband even uses it as a dip for Mexican food!

**—KATHERINE METZ** SHARPSBURG, GA

**PREP:** 1 HOUR • **PROCESS:** 10 MIN.
**MAKES:** 7 HALF-PINTS

- 6 **jalapeno peppers, halved lengthwise and seeded**
- 1 **medium sweet red pepper, halved lengthwise and seeded**
- 1 **habanero pepper, halved lengthwise and seeded**
- 1¼ **cups white vinegar, divided**
- 6 **cups sugar**
- ¾ **cup unsweetened pomegranate juice**
- 2 **pouches (3 ounces each) liquid fruit pectin**

**1.** Place peppers in a food processor; pulse until combined. Add 1 cup vinegar; process until peppers are finely minced. Transfer to a 6-qt. stockpot. Stir in sugar, pomegranate juice and remaining vinegar. Bring to a full rolling boil over medium heat, stirring constantly. Boil 10 minutes. Remove from heat. Stir in pectin. Return to a boil, stirring constantly. Remove from heat; skim off foam.

**2.** Ladle hot mixture into seven hot half-pint jars, leaving ¼-in. headspace. Remove air bubbles and adjust headspace, if necessary, by adding hot mixture. Wipe rims. Center lids on jars; screw on bands until fingertip tight.

**3.** Place jars into canner with simmering water, ensuring that they are completely covered with water. Bring to a boil; process for 10 minutes. Remove jars and cool.

**NOTE** *Wear disposable gloves when cutting hot peppers; the oils can burn skin. Avoid touching your face. The processing time listed is for altitudes of 1,000 feet or less. Add 1 minute to the processing time for each 1,000 feet of additional altitude.*

# Bourbon Caramel Popcorn

I took my great-aunt's caramel corn recipe and added a touch of my Kentucky-born husband's home state—bourbon. If you don't have a large enough bowl for stirring the popcorn, use a turkey roaster.

—**LISA HENDRICKS** CHICAGO, IL

**PREP:** 15 MIN. • **BAKE:** 1 HOUR • **MAKES:** 5 QUARTS

- 5 **quarts popped popcorn**
- ⅓ **cup bourbon**
- 1 **cup unsalted butter, cubed**
- 2 **cups packed light brown sugar**
- ½ **cup light corn syrup**
- ¼ **teaspoon cream of tartar**
- ¼ **teaspoon salt**
- ½ **teaspoon baking soda**

**1.** Preheat oven to 250°. Place popcorn in a large bowl. In a large saucepan, bring bourbon to a boil. Reduce heat; simmer, uncovered, 2 minutes. Add butter; cook on low until melted. Stir in brown sugar, corn syrup, cream of tartar and salt. Bring to a boil; cook 5 minutes longer, stirring occasionally. Remove from heat; stir in baking soda. Quickly pour over popcorn and mix well.

**2.** Transfer to two greased 15x10x1-in. baking pans. Bake 1 hour or until dry, stirring every 15 minutes. Remove from pans to waxed paper to cool. Store in airtight containers.

# Hazelnut Almond Biscotti

Pour a cup of coffee and indulge! Crisp, crunchy biscotti cookies are perfect for dunking. Hazelnuts and almonds make my favorite version even better.

—**JOHNNA JOHNSON** SCOTTSDALE, AZ

**PREP:** 30 MIN. • **BAKE:** 30 MIN. + COOLING • **MAKES:** 2 DOZEN

- 1⅔ **cups all-purpose flour**
- ¾ **cup sugar**
- ½ **teaspoon baking soda**
- ¼ **teaspoon salt**
- 3 **large eggs**
- 2 **teaspoons vanilla extract**
- ¾ **teaspoon almond extract**
- ⅔ **cup chopped hazelnuts, toasted**
- ¼ **cup sliced almonds, toasted**

**1.** Preheat oven to 325°. In a large bowl, combine flour, sugar, baking soda and salt. In a small bowl, whisk eggs and extracts; stir into dry ingredients. Stir in nuts (dough will be sticky).

**2.** Divide dough in half. Using lightly floured hands, shape each portion into a 9x2-in. rectangle on a parchment paper-lined baking sheet. Bake 20-25 minutes or until lightly browned.

**3.** Cool on pan on a wire rack. Transfer baked rectangles to a cutting board. Using a serrated knife, cut diagonally into ¾-in. slices. Place on ungreased baking sheets, cut side down.

**4.** Bake 6-9 minutes or until lightly browned. Remove from pans to wire racks to cool completely. Store in an airtight container.

**NOTE** *To toast nuts, bake in a shallow pan in a 350° oven for 5-10 minutes or cook in a skillet over low heat until lightly browned, stirring occasionally.*

# Rosemary-Lemon Sea Salt

Making flavored sea salt is so easy. Mix in grated lemon peel and minced rosemary for a delicious way to enhance chicken, fish and salads.

—**SHELLEY HOLMAN** SCOTTSDALE, AZ

**PREP:** 5 MIN. + STANDING • **MAKES:** ABOUT ⅔ CUP

- ½ **cup sea salt, fine grind**
- 1 **tablespoon grated lemon or orange peel**
- 1 **teaspoon minced fresh rosemary or thyme**

In a small bowl, combine all ingredients. Spread onto a parchment paper-lined pan. Let stand overnight. Store in an airtight container in a cool, dry place for up to 3 months.

# French Mustard

**PREP:** 15 MIN. • **COOK:** 30 MIN. + CHILLING
**MAKES:** 1 CUP

- **1** teaspoon whole allspice
- **¾** cup plus 3 tablespoons water, divided
- **½** cup white vinegar
- **¼** cup maple syrup
- **1** tablespoon all-purpose flour
- **1** tablespoon cornstarch
- **2** teaspoons ground mustard
- **1** teaspoon ground turmeric
- **¾** teaspoon salt

**1.** Place allspice on a double thickness of cheesecloth. Gather corners of cloth to enclose seasoning; tie securely with string.

**2.** In a small bowl, mix ¾ cup water, vinegar and maple syrup until blended. In a small saucepan, mix flour, cornstarch, mustard, turmeric, salt and remaining water until smooth. Gradually whisk in vinegar mixture. Add spice bag; bring to a boil. Reduce heat; simmer, uncovered, 25-30 minutes or until thickened, stirring occasionally.

**3.** Discard spice bag. Transfer to a covered container; cool slightly. Refrigerate until cold. Store in refrigerator for up to 1 month.

## Holiday Helper

Package this condiment with a bag of pretzels for a great gift anyone would enjoy! If the mustard is going to a grilling enthusiast, consider pairing it with a gift certificate to a local butcher shop or grocery store so he or she can pick up some burgers or sausages to grill.

*"Have grill masters on your* Christmas list? Consider giving them a special homemade mustard flavored with maple syrup, allspice and turmeric. Everyone loves it."

—**LORRAINE CALAND** SHUNIAH, ON

## Coffee Cake Muffin Mix

Our local home-school group has an annual Christmas craft breakfast. Forty children signed up to come to my table and make this mix. It was so rewarding to see their excitement as they created a special gift to give.

**—TAMERA SERAFIN** NEW WINDSOR, MD

**PREP:** 15 MIN. • **BAKE:** 20 MIN.
**MAKES:** 1 DOZEN

- 1½ cups all-purpose flour
- ½ cup sugar
- 2 teaspoons baking powder
- ½ teaspoon salt
- ¼ cup packed brown sugar
- ¼ cup chopped walnuts or pecans, toasted
- 1 teaspoon ground cinnamon

**ADDITIONAL INGREDIENTS**
- ½ cup shortening
- 1 large egg
- ½ cup 2% milk
- 1 tablespoon butter, melted

In a large bowl, whisk flour, sugar, baking powder and salt. Transfer to a 1-qt. resealable plastic bag. In a snack-size plastic bag, combine brown sugar, walnuts and cinnamon. Store bags in a cool, dry place or in a freezer for up to 3 months.

**TO PREPARE MUFFINS** *Preheat oven to 350°. Place flour mixture in a large bowl. Cut in shortening until crumbly. In a small bowl, whisk egg and milk until blended. Add to flour mixture; stir just until moistened. In a small bowl, mix brown sugar mixture with melted butter.*

*Fill greased or paper-lined muffin cups half full. Sprinkle with brown sugar mixture. Bake 18-22 minutes or until a toothpick inserted into center comes out clean. Cool 5 minutes before removing from pan to a wire rack. Serve warm.*

## Festive Holiday Fruitcake Bark

Every year, I make brandy-soaked dried fruit for fruitcake, but I always make too much. When I tried turning the extras into candy, the result was a sweet and colorful bark for grown-ups.

**—SUSAN BICKTA** KUTZTOWN, PA

**PREP:** 25 MIN. + STANDING
**MAKES:** 2 POUNDS

- ⅔ **cup chopped mixed candied fruit**
- 2 **tablespoons brandy**
- ½ **cup walnut pieces, toasted, divided**
- 20 **ounces white candy coating, coarsely chopped**
- ⅔ **cup miniature marshmallows**
- 10 **shortbread cookies, coarsely chopped**

**1.** In a small bowl, combine candied fruit and brandy. Refrigerate, covered, 2 hours, stirring occasionally.

**2.** Line a 15x10x1-in. baking pan with waxed paper. Reserve 2 tablespoons of candied fruit and 2 tablespoons walnuts for topping. In a microwave-safe bowl, melt candy coating; stir until smooth. Stir in marshmallows, cookie crumbs and remaining fruit and walnuts.

**3.** Spread into prepared pan (pan will not be full). Sprinkle with reserved fruit and walnuts; press into candy coating. Let stand until set. Break or cut bark into pieces. Store in an airtight container.

## Hazelnut Dream Cookies

I sampled these goodies at a Bible study and knew from the first bite that I had to have the recipe. To my surprise, the rich cookies require just four ingredients.

**—JULIE PETERSON** CROFTON, MD

**START TO FINISH:** 25 MIN.
**MAKES:** 2 DOZEN

- 1 **cup Nutella**
- ⅔ **cup all-purpose flour**
- 1 **large egg**
- ½ **cup chopped hazelnuts**

**1.** Preheat oven to 350°. In a large bowl, beat Nutella, flour and egg until blended. Stir in hazelnuts.

**2.** Drop by tablespoonfuls 2 in. apart onto ungreased baking sheets. Bake 8-10 minutes or until set. Remove from pans to wire racks to cool.

## Holiday Cookie Kit

Looking for a change-of-pace surprise? Bake up some simple cutout cookies and use them to create a Holiday Cookie Kit. Alongside the cookies, pack colored sugars, Christmas sprinkles, decorative candies or anything you think would make for a fun day of cookie decorating. Presented in a tin or on a platter, it's one sweet gift they're sure to remember!

## Butterscotch Brownie Mix

Most people have butter, eggs and vanilla on hand, and those ingredients are all you'll need to turn this mix into a panful of butterscotch brownies.

—**MACEY ALLEN** GREEN FOREST, AR

**PREP:** 15 MIN. • **BAKE:** 20 MIN. + COOLING
**MAKES:** 2 DOZEN BROWNIES (4 CUPS MIX)

- 2 **cups all-purpose flour**
- 3½ **teaspoons baking powder**
- ¼ **teaspoon salt**
- ¾ **cup chopped pecans, toasted**
- 1½ **cups packed brown sugar**
- ½ **cup butterscotch chips**

**ADDITIONAL INGREDIENTS**

- ¾ **cup butter, cubed**
- 2 **large eggs**
- 2 **teaspoons vanilla extract**

In a small bowl, mix flour, baking powder and salt. In a 1-qt. glass jar, layer flour mixture, pecans, brown sugar and butterscotch chips in the order listed. Cover and store in a cool, dry place for up to 3 months.

**TO PREPARE BROWNIES** *Preheat oven to 350°. In a large saucepan, heat butter over medium heat until just melted. Remove from heat. Whisk in eggs and vanilla until blended. Gradually add brownie mix, mixing well. Spread into a greased 13x9-in. baking pan.*

*Bake 20-25 minutes or until a toothpick inserted in center comes out with moist crumbs (do not overbake). Cool completely in pan on a wire rack.*

### Holiday Helper

Not only are the Butterscotch Brownies easy, but you can customize them as well. Swap out the butterscotch chips for chocolate chips or replace the pecans with macadamia nuts. You can even toss a handful of coconut into the batter for a textured taste sensation.

## Kumquat Marmalade

I didn't even know what a kumquat was until my husband and I discovered them in southern Florida. Now I love using them for marmalade. I always get carried away making it and am happy to share!

—**FAYE ROBINSON** PENSACOLA, FL

**PREP:** 50 MIN. • **PROCESS:** 10 MIN.
**MAKES:** 7 HALF-PINTS

- 1¾ **pounds kumquats**
- 1 **cup water**
- 1 **package (1¾ ounces) powdered fruit pectin**
- 6½ **cups sugar**

**1.** Rinse kumquats; cut in half and remove seeds. Place in a food processor; process until fruit is coarsely chopped.
**2.** In a Dutch oven, combine the kumquats and water. Stir in pectin.

Bring to a full rolling boil over high heat, stirring constantly. Stir in sugar; return to a full rolling boil. Boil and stir 1 minute.
**3.** Remove from heat; skim off foam. Ladle hot mixture into seven hot half-pint jars, leaving ¼-in. headspace. Remove air bubbles and adjust headspace, if necessary, by adding hot mixture. Wipe rims. Center lids on jars; screw on bands until fingertip tight.
**4.** Place jars into canner with simmering water, ensuring that they are completely covered with water. Bring to a boil; process for 10 minutes. Remove jars and cool.
**NOTE** *The processing time listed is for altitudes of 1,000 feet or less. Add 1 minute to the processing time for each 1,000 feet of additional altitude.*

# Indian-Spiced Snack Mix

Use your microwave to make a big batch of snack mix in just 20 minutes. It's ideal for anyone who likes a little spice. What a great change of pace from sweets!

—JILL POKRIVKA YORK, PA

**START TO FINISH:** 20 MIN.
**MAKES:** 2½ QUARTS

- 3 cups Rice Chex
- 3 cups Corn Chex
- 3 cups Wheat Chex
- 1 cup salted cashews
- ½ cup sliced almonds
- ½ cup shelled pistachios
- 3 tablespoons corn syrup
- 3 tablespoons honey
- 4½ teaspoons butter
- 1½ teaspoons salt
- 1½ teaspoons ground cardamom
- ½ teaspoon ground ginger
- ⅛ teaspoon cayenne pepper

**1.** In a large bowl, combine cereals and nuts. In a small microwave-safe bowl, combine corn syrup, honey and butter; microwave, uncovered, on high for 30-45 seconds or until bubbly. Stir in salt and spices; pour over cereal mixture and toss to coat.

**2.** Microwave in batches on high for 2 minutes, stirring once. Spread onto a baking sheet to cool. Store in an airtight container.

**NOTE** *This recipe was tested in a 1,100-watt microwave.*

# Orange-Almond Choclava

A twist on classic baklava, this recipe adds semisweet chocolate to the nut filling and drizzles even more on top. Christmas gift-giving has never been yummier!

—NELLA PARKER HERSEY, MI

**PREP:** 1 HOUR • **BAKE:** 50 MIN. + CHILLING
**MAKES:** ABOUT 6 DOZEN

- 1 pound slivered almonds
- 1 cup (6 ounces) semisweet chocolate chips
- ¾ cup sugar
- 2 tablespoons grated orange peel
- 1½ cups butter, melted
- 1 package (16 ounces, 14x9-inch sheets) frozen phyllo dough, thawed

**SYRUP**
- 1¼ cups orange juice
- ¾ cup sugar
- ½ cup honey
- 2 tablespoons lemon juice

**DRIZZLE**
- 2 ounces semisweet chocolate, chopped
- 3 tablespoons water

**1.** Preheat oven to 325°. Place the almonds and chocolate chips in a food processor; pulse until finely chopped. In a large bowl, combine the almond mixture, sugar and orange peel. Brush a 15x10x1-in. baking pan with some of the butter.

**2.** Unroll the phyllo dough. Layer 10 sheets of phyllo in prepared pan, brushing each with butter. Keep remaining phyllo covered with plastic wrap and a damp towel to prevent it from drying out. Sprinkle with a third of the almond mixture. Repeat layers twice. Top with remaining phyllo sheets, brushing each with butter. Cut into 1-in. diamonds. Bake for 50-60 minutes or until golden brown. Meanwhile, in a saucepan, combine syrup ingredients; bring to a boil. Reduce heat; simmer, uncovered, for 20 minutes.

**3.** In a small heavy saucepan, heat chocolate and water over very low heat until melted and smooth, stirring constantly. Pour syrup over warm baklava; drizzle with the chocolate mixture. Cool completely in pan on a wire rack. Refrigerate, covered, several hours or overnight. Serve at room temperature.

## Mulled Wine Cordial

Give festive bottles of your own mulled wine to family and friends this Christmas season. They'll love it! You might want to double the recipe and keep a bottle on hand for parties at home, too.

—JAMES SCHEND PLEASANT PRAIRIE, WI

**PREP:** 15 MIN. • **COOK:** 1 HOUR + CHILLING
**MAKES:** 22 SERVINGS (1½ OUNCES EACH)

- 1  **large orange**
- 1  **medium lemon**
- 4  **cups dry red wine**
- 1  **cup sugar**
- 1  **cinnamon stick**
- 4  **whole cloves**
- 1  **vanilla bean**
- 1  **cup brandy**
   **Ice cubes, optional**

**1.** Using a vegetable peeler, remove colored layer of peel from orange and lemon in strips, leaving the white pith. Cut fruit crosswise in half; squeeze juice into a large saucepan.

**2.** Add wine, sugar, cinnamon, cloves and citrus peels to pan. Split vanilla bean lengthwise. Using the tip of a sharp knife, scrape seeds from the center into wine mixture.

**3.** Cook over medium-low heat 1 hour to allow flavors to blend, stirring occasionally. Transfer to a large bowl; cool completely. Let stand, covered, 24 hours.

**4.** Strain wine, discarding solids. Stir in brandy. Pour into glass bottles; seal tightly. Refrigerate at least 1 week. If desired, serve over ice.

# Best Bacon Jam

After sampling bacon jam at a restaurant, I just had to try making it at home. My family loved the result! Spread it on sandwich bread, hamburger buns, crackers, muffins—you name it.

—PAULA MARCHESI LENHARTSVILLE, PA

**PREP:** 15 MIN. • **COOK:** 1¾ HOURS
**MAKES:** 3½ HALF-PINTS

- 2 pounds bacon strips, cut into ½-inch pieces
- 2 large Vidalia onions, chopped
- 4 garlic cloves, minced
- 2 cups strong brewed coffee
- 1 cup cider vinegar
- 1 cup unsweetened pineapple juice
- ½ cup Nutella
- ¼ cup crushed pineapple, drained
- 2 tablespoons brown sugar
- ½ teaspoon ground cinnamon
- ¼ teaspoon pepper
- ⅓ cup peach nectar

**1.** Rinse four 1-cup plastic or freezer-safe containers and lids with boiling water. Dry thoroughly.

**2.** In a 6-qt. stockpot, cook bacon in batches over medium heat until it starts to brown, stirring occasionally. Remove with a slotted spoon; drain on paper towels. Discard drippings, reserving 3 tablespoons in pan.

**3.** Add onions to drippings; cook and stir over medium heat 5-6 minutes or until tender. Add garlic; cook 1 minute longer. Return bacon to pan. Stir in the coffee, vinegar, pineapple juice, Nutella, pineapple, brown sugar, cinnamon and pepper; bring to a boil. Reduce heat; simmer, uncovered, 45 minutes, stirring occasionally. Cool slightly. Transfer to a blender in batches; cover and pulse until chopped.

**4.** Return mixture to pan; bring to a boil. Simmer, uncovered, 15 minutes longer, stirring occasionally. Add peach nectar; simmer, uncovered, 20-30 minutes longer or until jam is thickened. Cool slightly. Store in airtight containers in the refrigerator for up to 2 weeks.

# Salted Peanut Rolls

A Christmas gift of homemade candy is always a hit with sweet tooths. I dip these peanut rolls in chocolate, but they're yummy plain, too.

—ELIZABETH HOKANSON ARBORG, MB

**PREP:** 1 HOUR + FREEZING
**MAKES:** ABOUT 5 DOZEN

- 1 jar (7 ounces) marshmallow creme
- 2 to 2¼ cups confectioners' sugar, divided
- 1 package (14 ounces) caramels
- 2 tablespoons water
- 4 cups salted peanuts, chopped
- 2 cups (12 ounces) semisweet chocolate chips
- 2 teaspoons shortening

**1.** Line two 15x10x1-in. pans with waxed paper. In a large bowl, beat marshmallow creme and 1 cup confectioners' sugar until blended.

Knead in enough remaining confectioners' sugar until mixture is smooth and easy to handle.

**2.** Divide mixture into four portions. Roll each portion into ½-in.-thick logs. Cut crosswise into 1½-in. pieces; place on one prepared pan. Freeze 15 minutes or until firm. Meanwhile, heat caramels and water over low heat until melted, stirring occasionally. Working with one-fourth of the logs at a time, dip in melted caramel; roll in peanuts. Place on remaining prepared pan. Repeat with remaining logs; freeze coated logs until set.

**3.** In top of a double boiler or a metal bowl over barely simmering water, melt chocolate chips and shortening; stir until smooth. Dip bottom of rolls into melted chocolate; allow excess to drip off. Return to prepared pans. Refrigerate until set. Store between layers of waxed paper in an airtight container at room temperature.

# Sugar Plum Phyllo Kringle

Thanks to store-bought phyllo dough, this pastry is easier to make than it looks. Serve it not only for breakfast, but also for dessert with a scoop of ice cream.

**—JOHNNA JOHNSON** SCOTTSDALE, AZ

**PREP:** 30 MIN. • **BAKE:** 20 MIN. + COOLING
**MAKES:** 6 SERVINGS

- ¾ **cup chopped dried apricots**
- ½ **cup dried cherries**
- ⅓ **cup water**
- ¼ **cup sugar**
- ¼ **cup raisins**
- ¾ **cup chopped walnuts**
- 1 **tablespoon lemon juice**
- 1 **package (8 ounces) cream cheese, softened**
- 12 **sheets phyllo dough (14x9 inches)**
  **Butter-flavored cooking spray**
  **Confectioners' sugar**

**1.** Preheat oven to 375°. In a large saucepan, bring apricots, cherries, water, sugar and raisins to a boil. Reduce heat; simmer, uncovered, 6-8 minutes or until the liquid is thickened. Stir in the walnuts and lemon juice. Remove from heat; cool completely.

**2.** In a small bowl, beat cream cheese until smooth. Place one sheet of phyllo dough on a work surface; spritz with cooking spray. Layer with remaining phyllo, spritzing each layer. Spread cream cheese over phyllo to within 2 in. of edges; top with dried fruit mixture. Fold in edges; roll up, starting with a long side.

**3.** Place in a parchment paper-lined 15x10x1-in. baking pan, seam side down. Spritz top with cooking spray. Bake 20-25 minutes or until golden brown. Cool on a wire rack. Sprinkle with confectioners' sugar.

# Turtle Snack Mix

A decadent turtle sundae I had at a restaurant inspired this sweet-salty snack mix. Just try to stop at one handful!

—**PRISCILLA YEE** CONCORD, CA

**PREP:** 10 MIN. • **COOK:** 5 MIN. + CHILLING
**MAKES:** 3½ QUARTS

- 1 **package (14¼ ounces) Chocolate Chex**
- 1 **cup pecan halves, toasted**
- ¾ **cup packed brown sugar**
- 6 **tablespoons butter, cubed**
- 3 **tablespoons light corn syrup**
- ¼ **teaspoon salt**
- ¼ **teaspoon baking soda**
- 1 **cup (6 ounces) semisweet chocolate chips**
- 1 **cup Kraft caramel bits**
- 1 **cup miniature pretzels**

**1.** In a large microwave-safe bowl, mix cereal and pecans. In a 2-cup glass measuring cup, combine brown sugar, butter, corn syrup and salt; microwave, uncovered, on high for 1-2 minutes or until smooth, stirring once.

**2.** Whisk in baking soda. Pour over cereal mixture; toss to coat. Microwave, uncovered, on high 3 minutes, stirring every minute.

**3.** Spread onto a parchment paper-lined baking sheet; immediately sprinkle with chocolate chips and caramel bits (do not stir). Refrigerate until chocolate is set. Break into pieces. Stir in pretzels. Store in an airtight container.

## Holiday Helper

When it comes to gifting, think outside the box! Holiday tins are delightful, but most craft stores also sell cardboard tubes, "Chinese takeout" cartons and other containers that make ideal presentations for cookies and snack mixes.

# HOMEMADE GIFTS & DECOR

# Geometric Holiday Hand Towels

The perfect gift for holiday bakers, these printed towels take advantage of simple stamps and sponges. Include the set of three with a platter of cookies or a loaf of freshly baked bread.

## MATERIALS

**3 white dish towels**
**Fabric paint—gold, green and red**
**Palette or plastic plate**
**Smooth kitchen sponge**
**Narrow masking tape**
**2 triangular sponges**
**Glue gun**
**10 small diamond-shaped wood pieces**
**Acrylic stamp block or wood block**
**Foam pouncer**
**Scrap paper (see Note)**

## NOTE

Before painting towels, practice stamping the designs on scrap paper.

## DIRECTIONS

**1.** Wash, dry and iron towels.
**2.** For gift box design, spread gold paint onto palette or plate. Cut a sponge into a square shape for gift box. Attach two pieces of crisscrossing tape to sponge for the ribbons on box. Place sponge into paint, gently patting up and down to ensure coverage. Remove tape (if paint leaked through, apply fresh tape, keeping it on while stamping). Firmly press sponge onto towel.
**3.** Place a triangular sponge into gold paint, gently patting up and down to ensure coverage. Firmly press sponge off-center above gift box for one side of the bow. Repeat for the remaining side of the bow.
**4.** For tree design, spread green paint onto palette or plate. Place a triangular sponge into paint, gently patting up and down to ensure coverage. Firmly press sponge onto towel. Repeat to create five rows of three trees.
**5.** For poinsettia design, use a small amount of glue to adhere the wood diamond shapes in a circle on the acrylic or wood block, creating a poinsettia-shaped stamp. Let dry.

**6.** Using pouncer, carefully apply red paint to the top of the diamond shapes until entire poinsettia design is covered. Firmly press stamp onto the towel.

**7.** Let towels dry completely.
**8.** To heat-set paint, run towels through dryer for 30-40 minutes on the highest setting.

# Trimmed Ornaments

Make you holidays merry and bright with these elegant ornaments. No one will suspect you made the set of three decorations with leftover trimming and fringe.

## MATERIALS

**Hot glue gun**
**Decorative fabric trim—2-3 yards each of white ruffle, gold sequin fringe and small white pom-pom**
**3 small plastic foam shapes—ball, egg and cone**
**Coordinating ribbon or fabric trim for hanging loops**
**3 decorative pins**
**Additional embellishments, optional**

## DIRECTIONS

**1.** Before gluing trim to foam shapes, practice wrapping trim around each shape to determine how to space the layers. Layers on the tree and pinecone should overlap.
**2.** For the tree, slowly begin wrapping the ruffle trim tightly around the bottom edge of foam cone, gluing as you go. Continue gluing the trim in the same way until you reach the top of the tree. Cut excess trim and let dry.
**3.** For the pinecone, glue sequin trim to foam egg the same as for tree. Let dry.
**4.** For the snowball, glue pom-pom trim to foam ball the same as for tree. Let dry.
**5.** For each ornament, cut a short length of ribbon or extra trim, and pin the ends to the top of the ornament, creating a hanging loop.
**6.** Glue additional embellishments to ornaments as desired. Let dry.

# Gold Glitter Branches

Tired of the same holiday centerpieces? Enhance Christmas table arrangements and outdoor flora with these pretty additions. Simply transform twigs and branches from your own backyard into magical metallic accents.

## MATERIALS

**Natural branches of desired sizes**
**Scotch Super 77 Spray Adhesive**
**Box or box top (to work over when adding glitter)**
**Gold glitter**
**Krylon Triple-Thick Crystal Clear Glaze**

## DIRECTIONS

**1.** Remove any dirt from branches. Cut branches to desired length.
**2.** Following adhesive manufacturer's directions, spray each branch generously with adhesive, making sure to cover all sides of branch.
**3.** Hold each branch over the box or box top and generously sprinkle glitter on all sides of branch. Prop up branches and let dry completely.
**4.** Following glaze manufacturer's directions, spray glitter-covered branches with clear glaze to help secure glitter on branches. Let dry. Add additional coats if needed, letting glaze dry after each application.
**5.** When branches are dry, add them to the desired floral arrangement.

# Paper Ornament Gift Tags

This year, add a personal touch to your wrapped gifts. Create cute ornament-shaped tags using decorative scrapbook paper, card stock or whatever paper you might have on hand.

## MATERIALS

**Ornament patterns on opposite page**
**Tracing paper**
**Scrapbook paper or card stock in assorted solid colors and patterns**
**Coordinating narrow ribbon**
**Craft glue**

## DIRECTIONS

**1.** Trace ornament patterns onto tracing paper and cut out.

**2.** Trace each pattern onto the back of 2 coordinating sheets of scrapbook paper or card stock. Cut out shapes.

**3.** For each ornament, choose one of the two cutouts to be used as the background piece. Cut the remaining shape horizontally in half or in 3 pieces. Glue 1 or 2 pieces to the background piece so that part of the background remains visible, aligning the outer edges. Let dry.

**4.** On each ornament, glue a short length of ribbon horizontally across the edges where the different paper pieces meet, concealing the edges. Let dry. Trim ribbon even with the outer edges of ornaments.

**5.** Cut a short length of ribbon for each ornament. Glue it in a loop at the top of each ornament.

**6.** Write on back or front of tags as desired, and attach to packages.

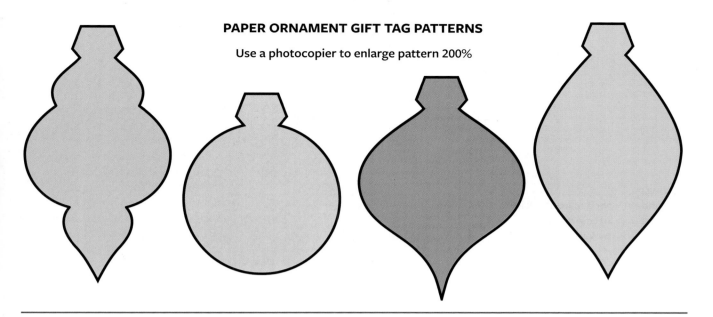

# Bleached Pinecone Centerpiece

Showcase nature's beauty all winter long with this idea. It's fun to tell your family and friends you created the conversation piece on your own.

## MATERIALS

**Pinecones (see Note)**
**Bleach**
**Large bucket**
**Rubber gloves**
**Paper towels**
**Baking sheets**
**Piece of natural burlap**
**Decorative platter**
**2 glass cylinder vases of the same height—one wide and one narrow**
**Pillar candle**
**Evergreen sprigs**

## NOTE

If using store-bought pinecones, choose unscented pinecones without any coating.

## DIRECTIONS

**1.** Place pinecones in bucket. Using 2 parts bleach to 1 part water, pour enough bleach and water into bucket to cover pinecones. To keep cones from floating, place a plate on top to weigh them down. Keep pinecones in mixture for at least 24 hours.
**2.** Line baking sheets with paper towels. Wearing gloves, carefully remove pinecones from bleach and place them on paper-towel lined baking sheets. (Pinecones will have closed up and some may not appear bleached.) Let pinecones dry and repoen indoors, or place them outdoors in sunlight to speed drying. Drying may take 1-3 days.
**3.** Set the burlap piece onto the platter as desired. Set wide vase on top. Place the narrow vase inside the wide vase, and place candle inside narrow vase.
**4.** Arrange the bleached pinecones inside the wide vase and on platter. Tuck evergreen sprigs into additional pinecones placed on the platter around the wide vase as desired.

making hole large enough to insert a ribbon for hanging. Wipe off any dust or dirt on wood slices.

**2.** Using a paper punch or scissors, cut a circular or oval shape from each photo, making sure the shape will fit below the hole on the wood slice.

**3.** With a paintbrush, apply a thin, even coat of decoupage glue to the back of a wood slice; let dry. Apply an even coat to the front, quickly adhering a photo below the hole, making sure photo lays flat. Apply 2-3 more thin coats over photo and front of wood slice, letting glue dry between applications.

**4.** Repeat with remaining photos and wood slices. Let all pieces dry completely, overnight if needed.

**5.** Spray a thin coat of adhesive onto the front of each thin wood shape, then cover sprayed side with metallic glitter. Shake off excess glitter. Let dry completly.

**6.** Apply a thin line of craft glue around the edge of an ornament photo and sprinkle with glitter. Shake off excess glitter. Use a soft brush or small piece of paper towel to carefully wipe away any remaining glitter.

**7.** In the same way, add a glitter border to each ornament if desired. Let ornaments dry completely.

**8.** Using wood glue, adhere desired glittered wood shape onto the back of each ornament. Let dry.

**9.** If desired, spray each ornament with sealer following manufacturer's directions for use.

**10.** Thread a piece of ribbon through each ornament hole and tie to create a hanging loop.

## Wooden Photo Ornaments

Bring the outdoors inside with these custom-made accents. Perfect for decorating the Christmas tree, they also make handsome additions to centerpieces and wrapped gifts.

### MATERIALS

**Coaster-size wood slices**
**Matte-finish photo for each ornament**
**Thin wood shape for each ornament,
    such as monogram letter, snowflake
    or dog bone as pictured below**
**Gloss-finish decoupage glue**
**Ribbon for hanging loops**
**Metallic glitter**
**Small paintbrushes**
**Spray adhesive**
**Craft glue**
**Wood glue**
**Circle or oval paper punch for punching
    out photos, optional**
**Clear coat spray sealer, optional**

### DIRECTIONS

**1.** If wood slices do not have holes, drill a hole through the top of each,

*Get creative this holiday!*
*Give pingpong balls and a string*
*of LED lights a festive cafe-style*
*treatment with this delightful idea.*

## Pingpong Ball Lights

**MATERIALS**
**Craft knife or utility knife**
**White pingpong balls**
**Liner paintbrush**
**Acrylic craft paint in desired color**
**Strand of small LED lights (see Note)**
**Toothpicks**
**Foam block**

**NOTE**
Use only LED light strands for this craft,
not traditional Christmas lights which may
become too hot for the pingpong balls.

**DIRECTIONS**
**1.** Using craft knife, carefully make
a slit measuring roughly ¼ in. along
the seam of a pingpong ball. Make
another cut across the first, creating
a plus-sign shape just large enough
for one LED bulb to be inserted.
Repeat with remaining balls.

**2.** Using liner brush, write "Let It
Snow" or another message by painting
a letter on each ball. Paint snowflakes
or other designs on additional balls
as desired.
**3.** Allow the paint to dry by placing
each ball onto a toothpick and then
inserting it into a foam block to hold
it upright. Dry completely.
**4.** Remove pingpong balls from
toothpicks Insert each LED bulb
into a painted ball.

## Vellum Photo Library

Showcase special photos in this three-sided, illuminated tabletop display. It's perfect for any decor—home or office.

**MATERIALS**
**Three 5X7-inch photos**
**Vellum paper**
**Three 5x7-in. tabletop photo frames**
   **with straight edges**
**Adhesive roller or small adhesive dots**
**Invisible tape**
**Medical cloth tape**
**Small battery-operated candle**

**DIRECTIONS**
**1.** Print 3 separate 5x7-in. photos onto vellum paper.
**2.** Remove backs from frames. Place a very small amount of adhesive in each corner of the glass on one frame. Gently press a front-facing vellum photo onto the glass, adhering the photo to each corner. Apply invisible tape along the edges in back of frame so that the tape overlaps the photo, securing the photo and glass to frame. Repeat with remaining vellum photos and frames.
**3.** Lay the 3 frames down side by side with the back sides facing up.

**4.** Cut a piece of cloth tape that is long enough to tape the sides of two frames together. Making sure the frames are touching one another, press the tape over the adjacent edges of the first and second frame, taping the frames together.
**5.** In the same way, tape the second and third frames together.
**6.** Carefully stand up the connected frames; bend in the two outer frames so their edges touch, forming a three-sided luminary.
**7.** Turn on battery-operated candle and place in the center of luminary.

# Monogram Door Hanger

Whether used to dress up a doorway or jazz up a wrapped gift, this crafty monogrammed hanger makes a cute and clever surprise.

## MATERIALS

**12-gauge decorative wire**
**Wire cutters**
**Tape**
**Natural jute twine**
**4¾-in. flat finished wood ornament (see Note)**
**Glue gun**
**Christmas-print ribbon**
**Two 1½-in. silver sleigh bells**
**2½-in. flat white wood letter for monogram**
**Artificial holly stem with berries and pinecones**

## NOTE

If your ornament does not have a hole at the top, drill a small hole through the top for tying the hanger to the ornament.

## DIRECTIONS

**1.** Shape wire into a 3-in. circle and cut off the excess using wire cutters. Overlap the ends of circle and tape securely together.

**2.** Tie one end of twine to the taped area of the wire circle. Wrap the twine all the way around the circle, covering it completely and leaving a tail of twine at the end.

**3.** Using the tail of twine, tie the wood ornament to the wrapped hanger. Glue twine knots to secure. Let dry.

**4.** Use the ribbon to tie a bow to the twine between the wrapped hanger and the wood ornament.

**5.** With twine, tie the sleigh bells to the wrapped circle so that the bells hang in front of the wood ornament.

**6.** Glue the letter to the wood ornament where desired. Let dry.

**7.** If needed, use wire cutters to trim the holly stem. Glue stem to the wood ornament, positioning stem so that it overlaps the ribbon bow. Let dry.

# Christmas Cactus Pots

Perfect for the gardener on your gift list, these clay pots couldn't be easier or more adorable. Choose colors that best reflect the decor of the recipient.

## MATERIALS

**3 clay pots with saucers**
**Sandpaper**
**Sponge or soft rag**
**Sponge brush**
**Acrylic craft paints—white, metallic gold, green and red**
**Paintbrushes**
**Soft tape measure, optional**
**Painter's tape**
**3 plastic pot liners or clear acrylic spray varnish**
**3 plants of choice**

## DIRECTIONS

**1.** Clean and soak pots and saucers in warm water for 1 hour. Sand any rough edges and wipe clean with sponge or rag. Let dry completely.
**2.** Use a sponge brush to apply 2-3 coats of white acrylic paint to saucers and exterior of pots, letting paint dry after each application.
**3.** Use a paintbrush to adorn the top edge or rim of desired pots and saucers with metallic gold paint.
**4.** If desired, use soft tape measure to measure the circumference of pots. Use this measurement as a guide for determining the size and number of painted designs that will fit around each pot.

**HERRINGBONE DESIGN:** Use pencil to mark angled lines in a continuous pattern around the center of pot. Use desired paintbrush to paint metallic gold and green lines where marked.

**TRIANGLE DESIGN:** Use pencil to mark a continuous triangle pattern around the bottom of a pot. Attach painter's tape along the sides of one triangle and paint with metallic gold. Dry completely; remove tape. Repeat until pattern is complete.

**RANDOM–DIAMOND DESIGN:** Use a fine paintbrush to paint red diamond shapes freehand at random places around a pot. When dry, use fine paintbrush to paint a metallic gold border around each diamond.

Let pots dry completely. Line pots with plastic liners or follow varnish manufacturer's directions to apply 2-3 coats of varnish to inside of pots, letting varnish dry after each application. Plant desired plant in each pot.

# Dried Fruit Garland

Spruce up your kitchen with a lovely, aromatic garland of cinnamon sticks, bay leaves and a variety of dried delights.

## FINISHED SIZE
Approximately 30 inches in length

## MATERIALS

**3 navel oranges**
**2 lemons**
**2 limes**
**2 Bartlett pears**
**3 Red Delicious apples**
**1 package brown 20-gauge craft wire**
**1 bag small to medium pinecones**
**1 spool twine or jute**
**1 leather upholstery needle**
**5 cinnamon sticks (about 3½ in. each)**
**Hot glue**
**1 jar (.16 ounces) whole bay leaves**

## DIRECTIONS

**1.** Preheat oven to 220°. Using a sharp knife, carefully slice the oranges, lemons, limes, 1 pear and 2 apples, horizontally, about ¼-in. thick. Slice remaining pear and apple vertically, about ¼-in. thick. Place slices on parchment covered cookie sheet. Place sheets in oven and bake for 2½ hours. Turn fruit slices and bake an additional 2½ hours or until fruit slices appear dry and edges of apple slices begin to curl. Remove from oven; cool.

**2.** Cut craft wire into six 5-in. pieces. Wrap a piece of wire around the inside center of each of 6 pinecones, twisting wire to secure.

**3.** Cut a 55-in. section of twine. Tie a loop at one end. Thread the twine through upholstery needle. Thread twine through the wire of a pinecone. Alternately thread 1-2 fruit slices onto the twine.

**4.** Wrap twine around a cinnamon stick. With a hot glue gun, secure twine on cinnamon stick and cover spot of glue with a bay leaf. Thread 1-2 fruit slices onto twine, alternating different types of fruit and directions of slices.

**5.** Continue threading with the pinecones, fruit slices and cinnamon sticks; reserving one pinecone.

**6.** Finish garland with remaining pinecone and tie a loop in the remaining twine.

## Recycled Sweater Mittens

Just can't bring yourself to get rid of your favorite worn-out wool sweater? Recycle it into these cozy mittens!

### FINISHED SIZE

This pattern will fit a medium hand. Measure your hand and adjust the pattern size if needed.

### MATERIALS

**Patterns on opposite page**
**Tracing paper**
**Wool sweater with ribbed sleeves**
**¼ yd. fleece for lining**
**Coordinating all-purpose thread**
**Coordinating buttons (optional)**

### DIRECTIONS

**1.** Trace the enlarged patterns onto tracing paper, and cut out. Position the patterns on sweater. Pin patterns and cut out. Position the patterns on fleece; pin and cut out.
**2.** For the cuff, cut off the bottom of a ribbed sweater sleeve plus ¾ in. of the sweater, cutting through both layers. Adjust cuff width to fit patterns.

**3.** To create back of mitten, place back bottom and back top sweater pieces right sides together, and pin. Leaving a 1/4-in. seam allowance, stitch together around the thumb and across to edge of mitten.

**4.** Place the back and front sweater pieces right sides together. Pin with 1/2-in. seam allowance. Stitch around mitten, leaving lower edge open.

**5.** Repeat steps 3 and 4 with fleece pieces, leaving 1/4-in. seam allowance in step 4. Turn wool mitten inside out. Insert fleece mitten into wool mitten.

**6.** With the right side facing out, insert the whole ribbed sleeve portion of the sweater inside the mitten, finished edge first. Align the sleeve's raw edge with the mitten's bottom edge. Pin the edges together, leaving a 1/2-in. seam allowance, and stitch. Fold cuff to outside over the wool mitten. If desired, sew a button to the middle of the cuff, stitching through the cuff, wool mitten and fleece mitten.

**7.** To create other mitten, flip back bottom patterns and back top pattern to opposite side, and repeat steps 1 through 6.

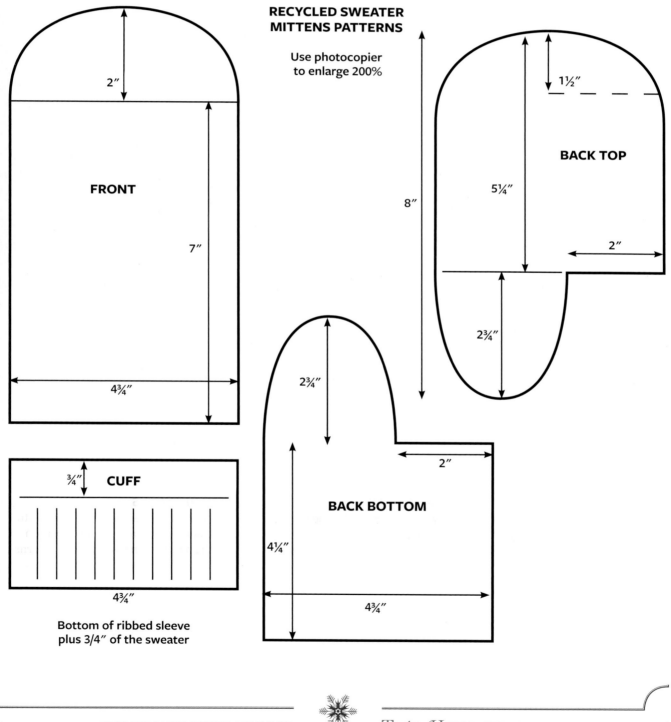

**RECYCLED SWEATER MITTENS PATTERNS**

Use photocopier to enlarge 200%

**FRONT**

2"

7"

4¾"

**BACK TOP**

1½"

5¼"

8"

2"

2¾"

**CUFF**

¾"

4¾"

Bottom of ribbed sleeve plus 3/4" of the sweater

**BACK BOTTOM**

2¾"

2"

4¼"

4¾"

# Fun Felt Christmas Stockings

You'll put a smile on St. Nick's face when he fills these whimsical keepsakes!

## MATERIALS

**Patterns on opposite page**
**Tracing paper**
**⅓ yard each light blue , white and green felt**
**One 9x12-in. sheet each of red glitter, green, brown, yellow, white, black and orange felt**
**2 strands green embroidery floss**
**4 strands white embroidery floss**
**1 bottle (4 ounces) premium craft and fabric glue**
**1 stipple paint brush**
**1 white fine line paint pen**
**1 black fine line paint pen**

## DIRECTIONS

**1.** Trace enlarged stocking pattern onto tracing paper with pencil. Pin pattern to a double thickness of the light blue felt. Cut pattern piece from felt. Repeat with white and green felt.

**2.** Thread a needle with 2 pieces of white embroidery floss. Sew around the blue stocking's outside edge using a blanket stitch. See Fig. 1 for stitch illustration. Turn stocking inside out. Repeat, using the white floss for the white stocking and green floss for the green stocking.

**3.** Trace the enlarged hanger loop pattern onto tracing paper with pencil. Pin pattern to scrap of blue felt. Cut pattern piece from felt. Make a loop and sew onto the inside seam of blue stocking. Repeat with scraps from white and green felt for each applicable stocking.

**BLUE STOCKING:** Trace snowflake patterns onto tracing paper with a pencil. Pin patterns to sheet of white felt. Cut patterns from felt. Repeat with pattern for snowman head. Trace headband pattern on tracing paper with a pencil. Pin pattern on sheet of black felt. Cut pattern from felt. Repeat with nose pattern on sheet of orange felt and earmuff pattern on remaining red glitter felt sheet. Glue snowflakes and snowman head in desired design on stocking. Glue headband slightly above snowman head. Glue nose in middle of the snowman head, pointing upward. Glue the earmuffs to each side of headband. Once dry, draw eyes and mouth onto snowman with black paint pen. Draw highlights on nose and earmuffs with white paint pen.

**WHITE STOCKING:** Trace tree patterns onto tracing paper with a pencil. Pin patterns to sheet of green felt. Cut pattern pieces from felt. Trace trunk pattern onto tracing paper with a pencil. Pin pattern to sheet of brown felt. Cut pattern piece from felt. Repeat twice. Repeat with star pattern and yellow felt, creating three stars. Trace ornament patterns onto tracing paper with a pencil. Pin patterns to remaining red glitter felt sheet. Cut pattern pieces from felt; repeat as desired. Glue trees in desired design on stocking. Glue tree trunks beneath each tree. Glue stars and ornaments to trees. Once dry, draw highlights on stars and ornament with white and black paint pens.

**GREEN STOCKING:** Trace large and small poinsettia patterns onto tracing paper with a pencil. Pin patterns to sheet of red glitter felt. Cut patterns pieces from felt. Repeat twice. Cut nine small circles from sheet of white felt. With glitter side facing out, glue large poinsettias to stocking in desired design With glitter side facing out,

glue the small poinsettias at center of large poinsettias. Glue three white circles in the center of each poinsettia. Once dry, draw dots onto the centers of white circles with black paint pen.

**FIG. 1** Blanket stitch

## FELT STOCKING PATTERNS

Use a photocopier to enlarge patterns 200%

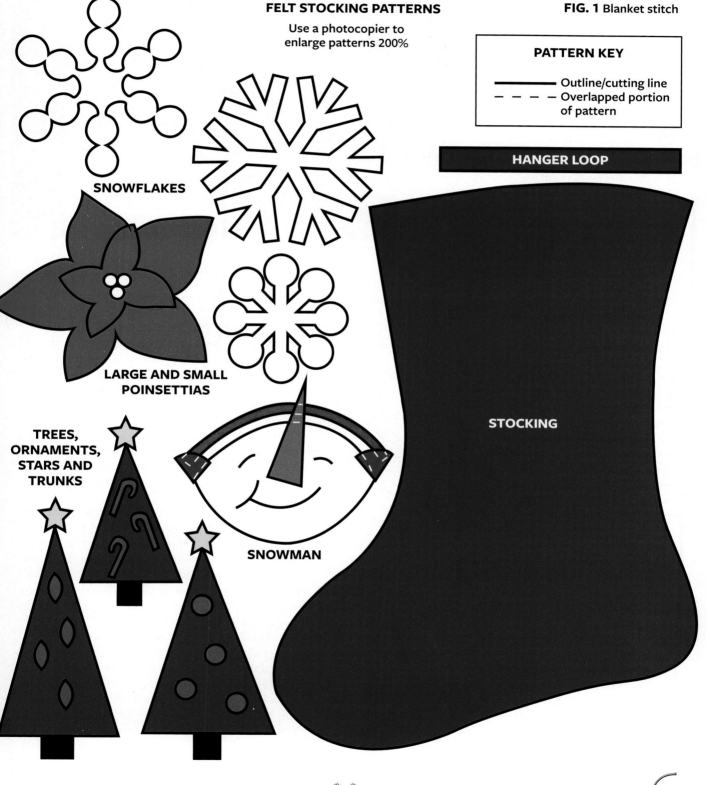

SNOWFLAKES

LARGE AND SMALL POINSETTIAS

TREES, ORNAMENTS, STARS AND TRUNKS

SNOWMAN

**PATTERN KEY**

——— Outline/cutting line
– – – – Overlapped portion of pattern

**HANGER LOOP**

**STOCKING**

# Beaded Key Chains

Steer your jewelry-making skills in a new direction with these attractive key chains.

## FINISHED SIZE
7½ in. long, each

## MATERIALS FOR SILVER KEY CHAIN (SEE NOTE)
11½ in. of silver oval-link chain
1 silver jump ring
1 silver swivel hook clasp with medium key ring
Ten or eleven 2-in. silver head pins
1 package assorted seed beads
1 package silver bead caps
Assorted beads in various sizes and colors
1 silver medium charm with jump ring
1 silver lobster claw clasp

## MATERIALS FOR GOLD KEY CHAIN (SEE NOTE)
1 gold jump ring
1 gold swivel hook clasp with medium key ring
8½ in. of gold oval-link chain
Eight 2-in. gold head pins
1 package assorted seed beads
1 package gold bead caps
Assorted beads in various sizes and colors
1 gold medium charm with jump ring
2 gold small charms with jump rings
3 gold lobster claw clasps

## NOTE
Both key chains require the use of a side cutter as well as chain-nose, bent-nose and round-nose pliers.

## DIRECTIONS FOR SILVER KEY CHAIN
**1.** Measure 7½ in. from the top of the chain. Cut and open the link to create two chains. (To open a chain link or jump ring: Position chain-nose and bent-nose pliers on each side of the cut. Bring the tips of one pliers toward you, and push the tips of the other pair away—do not pull the ring side to side. To close the link or ring, reverse the process.)
**2.** Open the jump ring, and attach the key ring of the hook clasp and one end of the shorter chain. Measure 4 in. from one end of the longer chain; slide that link onto the jump ring so one end of that chain hangs longer than the other. Close the jump ring.
**3.** To make a bead unit: On a head pin, string a seed bead or bead cap. String assorted beads as desired, and make a loop. (To make a loop: Leaving ⅜ in. of pin above the top bead, use side cutters to trim the excess. Using chain-nose pliers, bend the pin to a 90-degree angle. Use round-nose pliers to grasp the end of the pin and roll it toward the bead. Reposition the pliers and continue rolling to complete the loop.) Repeat to make 10 or 11 bead units.
**4.** Open the jump ring of a charm, and attach it to the loop of the lobster claw clasp. Attach the lobster claw clasp to the end of the longest chain. Open the loop of the largest bead unit as you would a jump ring (see step 1), and attach it to the end of the shortest chain. Close the loop. Continue attaching bead units, varying sizes and spacing them along the chain as desired.

## DIRECTIONS FOR GOLD KEY CHAIN

**1.** Open a jump ring, and attach the key ring of the hook clasp. (To open a jump ring: Position chain-nose and bent-nose pliers on each side of the cut. Bring the tips of one pliers toward you, and push the tips of the other pair away—do not pull the ring side to side. To close the ring, reverse the process.) Measure 4 in. from the top of the chain; slide that link onto the jump ring so one end of the chain hangs longer than the other. Close the jump ring.

**2.** To make a bead unit: On a head pin, string a seed bead or bead cap. String assorted beads as desired, and make a loop. (To make a loop: Leaving ⅜ in. of pin above the top bead, use side cutters to trim the excess. Using chain-nose pliers, bend the pin to a 90-degree angle. Use round-nose pliers to grasp the end of the pin and roll it toward the bead. Reposition the pliers and continue rolling to complete the loop.) Repeat to make 8 bead units.

**3.** To make a charm unit: Open the jump ring of each charm, and attach it to the loop of a lobster claw clasp. Close each jump ring.

**4.** Open the largest charm's lobster claw clasp, and attach it to the end of the shortest chain. Attach another charm unit to the middle of the short chain, and attach another toward the top of the longest chain.

**5.** To attach bead units: Open the loop of the largest bead unit as you would a jump ring, and attach it to the end of the longest chain. Continue attaching bead units, varying sizes and spacing them along the chain as desired.

## Outdoor Ball Ornament

Take your love of crafting to the outdoors with a sturdy jumbo-size ornament. Decorate an evergreen or hang it from a balcony for a little holiday cheer.

### MATERIALS

**Two 8-in.-diameter clear acrylic prismatic ribbed dome clip-on lamp shades**
**Gloss enamel craft paint—red or green**
**Red or green glitter**
**Loctite GO2 Gel glue**
**22-gauge wire**
**Ribbon for hanging loop**

### DIRECTIONS

**1.** Remove light bulb clip from inside each acrylic dome.

**2.** Paint the interior of each dome with gloss enamel craft paint. While paint is still wet, generously sprinkle glitter around the interior of each dome. Let dry.

**3.** Gently shake excess glitter out of domes. Replace the light bulb clip inside each.

**4.** Spread gel glue all the way around the top edge of one dome. Place the second dome on top with the edges matching to adhere, forming a ball shape. Following glue manufacturer's directions, let dry completely.

**5.** Cut a 6-in. length of wire. Twist wire piece tightly around the ornamental bulb clip on one end of ball ornament, creating a small wire loop at the top for the hanger. Trim any excess wire.

**6.** Thread desired length of ribbon through the hanger and tie to create a loop for hanging.

## Ball Ornament Wreath

Don't toss your old ornaments! Recycle them into this striking salute to the merriest season of them all. Use the color combination you like best or simply use an assortment of whatever ornaments you have on hand. Regardless, the result will be a truly impressive sight.

### MATERIALS

Wire cutters

12-gauge aluminum floral wire for wreath hook

14-in. plastic foam flat-face circle wreath form

Glue gun

Wide ribbon to wrap around wreath form

Shatter-proof ball ornaments of desired colors in a variety of sizes

Coordinating miniature ornament clusters

### DIRECTIONS

**1.** With a wire cutters, cut a 6-in. length of wire. Shape wire piece into a small loop, twisting one end of wire several times around the base of loop. Insert the other end into back of wreath form as deeply as possible without penetrating the front. If needed, add glue to hook to secure. Let dry completely.

**2.** Wrap ribbon tightly around wreath form, covering it completely and leaving the wire hook exposed. Glue the ribbon ends on the back of wreath to secure. Let dry.

**3.** Remove the metal tops from ball ornaments. Attaching the ornaments with the top down, glue medium-to-larger ornaments around the outer edge of the wreath form. Let wreath dry completely.

**4.** In the same way, glue ornaments of all sizes to the wreath form, creating a layered look. Fill gaps by gluing in miniature ornament clusters.

**5.** Let the wreath dry completely before hanging.

## Rustic Christmas Tree

Ask the kids to gather sticks and twigs from the yard for this earthy decoration.

### FINISHED SIZE

Wall hanging measures 13 in. high x 9 in. wide, approximately.

### MATERIALS

13x9-in. rectangular piece of barnwood or rustic wood for background

White acrylic craft paint

Wood stain

Small star-shaped wood cutouts in a variety of sizes

Variety of thin natural tree branches and twigs

Glue gun

White snowflake novelty buttons

Sawtooth hanger, optional

### DIRECTIONS

**1.** Wipe the rectangular wood background piece clean. Mix 1 part white paint with 1 part water and brush over background piece. Wipe paint with cloth, creating an aged look. Let dry.

**2.** Following stain manufacturer's instructions, apply stain to desired wood stars. Let dry.

**3.** From a branch or twig, cut a piece measuring about 7-in. long for the widest part of tree. Cut about 22 more pieces, making sure each piece is slightly shorter than the last; Lay out the pieces in a tree pattern.

**4.** Cut two 2¼-in. pieces for the tree trunk. Cut one 2-in. piece and four 1-in. pieces for the tree topper.

**5.** Glue the cut branch and twig pieces to the painted wood background piece in the planned Christmas tree shape. Let dry.

**6.** Glue snowflake buttons and wood star shapes to the tree and background where desired. Let dry.

**7.** Add sawtooth hanger to the back of piece for hanging if desired.

# Snowflake Package Trims

Take paper crafting to new heights with nine intricate snowflakes. Tape the impressive cutouts to wrapped packages or hang them from gift bags!

## FINISHED SIZES

Large Round: 12 in.
Medium Round: 9 in.
Square: 10 in.
3-D: 9½ in.

## MATERIALS

**Large Round Snowflake (1)**
 1 sheet (12-in. square) one-sided
  scrapbook paper
 Pattern on page 216
 Tracing paper

**Medium Round Snowflakes**
 **(2, 3, 4, 5, 6)**
 1 sheet copy paper
 3 sheets construction paper
 1 sheet vellum paper
 Patterns on page 216
 Tracing paper

**Square Snowflakes (7, 8)**
 1 sheet vellum paper
 1 sheet suede paper
 Patterns on pages 217
 Tracing paper

**3-D Snowflake (9)**
 Cutting pattern on page 217
 2 sheets one-sided scrapbook
  paper
 2 sheets double-sided scrapbook
  card stock
 1 can (5.75 ounces) Krylon Glitter
  Blast Golden Glow spray paint
 Glue gun

# DIRECTIONS

## LARGE ROUND SNOWFLAKE

**1.** Fold the 12-in. square of scrapbook paper as shown in Folding Steps, below right. Run the edge of a ruler along the folds to smooth them.

**2.** Trace pattern 1, page 216, onto tracing paper, and cut out. Align the pattern along the folded edge of the snowflake paper, and trace pattern with a pencil.

**3.** Cut out the traced pattern, being careful not to cut through the folded edge or tip. Carefully unfold to reveal the snowflake.

## MEDIUM ROUND SNOWFLAKES

**1.** Cut copy paper, construction papers and vellum paper into 8½-in. squares. Fold as shown in Folding Steps, right. Run the edge of a ruler along the folds to smooth them.

**2.** Trace patterns 2, 3, 4, 5 and 6 on page 216 onto tracing paper, and cut out. Align one pattern along the folded edge of a snowflake paper, and trace the pattern with a pencil.

**3.** Cut out the traced pattern, being careful not to cut through the folded edge or tip. Carefully unfold the paper to reveal the snowflake. Repeat with the remaining patterns and papers.

## SQUARE SNOWFLAKES

**1.** Using 8½-in. square vellum paper, fold in half to make a triangle. Fold triangle in half to make a smaller triangle. Run the edge of a ruler along the folds to smooth them.

**2.** Trace pattern 7 from page 217 onto tracing paper. Align the pattern along the folded edge of the vellum, and trace the pattern with a pencil.

**3.** Cut out the traced pattern, being careful not to cut through the folded edge. Unfold the snowflake carefully. Repeat with the suede paper and pattern 8 from page 217.

## 3-D SNOWFLAKES

**1.** Copy and enlarge the cutting pattern on page 217 as directed. Tape the pattern to an 8½-in. sheet of scrapbook paper. Use a craft knife to

cut through the pattern's L-shaped lines. Follow the pattern to cut the scrapbook paper into four squares. Remove the cutting pattern. Use the cutting pattern and a second sheet of scrapbook paper to make a fifth square.

**2.** For each square, lift the tips of the innermost flaps, and curl them around a pencil to form a tube shape. Secure flaps with small pieces of transparent tape. Flip the square over, and lift the next pair of flaps. Bend

them around the pencil and secure with tape to form this tube opposite the first. Continue with the remaining flaps. Repeat with the remaining four squares.

**3.** Use tape to secure five points, one from each piece, together to form a snowflake.

**4.** Repeat with scrapbook card stock, using hot glue to secure the flaps

**5.** Lightly spray one side of the card stock snowflake with glitter spray paint. Let dry completely.

## FOLDING STEPS

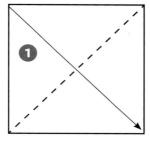

**Fold square in half to make triangle.**

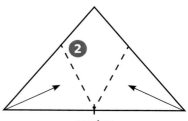

center

**With folded edge at bottom, fold right point and left point up, fine-tuning until triangle is divided into thirds and all edges are flush.**

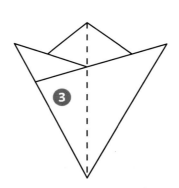

**You should now have three peaks at top and one at bottom. Fold straight along center.**

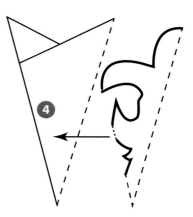

**Pattern 2 (for example) ready for tracing!**

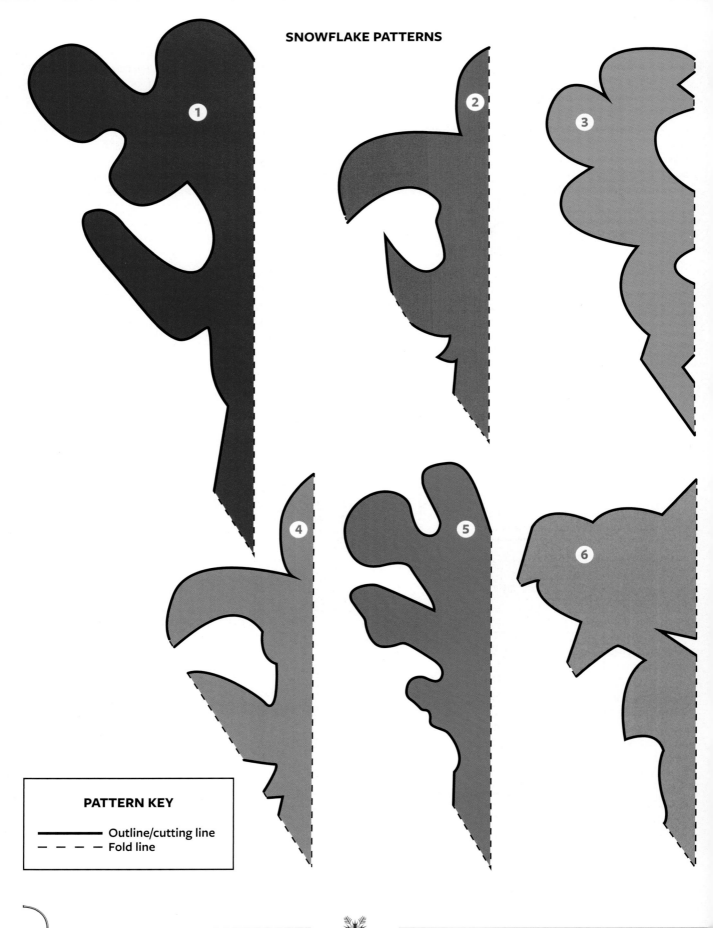

**PATTERN KEY**

——— Outline/cutting line
– – – Fold line

Use a photocopier to enlarge
patterns on this page 200%

**7**

**8**

**9** CUTTING PATTERN

## Snowflake String Art

Use a string-art technique to create a peaceful piece of wall decor that makes a truly impressive gift. The snowy wall scene is a lovely accent to any room.

**FINISHED SIZE**
12 in. square

**MATERIALS**
**Acrylic white craft paint**
**12x12-in. unfinished basswood canvas**
**Acrylic teal craft paint**
**Clear gloss paint**
**Pattern on opposite page**
**Tracing paper**
**1-in. nails (see Note)**

**White crochet thread**
**Spray adhesive**

**NOTE**
The points of the nails will be visible on back of the canvas. If desired, carefully cover the back of the canvas with card stock or desired material.

## DIRECTIONS

**1.** Add water to white paint to create a whitewash. Brush whitewash onto the front and sides of wood canvas. Let whitewash dry.

**2.** Repeat, using water and the teal paint. Let dry.

**3.** Apply 3 coats of gloss to front and sides of canvas, drying between coats. Let dry a total of 24 hours.

**4.** Trace the enlarged snowflake pattern onto tracing paper and cut out. Following the manufacturer's directions on the adhesive, spray one side of pattern with adhesive and adhere to the center front of canvas.

**5.** Pound nails about halfway into the wood along the edges of entire pattern, spacing nails about ½- to ⅝-in. apart. Remove pattern.

**6.** Tie the end of the thread around a nail. Working from one nail to the next, wrap thread around each nail to create the outline of the snowflake. Continue wrapping thread from nail to nail in a zigzag pattern until pleased with the design.

**7.** Tie off the thread in a knot around a nail. Trim tail of the thread close to the knot.

## SNOWFLAKE STRING ART PATTERN

**Use a photocopier to enlarge pattern 200%**

# Snowy Etched Candle Vases

## MATERIALS

3 clear glass cylinder vases
Desired adhesive-backed etching
   stencils
Painter's tape
Newspaper
Protective gloves
Glass etching cream
Small paintbrush
Clean sponge or paper towel
3 pillar candles
Clear glass bead vase filler

## DIRECTIONS

**1.** Clean vases with soapy water. Let dry completely. Keep areas to be etched clean of all fingerprints and smudges.

**2.** Adhere a stencil onto a vase where desired, pressing firmly. Rub stencil to make sure there are no air bubbles or wrinkles.

**3.** Tape down outside edges of the stencil with painter's tape. Rub tape to smooth it down on the glass.

**4.** In a well-ventilated area, cover the work surface with newspaper. Wearing gloves, follow the cream manufacturer's directions and use a small paintbrush to apply etching cream generously onto open area of the stencil. Brush in at least two directions to avoid showing brush strokes. Leave the cream on for 15 minutes.

**5.** Wipe off cream with a damp sponge or damp paper towel, removing the cream completely.

**6.** Remove stencil and tape from vase. Immediately wash vase with warm water, using a clean sponge or paper towel. Wash vase with soapy water, rinse and dry.

**7.** Repeat the etching process as needed to add desired etched designs to each vase. Let vases dry completely.

**8.** Place candle in each vase; pour glass bead vase filler around candles.

*Enjoy the beauty*
of a snowy day with these lovely candle vases.
A basic etching technique makes them easy.

## Noel Marquee Light Letters

These show-stopping letters promise to light up your holiday celebrations! Made easily with paper mache letters and pingpong balls, the letters can be custom made to spell out any yuletide word or phrase you'd like.

### MATERIALS

**12-inch paper mache letters:**
   **N, O, E and L (see Note)**
**Utility knife or box cutter (see Note)**
**1 can (11.5 ounces) Krylon Craft Series**
   **Shimmer Metallic red spray paint**
**4 sets (20 lights each) connectable**
   **electric clear indoor LED mini-lights**
**48 ping-pong balls**

### NOTE

We created a marquee spelling "Noel," but you could use this technique for the marquee of your choice. Adjust the number of light sets and pingpong balls accordingly. A craft knife could also be used in place of a utility knife or box cutter for this craft. Use LED lights: they run cooler and are safer.

### DIRECTIONS

**1.** Use a ruler and pencil to measure and mark approximately 1 in. from the top and approximately 1 in. from the left side of the front of the letter N. Draw a small "x" for the placement of the first bulb. Measure approximately 2 in. below this first mark and place the second "x." Continue downward until you have five such markings. Using the same method, mark the right vertical part of the letter, making sure that the all marks are horizontally even. Create three such marks on the diagonal part of the letter, centered in the middle and spaced approximately 2 in. apart. There should be 13 marks on the letter N.

**2.** Continue the same measurement and marking method on the front of the other three letters. There should be 14 marks on the O, 13 marks on the E, and 8 marks on the L. Use the tip of a utility knife to carefully cut each "x," noting that the smaller the cut the tighter the bulb will fit.

**3.** To remove back of letters, turn the letters over and use a utility knife to carefully cut through the back of each letter, leaving a 1/4-in. border around the top back side. Do not to cut through the side or the front of the letters. Carefully cut until the back of the letter is loose and removable. Remove any inside cardboard supports.

**4.** In a well-ventilated area, set the letters down, front side facing up. Evenly spray the front and sides of all four letters with spray paint. Spray two coats, allowing 15-20 minutes dry time between coats.

**5.** To position the lights, gently poke the light bulb nearest the plug end of a strand of lights through the bottom "x" through the backside of the letter N. Continue until all of the "x" holes are filled with a light bulb. Repeat with other remaining letters.

**6.** Using the tip of a utility knife, carefully cut a small "x" into each pingpong ball. If the balls have a logo, cut the "x" in the middle of the logo. Hold each light bulb from the back of the letter and gently push each pingpong ball over each light bulb. Plug each light strand into the next and plug the final strand into the wall outlet.

## Snow Scene Ornament

Capture the whimsical spirit of the season with this simply enchanting, scene-stealing keepsake.

### MATERIALS

**Plastic foam ball that will fit inside ornament**
**Two-piece clear plastic fillable ball ornament**
**Artificial snow**
**Coarse clear glitter**
**Desired miniature Christmas figurines and decorations for snow scenes**
**Narrow ribbon for ornament hangers**
**Spray adhesive**
**Craft knife**
**Glue gun**

### DIRECTIONS

**1.** Use a craft knife to cut a small section off the top of the foam ball, creating a shape that resembles a hill to form the base of the snow scene.

**2.** Spray a thin, even coat of spray adhesive onto the foam base; quickly sprinkle it with artificial snow and glitter. Let dry. If needed, add a second coat of snow and glitter in the same way and let dry.

**3.** Attach desired figurines and decorations to base to create a Christmas scene, inserting items into the base or gluing them on top.

**4.** Sprinkle a small amount of artificial snow and glitter into the bottom section of the ornament. Carefully place snow scene on top of snow, positioning scene so it faces the front of ornament; snap ornament closed. If needed, open ornament and reposition scene or add more snow.

**5.** Thread a piece of ribbon through the top loop on ornament. Tie ribbon in a loop for hanging.

# Sparkle Snowflake Mobile

Add a little beauty to a quiet corner in your home with these glittery paper snowflakes. Hanging from branches, the pretty flakes are the perfect way to brighten up any room this season. Choose the card stock color that best matches your decor.

## MATERIALS

**3 small natural tree branches or sticks**
**12-in.-square sheets of glitter card stock—one each of blue, gold and white**
**Gold metallic all-purpose thread**
**White 6-strand embroidery thread**
**White spray paint**
**Craft glue**
**3-inch snowflake paper punch**

## DIRECTIONS

**1.** Cut branches or sticks into three 9-in. pieces. Following paint manufacturer's directions, spray pieces with white spray paint. Let dry.

**2.** For mobile top, stack the painted branches on top of each other so that they fan out in a star shape and overlap in the center.

**3.** Tie white thread around the center of the bottom branch. Wrap the thread around the branch several times, then lay the second branch on top in the planned position and tightly wrap the thread around the center of both branches, attaching them together. Attach the remaining branch on top in the same way, wrapping all three of the branches tightly together.

**4.** Using the paper punch and the glitter card stock, make 12 white snowflakes, 10 blue snowflakes and 8 gold snowflakes.

**5.** Cut fifteen 3-ft. pieces of gold thread. Add glue to the back of two matching snowflakes. Lay the end of a thread piece in the glue on one snowflake and press the glued side of the remaining snowflake over the thread, carefully aligning the edges of the snowflakes.

**6.** Continue attaching a snowflake pair to each piece of gold thread in the same way.

**7.** Wrap the unglued end of each thread piece to the mobile top, staggering the snowflakes at different heights and positioning them so that the arrangement balances the mobile. When pleased with the arrangement, tie the thread to the sticks to secure.

**8.** Tie a loop of white thread to the mobile top for a hanger.

# Taped Tree Card Display

Using washi tape, it's a snap to decorate a plain wall in your house with a simple Christmas tree design. As you receive them, add your holiday cards for a fun and festive display.

## MATERIALS

**Washi tape—gold, green prints and red prints**
**Ruler, yardstick or tape measure**
**Desired jar lids for circle ornament patterns**
**Greeting cards**

## DIRECTIONS

**1.** Measure wall space and determine desired tree size.

**2.** With a pencil, lightly mark the desired top and bottom points of tree on wall, leaving space for a star at the top and a planter at the bottom.

**3.** Measure the length needed for the vertical center line of tree and cut a green piece of tape this length. Adhere tape to wall in a straight vertical line.

**4.** Determine the desired number of horizontal tree branch pieces and lightly mark their locations along the center of tree.

**5.** Cut green tape to the desired length for the bottom tree branch. Tape the piece in a straight horizontal line on the wall where planned so that the center of the piece overlaps the vertical center line of tree.

**6.** Continue adding branch pieces to the tree in the same way, working from the bottom of the tree to the top; making each branch piece slightly shorter than the last.

**7.** Lightly mark the desired height of the star on the wall. From gold tape, cut 4 pieces of this length. Tape 2 pieces to the wall in a plus-sign shape, then tape the remaining 2 pieces in an X- shape over the plus sign.

**8.** For the planter, lightly mark a trapezoid shape centered underneath the tree. Tape pieces of gold tape to the wall where marked.

**9.** For each circle ornament, tape a series of red strips to a jar lid and

cut along the edges to remove excess. Carefully remove the tape strips from the lid, piece by piece. Tape the strips to the wall one piece at a time to form the ornament shape, adding a small piece of contrasting red tape at the top to resemble a hanger.

**10.** For each remaining ornament, tape a series of red strips to the wall in a staggered pattern as desired and add a hanger to the top the same as before.

**11.** Tape the center top of each card to the wall so that the cards resemble ornaments hanging on the tree.

## Sweet Painted Mugs

Cheers! Easy-to-use paint pens create fun and colorful designs on white coffee mugs for these one-of-a-kind gifts

### MATERIALS

**2 white ceramic coffee mugs (see Note)**
**Cookie cutters to use as patterns—gingerbread man, large circle and small circle**
**Scrap paper**
**Temporary spray adhesive**
**Oil-based paint-pens—gold, pink, orange, yellow, green, blue and white**
**Goo Gone cleaner to remove adhesive**
**Cotton applicator or small sponge applicator**

### NOTE

Painted coffee mugs are not dishwasher or microwave safe.

### DIRECTIONS

**1.** Wash coffee mugs and let dry completely.
**2.** For patterns, trace gingerbread cookie cutter on scrap paper and cut out. Trace large circle cookie cutter onto paper, then trace small circle cookie cutter in the center to create a doughnut shape. Cut out doughnut.
**3.** Lightly spray temporary adhesive on back of gingerbread pattern and gently adhere the pattern to a coffee mug where desired, smoothing down the edges.
**4.** Randomly paint dots around gingerbread pattern using paint pens in a variety of colors, placing dots closer together along the edge of pattern. Continue adding dots until they form an obvious gingerbread man outline. Let dry. Carefully remove the pattern.

**5.** Repeat with doughnut pattern and remaining mug the same as before. Trace outline of doughnut using gold paint pen. Let dry. Remove pattern.
**6.** Use cotton or sponge applicator and Goo Gone to remove any remaining adhesive on both mugs.
**7.** Use white paint pen to paint the glaze on the doughnut, applying 3-4 coats and letting the paint dry after every application.
**8.** When painted glaze is dry, randomly add sprinkles on doughnut using paint pens in a variety of colors. Let dry.

## Winter Wonderland Teacups

It's fun to create magical gardens with vintage teacups. They're so easy!

### MATERIALS FOR ONE CUP

**China teacup and saucer**
**Glass decorator marbles**
**Sheet of artificial moss or large precut snowflake**
**Hot glue gun**
**Miniature accents and artificial snow as desired (see Note)**

### NOTE

Not sure what to put in your winter garden? Anything goes, including any plastic trinkets buried in your junk drawer! Look for tiny trees from model train sets, dollhouse miniatures or ceramic figurines from thrift and antique shops.

### DIRECTIONS

Wash and dry teacup and saucer. Fill cup with marbles. Trim moss or snowflakes to fit width of cup; set over marbles. Use a hot glue gun to decorate with miniature accents as desired. Sprinkle with artificial snow if desired.

# Handmade Heart Sachets

These sweet potpourri-filled sachets are perfect to give as gifts for Christmas or anytime. What a delightful way to use up extra scraps of fabric.

## FINISHED SIZE

Tall heart measures about 5½ in. tall and wide heart measures about 3½ in. tall.

## MATERIALS

**Heart patterns below right**
**Tracing paper**
**Fabric scraps**
**Coordinating all-purpose thread**
**Trims, optional**
**Pinking shears**
**Potpourri**
**Ribbon for hanging loop if desired**
**Coordinating button**
**Ribbon for hanging loop, optional**

## DIRECTIONS

**1.** Trace tall heart pattern or wide heart pattern onto tracing paper and cut out. Pin pattern to desired fabric and cut out fabric heart with straight scissors. Unpin pattern and repeat, creating a matching fabric heart.
**2.** If desired, using all-purpose thread to hand-sew trims to the right side of one fabric heart, leaving space to add button at the top center point of the heart.
**3.** Pin together the two fabric hearts with right sides out and edges matching. Leaving an opening at the top, machine-sew the fabric hearts together with a ¼-in. seam allowance. Trim edges with pinking shears.
**4.** Loosely fill heart with potpourri through the top opening.
**5.** To add a hanging loop, cut a 6-in. length of ribbon, fold in half and insert the ends into the center of the heart opening. Hand-sew the opening closed.
**6.** Hand-sew button to sachet at the top center point of heart.

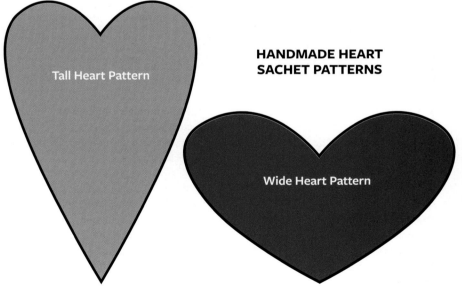

**HANDMADE HEART SACHET PATTERNS**

Tall Heart Pattern

Wide Heart Pattern

## Decoupage Coasters

Not sure what to get for the person who has everything? How about a set of these modern coasters?

### MATERIALS (FOR A SET OF 8)
**Compass**
**Two 12-in.-square sheets chipboard in color of choice**
**Sponge brush**
**Matte decoupage glue**
**Several 4½-in.-square scraps of patterned card stock**

**Polyurethane or waterproof clear sealer**

### DIRECTIONS
**1.** Using the compass, create four 4-in. circles on each chipboard sheet. Cut out all eight circles.

**2.** Using sponge brush, coat one side of each circle with a thin layer of decoupage glue. Adhere each circle to the back of a card stock scrap. Let glue dry. Trim card stock to the edge of each circle.

**3.** Coat the top (patterned) side of each coaster with at least two layers of decoupage glue. Let glue dry to the touch between each layer.

**4.** Coat the top side of each coaster with a thick layer of clear sealer. Let coasters dry 24 hours before using. To clean, wipe coasters with a damp cloth. Do not submerge in water.

# Off the Bee-Tin Path

Not only is it easy to make your own beeswax lip balm, but it's also a snap to design a cute container just perfect for the season of gift giving. Look for food-safe containers at your craft store or find them online.

## INGREDIENTS (FOR BALM)

- **2 tablespoons grated or finely chopped beeswax**
- **1 tablespoon coconut oil**
- **3 small vitamin E capsules**
- **1 - 2 drops essential oil, optional**

## MATERIALS (FOR CONTAINER)

**Small, lidded food-safe container**
**Scraps of patterned card stock**
**Scrapbook adhesive**
**Scrapbook embellishments, optional**

## DIRECTIONS (MAKES ABOUT 2 OZ.)

**1.** Combine beeswax, coconut oil and vitamin E oil in a glass measuring cup. (Use toothpick to puncture vitamin E capsules, squeezing out contents into cup. Discard capsule shells.)

**2.** Add water to a shallow pot. Set glass measuring cup in the water and set pot on the stovetop. Over medium heat, slowly bring the water around the measuring cup to a boil. Using a spoon, constantly stir ingredients in the measuring cup. When the ingredients are completely melted and combined into a light yellow liquid, remove all from stovetop.

**3.** If desired, add essential oil into mixture and stir. (Be careful not to add very much essential oil as it can hurt the skin if too concentrated.)

**4.** Using hot pads, carefully remove the measuring glass from the pot. Carefully pour mixture into container and let sit for at least an hour to cool and harden.

**5.** Cut a piece of patterned card stock to fit outside surface of the lid. Use scrapbook adhesive to adhere card stock, and other embellishments if desired, to the lid.

**6.** Place lid on container once lip balm has completely hardened.

# General Recipe Index

This index lists every recipe in the book by food category, major ingredient and/or cooking method, so you can easily locate recipes to suit your needs.

p. 11

p. 111

p. 91

p. 137

p. 9

p. 128

p. 138

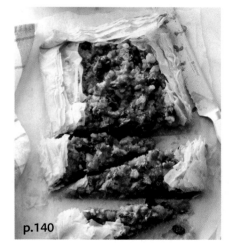

p.140

p. 171

p.133

## STEWS
Easy Pork Posole, 35
Shrimp & Cod Stew, 33

## STUFFING & DRESSING
Fancy Stuffed Pork Chops, 61
Sausage & Corn Bread Dressing, 52

## SWEET POTATOES
Coconut Mashed Sweet Potatoes, 116
Family-Favorite Sweet Potato Pie, 86
Sweet Potato Bisque, 23
Sweet Potato Praline Casserole, 84

## TOFFEE
Caramel Fluff & Toffee Trifle, 116

## TOMATOES
Cherry Tomato & Basil Focaccia, 27
Chicken Cacciatore with Polenta, 118
Chicken Thighs with Tomato-Vodka
  Sauce, 124
Sun-Dried Tomato Spinach-Artichoke
  Dip, 14
Tomato-Onion Green Beans, 122

## TORTILLAS
Anaheim Chicken Tortilla Soup, 28

## TURKEY & TURKEY
  SAUSAGE
Hearty Turkey 'n' Rice Soup, 31
Make-Ahead Turkey and Gravy, 49
Zesty Lemon Cream Turkey Pasta, 143

## VEGETABLES
*(also see specific kinds)*
Grandma's Collard Greens, 93
Hearty Beef & Vegetable Soup, 34
Warm Tasty Greens with Garlic, 52

## VEGETARIAN ENTREE
Broiled Cheese Stuffed Portobellos, 124

## WHITE CHOCOLATE
Festive Holiday Fruitcake Bark, 186
White Chocolate Maple Bacon
  Fudge, 147

## YEAST BREADS
Candied Lemon Christmas Bread, 139
Cherry Tomato & Basil Focaccia, 27
Garlic Potato Bread, 30
Italian Flatbread, 40
Scottish Oatmeal Rolls, 39

# Alphabetical Recipe Index

This index lists every recipe in the book in
alphabetical order. Just search for the titles
you want to easily find your favorites.

p. 45

p. 32

## Craft Index

This index lists every craft project in the book by craft category, technique and/or main materials, so you can easily locate the types of projects that interest you.

p. 200

Visual Geography Series®

# VENEZUELA

## ...in Pictures

Prepared by
Geography Department

Lerner Publications Company
Minneapolis

Independent Picture Service

**Animals trudge up a sandy incline in a desert area near Coro, northeast of Caracas.**

This book is an all-new edition in the Visual Geography Series. Previous editions were published by Sterling Publishing Company, New York City. The text, set in 10/12 Century Textbook, is fully revised and updated, and new photographs, maps, charts, and captions have been added.

Website address: www.lernerbooks.com

LIBRARY OF CONGRESS CATALOGING-IN-PUBLICATION DATA

**Venezuela in pictures.**

(Visual geography series)
Rev. ed. of: Venezuela in pictures / prepared by Lincoln A. Boehm.
Includes index.
Summary: An introduction to the land, history, people, economy, and government of the country with South America's largest known petroleum deposit.
1. Venezuela. [1. Venezuela] I. Boehm, Lincoln A. Venezuela in pictures. II. Lerner Publications Company. Geography Dept. III. Series: Visual geography series (Minneapolis, Minn.)
E2308.V52  1987  987       87–2794
ISBN 0–8225–1824–4 (lib. bdg.)

International Standard Book Number: 0–8225–1824–4
Library of Congress Catalog Card Number: 87–2794

## VISUAL GEOGRAPHY SERIES®

**Publisher**
Harry Jonas Lerner
**Associate Publisher**
Nancy M. Campbell
**Executive Series Editor**
Mary M. Rodgers
**Assistant Series Editor**
Gretchen Bratvold
**Editorial Assistant**
Nora W. Kniskern
**Illustrations/Editors**
Nathan A. Haverstock
Karen A. Sirvaitis
**Consultants/Contributors**
Dr. Ruth F. Hale
Nathan A. Haverstock
Sandra K. Davis
**Designer**
Jim Simondet
**Cartographer**
Carol F. Barrett
**Indexer**
Kristine S. Schubert
**Production Manager**
Gary J. Hansen

Independent Picture Service

**Waves crash against the rocks along Venezuela's Caribbean coastline.**

### Acknowledgments

Title page photo courtesy of Embassy of Venezuela, Washington, D.C.

Elevation contours adapted from *The Times Atlas of the World,* seventh comprehensive edition (New York: Times Books, 1985).

5  6  7  8  9  10  –  JR  –  03  02  01  00  99  98

Spanning the oil-rich basin of Lake Maracaibo, the General Rafael Urdaneta Bridge connects the city of Maracaibo with the Lara-Zulia motorway. An early Venezuelan independence leader, Urdaneta later became Simon Bolívar's chief of staff.

# Contents

CARIBBEAN SEA

LOS ROQUES ISLANDS        LOS HERMANOS ISLANDS

Amuay    Paraguaná
         Peninsula

Gulf of
Venezuela

Coro                              Juangriego   MARGARITA ISLAND
                                  CUBAGUA        Porlamar
         YARACUY    Puerto Cabello   CARACAS   La Guaira          Paria Peninsula
                          Morón        D.F.
FALCON                              La Guaira
                                              MIRANDA           SUCRE   Gulf of Paria
Maracaibo        LARA   Urachiche  Valencia  Las Tejerías  Guatire
         La Salina                  CARABOBO          San Francisco              Puerto La Cruz    TRINIDAD
ZULIA   Lake          Barquisimeto  Carabobo  Maracay  de Yare
        Maracaibo                          Lake Valencia                              ANZOATEGUI   MONAGAS
                 El Tocuyo                         ARAGUA
         TRUJILLO        COJEDES                                                     Ciudad
                                                                                    Guayana
                 PORTUGUESA          GUARICO                                              El Pao
Pan-American Highway                                              R.
         Mérida                    Portuguesa R.        Orinoco      Ciudad Bolívar
MERIDA   BARINAS        Apure R.              Manapire R.  Unare R.     Guri
San Cristóbal                                                                    El Callao
TACHIRA         Arauca R.                                          Caroni R.
                                   APURE                    Caura R.
                          Meta R.                                              Yuruari R.
                                                                    CANAIMA FALLS   Carrao R.
                                                    Orinoco                       DELTA AMACURO TERR
                                                              ANGEL FALLS
                                                                                    GUYANA
COLOMBIA
                                                    BOLIVAR

                 Orinoco R.

AMAZONAS TERR

                 Casiquiare Channel                                        BRAZIL

**VENEZUELA**   N ↑

—— State Boundaries

0 _____ 100 Miles
0 _____ 100 Kilometers

80°   60°   40°

EQUATOR                    0°

PACIFIC
OCEAN

                                          20°

**VENEZUELA**

SOUTH AMERICA

                           ATLANTIC
                           OCEAN        40°

0 ____ 1000 Miles
0 ____ 1000 Kilometers

## METRIC CONVERSION CHART
### To Find Approximate Equivalents

| WHEN YOU KNOW: | MULTIPLY BY: | TO FIND: |
| --- | --- | --- |
| **AREA** | | |
| acres | 0.41 | hectares |
| square miles | 2.59 | square kilometers |
| **CAPACITY** | | |
| gallons | 3.79 | liters |
| **LENGTH** | | |
| feet | 30.48 | centimeters |
| yards | 0.91 | meters |
| miles | 1.61 | kilometers |
| **MASS** (weight) | | |
| pounds | 0.45 | kilograms |
| tons | 0.91 | metric tons |
| **VOLUME** | | |
| cubic yards | 0.77 | cubic meters |
| **TEMPERATURE** | | |
| degrees Fahrenheit | 0.56 (*after* subtracting 32) | degrees Celsius |

The capital city of Caracas, founded in 1567, has developed into a major metropolis of the Western Hemisphere. The rapid growth of Caracas is due largely to the continuing importance of Venezuela's oil industry.

# Introduction

Venezuela, the wealthiest of the South American nations, ranks as the seventh largest producer of petroleum in the world. Oil became the focus in the economy soon after Venezuela's first commercial oil drilling in 1917.

By 1926 petroleum had replaced coffee as Venezuela's principal export. By 1928 Venezuela was ranked as one of the world's leading petroleum exporters. The dictatorship of Juan Vincente Gómez granted numerous concessions—including permission to operate and control the profits from secondary businesses—to foreign oil companies. Secret payments for these concessions were commonplace. Future political disagreement took root in public disgust with

the widespread abuse of power and of position to gain oil profits. Government corruption did not stop even in 1976, when Venezuela nationalized all of its oil fields.

Oil remains the core issue in Venezuelan affairs. Rising oil prices in world markets have created a boom in Venezuela's economy. The oil sector grew by 7.7 percent the first six months of 1995. The economy, which had fallen steadily in the early 1990s, has begun to turn around and was expected to rise nearly six percent in 1997.

Despite the positive economic outlook in the oil industry, however, Venezuelans are still worried. President Rafael Caldera won the 1993 election by campaigning vigorously to keep government control of most

5

of the business sector. In the months following Caldera's inauguration, bankruptcies rose dramatically and the banking system nearly collapsed. President Caldera eventually accepted assistance from the International Monetary Fund (an organization that provides short-term credit), but part of the deal involved lifting price controls, and laying off thousands of public workers. Unemployment rose, and inflation exploded to 103 percent.

Venezuelans also worry about the continuing drug traffic through their homelands. Venezuela's long, largely unprotected border with Colombia continues to be a relatively safe route to the cocaine markets of North America and Europe. Venezuelans suspect that drug gangs have bribed government officials into allowing the illegal shipments into Venezuela. Considering Venezuela's history of government corruption, and the still shaky economic outlook, the people are closely watching both President Caldera and their pocketbooks.

A side effect of Venezuela's petroleum industry is the pollution it causes. Here, a biologist at Simon Bolívar University attempts to control contaminated petroleum waste.

Pipelines follow the bends of a Venezuelan river en route to a refinery at Puerto La Cruz and waiting international oil tankers.

From the air, this section of Venezuela's western Andes is a panorama of land patches crossed by a long, snaking road that links villages and towns.

# 1) The Land

The Republic of Venezuela is located on the northern coast of South America and has a 2,000-mile coastline along both the Caribbean Sea and the Atlantic Ocean. To the west lies Colombia, with whom Venezuela shared its early history as a nation. To the south is Portuguese-speaking Brazil. Guyana, a former British colony, shares Venezuela's eastern border.

With 352,145 square miles of territory, Venezuela is larger than the states of Texas and Oklahoma combined. North to south, Venezuela stretches for more than 800 miles at its widest point. From west to east, it measures more than 900 miles. Within Venezuela, four main geographical regions are evident—the mountains, the Maracaibo Lowlands, the llanos, and the Guiana Highlands.

## The Mountains

The mountains of Venezuela—including the Andean Cordillera Mérida and the Cordillera de Venezuela—extend in an arc from Colombia to the tip of the Paria Peninsula along the Caribbean coastline. While representing only 12 percent of Venezuela's land area, this region contains two-thirds of the population and most of the country's major cities.

From the lowlands along the Caribbean, Venezuela's land rises quickly to great heights in several mountain ranges. The

7

highest point is Pico Bolívar at 16,427 feet in the Cordillera Mérida. The Sierra de Perijá—actually an extension of the Andes—has a rugged crest that marks the Colombian border, and its slopes form the western limits of the Lake Maracaibo Basin. The north-south Cordillera Mérida extends for 300 miles, but another Andean continuation—the Cordillera de Venezuela—is even longer. This range covers 310 miles west to east and extends 43 miles from north to south. Venezuela's largest cities are located on the slopes of its several mountain chains.

The interior ranges consist chiefly of rock, shale, sandstone, and limestone. The limestone creates spectacular formations, such as the San Juan Bluffs and the Cave of the Guácharos—named after birds that appear only in northern South America. The arid state of Falcón, which lies north of the Andes, is the only region resembling a desert in Venezuela.

## The Maracaibo Lowlands

The narrow strip of land between the mountains and the sea is the smallest geographical zone in Venezuela. It broadens out toward the west to form the Lake Maracaibo Basin—the heart of the oil industry—while far to the east the land flattens into the Orinoco Delta. More than 20 percent of the country's entire population lives in this region—on less than 7 percent of Venezuela's total amount of land. The warm valleys near the sea are important for growing cacao—from which chocolate is made—and farther from the coast coconut, sugarcane, and banana plantations thrive. Although the attractive Venezuelan islands of Margarita, Los Hermanos, and

Courtesy of Henry W. Haverstock

A small settlement is nestled between the sweeping heights of the Cordillera Mérida.

Los Roques are located near the coastal zone, their topography differs from the rest of the region.

### LAKE MARACAIBO

Lake Maracaibo, dotted with thousands of oil wells, lies in northwestern Venezuela. A 34-mile-wide channel connects the lake with the Gulf of Venezuela, which was so shallow that it had to be deepened to make way for the passage of oil tankers. Lake Maracaibo—75 miles wide and approximately 100 miles long—lies in hot, humid lowlands, which are encircled by the mountains of the Sierra de Perijá.

The great importance of Lake Maracaibo is its tremendous petroleum wealth, which developed from mud deposits millions of years ago. Even today, mud is still deposited at the bottom of the lake. Under most conditions, the lake would have filled up with sediment long ago. A remarkable geological balance is at work, however, in which the lake bed gradually sinks at the same speed at which the sediment is deposited. Centuries of sinkage and sedimentation have formed a layer of petroleum at the bottom of the lake. From this layer millions of barrels of oil are extracted each year.

## The Llanos

Flat, wide llanos—or plains—occupy more than one-third of Venezuela's territory and consist of both cleared savannas and untouched jungles. Attempts now are being made to turn the plains—traditionally cattle-raising country—into fields suited to the cultivation of rice and corn.

The plains are the result of mud and sand deposited by rivers over millions of years. Only a few mesas (flat-topped peaks), bits of scattered vegetation, and rivers, such as the Unare and the Manapire, break the landscape between the Andes and the Orinoco Delta.

Along the northern shore of the Orinoco River lies the Orinoco Heavy Oil Belt, a

Independent Picture Service

**An oil-drilling platform sits on the calm waters of Lake Maracaibo. The tall derrick *(right)* suspends and rotates a drill pipe, which is sunk in the lake's depths.**

Photo by Amandus Schneider

**Dense undergrowth and lush vegetation characterize Venezuela's jungle areas.**

9

Photo by Amandus Schneider

Venezuela's Gran Sabana occupies the southeastern corner of the state of Bolívar in the plains of the Guiana Highlands. The oddly shaped mountains are mixtures of sandstone, rock, and volcanic deposits.

vast expanse of petroleum deposits. These deposits have remained undeveloped because the oil is difficult to extract. In the late 1980s, the Venezuelan government formed a company to exploit these reserves, which are said to rival those of Saudi Arabia.

## The Guiana Highlands

The fourth major geographical division, the Guiana Highlands, is not to be confused with the three countries to the east. These nations are called collectively the Guianas and consist of Guyana (formerly British Guiana), Suriname (formerly Dutch Guiana), and French Guiana. The Largest of Venezuela's geographical divisions in size and the smallest in population, the Guiana Highlands includes all the land to the south and east of the Orinoco River. Still largely unexplored, the Guiana Highlands contain hilly, sparsely settled areas that are rich in mineral and forest resources. Striking mountains and gushing waterfalls mark the whole region. Indeed, most of Venezuela's rivers are found in this section of the country.

The Orinoco River separates two drastically different types of land. South and east of the Orinoco is a land of strange granite masses, vast plateaus, and sheer mountains in contrast to the extensive flatlands of the western plains. Sandstone-covered granite with a high content of pure iron makes up Cerro Bolívar and El Pao in Bolívar state. Farther south, beyond lowlands and jungles crossed by many rivers, is the Yuruari River, which is rich in gold. Finally, the spectacular Gran Sabana (Great Plain) comes into view. Its flat-topped mountains and sheer sides rise up one after another, like flights of steps, as they reach thousands of feet into the sky.

Dozens of rivers, which create magnificent waterfalls, tumble over the edges of the mountains. The extreme difficulty in reaching the Guiana Highlands has so completely hampered exploration that the headwaters of the Orinoco River were found only recently.

Unlike the Andean ranges, the mountains here consist of rocks overlaid by sandstone and volcanic deposits. The mineral deposits that they contain have never been fully tapped. Gold has lured prospectors to the Guiana Highlands for decades, and the search for diamonds is often successful.

The most important mineral resource of the Guiana Highlands is iron ore. The government began a crash project in 1974 to develop the iron-ore zone into a Venezuelan industrial resource area. A new steel industry is taking shape at Santo Tomé de Guayana, frequently known as Ciudad Guayana. Cement and metal-processing plants are now in operation, and a government-owned steel mill processes iron ore using nine electrical furnaces.

Venezuela's Amazon territory lies in the southern Guiana Highlands, near Brazil. The territory's thick jungles are crossed by numerous rivers, and its boundary lies less than 100 miles from the equator.

## Angel Falls

Angel Falls, the highest waterfall in the world, is located on a branch of the Carrao River—an upper tributary of the Caroní River. The total drop of 3,212 feet is more than 15 times longer than the descent of Niagara Falls. The falls was first observed from the air in 1935 by Jimmy Angel, a U.S. pilot who was exploring the mystery of El Dorado (the golden one)—a legendary treasure of gold said to be hidden in the area.

Uniquely, Angel Falls does not flow over the top of a cliff. The water gathers

Emerging from mountain crevices, Angel Falls drops more than 3,000 feet to a lush ravine. The long descent can be imagined by comparing the falls to the size of the airplane *(center)* flying across the middle of the cascading water.

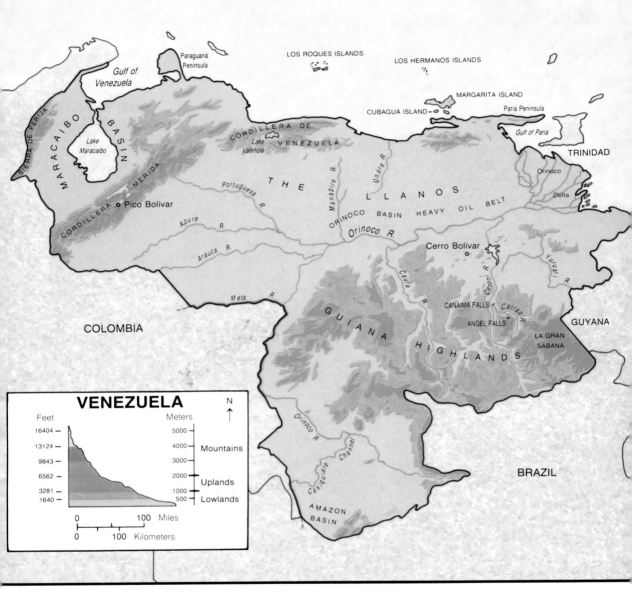

underground and erupts from several crevices located 300 feet below the top of the mountain. The Indians call the site of the falls Devil's Mountain because the area is often subject to fierce thunderstorms and mysterious cloud formations, which frequently hide Angel Falls from view. The falls can be seen from the air, and only recently has a person succeeded in scaling the steep sides of Devil's Mountain to reach its top.

## The Orinoco River

The Orinoco River, the eighth longest river in the world, has many tributaries along its 1,700-mile length. From the west flow large waterways—the Portuguesa, Apure,

The Orinoco River is shallow but wide at this point in its course, where many islands of greenery dot the waters.

Arauca, and Meta rivers—that originate in the Andes. These are streams of troubled waters and undefined courses that overflow their banks in the rainy season and flood great expanses of land. From the south and east, the Orinoco is enlarged by the dark waters of the Caroní and Caura rivers, which come from the mountains of the Gran Sabana.

Upstream and not far from their source, the waters of the Orinoco River divide, and one-third continues through the southern

Canaima Falls are located at the junction of the Carrao and Caroní rivers in the Guiana Highlands.

Casiquiare Channel to the mighty Amazon. Strangely, the point where the division takes place—777 miles from the sea by the Orinoco course and 1,864 miles from the sea by the Amazon route—is only 395 feet above sea level. In other words, the river's incline is so slight as to be inadequate for the water to flow for long distances. Seasonal rainfall—rather than the powerful runoff from melted Andean snow —causes the rivers to move.

Downstream from the dividing point, the Orinoco has a 25-mile-long course of rapids, which is the only barrier to continuous navigation from the Gulf of Paria to the mouth of the Amazon. On approaching the Caribbean Sea, the Orinoco divides itself again at the delta to distribute its waters through 26 outlets into the Atlantic Ocean.

Although the Orinoco River dominates Venezuela's waterway system, the nation has hundreds of lakes and beautiful lagoons in addition to its more than 1,000 rivers. During the wet season, the rivers swell and flood the lagoons, and the lakes rise so high that nearby cities are threatened by the overflowing waters.

## Climate

Venezuela's varied topography creates four distinct climatic zones. The tropical zone, or tierra caliente, ranges in altitude between sea level and 2,600 feet and has temperatures ranging from 76° F to 96 ° F. Included in this zone are the coastlines, the areas at the base of the mountains, and the plains, valleys, and deltas of the Orinoco River. Maracaibo is located in this zone and has an average temperature of 83° F and an average humidity of 77 percent, making it one of the hottest and most humid cities in South America.

The moderate zone, called the tierra templada, embraces the lower levels of the mountains, below 6,500 feet. The area's temperatures are mild, and the air is cool and moist at higher elevations. At lower

Independent Picture Service

The source of the Orinoco River lies deep within the Guiana Highlands. Throughout the river's long course, the Orinoco receives the waters of other rivers and occasionally spills over a cliff to form a powerful waterfall.

elevations, however, it can often be hot and humid.

The cool zone, or tierra fría, found only in the mountainous areas of the country, has temperatures ranging between 34° F and 75° F. Finally, the cold zone is the region where the snow never melts away. It is found in the Andean Cordillera Mérida, and the temperatures average as low as 17° F throughout the year.

The plains have an especially great moisture contrast between the rainy and the dry seasons. During the rainy season— from April to October—heavy rains fall, and the swollen rivers flood large stretches of land. Travel by land is difficult or impossible except on the main highways. In the dry season—from December through March—many of the rivers dry up, pastures wither, cattle find little to feed on, and even the rain forest loses its foliage.

Rainfall varies a great deal from region to region. Caracas averages 32 inches each year, while Ciudad Bolívar receives 41 inches or more. Despite Maracaibo's regularly high humidity, the city gets only about 23 inches of precipitation in an average year.

The variations of Venezuela's climate are illustrated by the contrast between the vegetation of the tropical rain forests *(above)* and the dry, cactus-studded land *(below)* near Coro.

Courtesy of Museum of Modern Art of Latin America

The busy and rapidly growing city of Caracas built a complex spiderweb of roads in the 1950s and 1960s to speed the traffic flow.

## Flora and Fauna

Venezuela is rich in unusual plant and animal life. The rivers and lagoons of the plains are full of crocodiles and strange fish. There are electric eels that can paralyze a bull with their electrical charges and ferocious piranhas that can eat an animal in a matter of seconds. Edible bagres, or catfish, can grow to over four feet long and can weigh up to 200 pounds.

Anteaters, *chiguires* (large rodents), jaguars, and peccaries (wild pigs) roam the land. The endless savanna, beautified by miriti palm trees, is full of birds. *Chenchenas* (small herons), scarlet ibis, and troupials fly overhead. Forests cover about half of Venezuela and feature stands of brazilwood and coral trees, as well as trees and shrubs that produce tropical fruits, such as mangoes and papayas.

## Major Cities

Caracas, the capital of Venezuela, is in a narrow valley 3,000 feet above sea level, bordered by steep mountains. In the last several decades, Caracas has changed dramatically from a provincial city to one of the richest and most modern capitals in the world. Many of its colonial structures have been replaced with tall apartment and office buildings. Its old dirt roads have been paved over by an *autopista*—a system of superhighways.

The city now has a metropolitan population of 3.4 million people—about 10 times its population in 1940. Growth has resulted in traffic jams on the autopista— only partially relieved by a new subway system. Insufficient housing is a problem, too, so that many poor people have built shacks, called *ranchos,* on the city's surrounding

**16**

Crocodiles inhabit many of the rivers and lagoons found throughout Venezuela.

Roughly-made ranchos cling to the hills surrounding Caracas. Made of various discarded materials, these dwellings often lack essential services, such as water and electricity.

hills, which are too steep for conventional construction. These communities of temporary housing are known as barrios (neighborhoods) and often lack essential services.

Caracas is rich in both history and natural marvels. The birthplace of Simon Bolívar—one of Venezuela's most famous sons—is within the city limits, as are many interesting museums, churches, and public buildings. La Guaira serves as the port for Caracas. Once linked by old mountain roads that took four hours to cross by car, Caracas and La Guaira are now connected by a six-lane superhighway that can be traveled in forty minutes. Maiquetía Airport, near La Guaira, handles international flights, while nearby Simon Bolívar Airport handles domestic flights.

The city of Maracaibo, which rivals Caracas in size, owes its importance to the oil industry that developed just beyond its shores in Lake Maracaibo, which is the largest lake in South America. The city has become a thriving industrial and commercial hub of about 1.4 million people.

A long time ago, Valencia (population 1.2 million) in northern Venezuela might have become the nation's capital. Unfortunately, disease-breeding marshes between the city and nearby Lake Valencia discouraged the early settlers. Valencia now lies in the middle of the leading agricultural region of Venezuela and is the country's most industrialized city.

## Secondary Cities

Barquisimeto, a large city with about 800,000 inhabitants, lies in good livestock-grazing country. Rebuilt completely after the earthquake of 1812, Barquisimeto is now a commercial center located on the Pan-American Highway about 150 miles from the Caribbean Sea.

Until surpassed in size by Ciudad Guayana, Ciudad Bolívar on the Orinoco River was the largest inland city in Venezuela. When Simon Bolívar headed Venezuela in the 1820s, Ciudad Bolívar was the capital of the eastern plains, the Orinoco Delta area, and the Guiana Highlands.

Northeast of Ciudad Bolívar at the junction of the Orinoco and Caroní rivers, the new city of Ciudad Guayana—the industrial capital of Venezuela's new iron and steel belt—was built. From a small village in 1960, it has grown into a bustling metropolis of 540,000 people.

Lake Valencia, which lies 75 miles west of Caracas, is separated from the Caribbean Sea by the peaks of the Cordillera de Venezuela.

When the Europeans arrived on the shores of northern Venezuela in the late fifteenth century, the coastal Indians lived in wooden houses built on stilts—dwellings that are still common among the nation's native groups. The style of housing reminded the explorer Alonso de Ojeda of Venice, Italy, and he christened the new land Venezuela—Spanish for "Little Venice."

# 2) History and Government

Christopher Columbus landed in Venezuela on August 1, 1498, during his third voyage to the New World. After reaching the island of Trinidad, he sailed along the coast toward the west and saw land that he mistook for another island. He named the area Isla de Gracia (Isle of Grace). Thus, it was on Venezuelan soil that Columbus first set foot on the South American continent.

The name Venezuela, which means "Little Venice," appeared for the first time shortly after Columbus's arrival. In about 1500 another explorer, Alonso de Ojeda, sailed along the northern coast of South America as far as Lake Maracaibo. He saw Indians living in groups of houses built on stilts over the waters of the lake, and these dwellings reminded him of the Italian city of Venice.

## Conquest of Venezuela

The Spaniards who followed Columbus to South America found several Indian groups in the country. Besides the Arhuaco and Goajiro, there were the Caribs—a warlike people who had spread to the farthest corners of the territory. The Betoya and Timote lived in the Cordillera Mérida and were believed to be descendants of the Chibcha Indians of Colombia.

The earliest known Spanish settlement was established in the sixteenth century in the northeastern part of Venezuela on Cubagua Island and was called Nuevo Cádiz. Fierce peoples inhabited most of the territory, but the Spaniards were determined to conquer the area. They sent expedition after expedition to subdue the local ethnic groups. By the end of the seventeenth century, the conquistadors had established settlements at El Tocuyo, Mérida, Caracas, Barquisimeto, and Coro.

Coro became important because of its business and political activities, especially after 1528, when representatives of a German banking firm set up headquarters in the town. The newly chosen Holy Roman emperor, Charles V—who was also known

**19**

as King Charles I of Spain—granted rights to this company to exploit the wealth of western Venezuela. In so doing, Charles V paid off his debt to the German firm, from whom he had borrowed heavily in his bid for the imperial crown.

Unsure of how long its rights would last, the company virtually looted the colony and slaughtered many of the native inhabitants. Two adventurers who worked as representatives for the company were especially famous—Ambrosio Alfinger and Nicholas Federmann. These men so abused their contract that Spain finally ended its agreement with the banking firm. The Spaniards, thereafter, undertook to colonize Venezuela themselves.

The Spanish found that conquering Venezuela was not a simple task. Although they encountered few pockets of resistance in the coastal areas, the central portion of the colony was not subdued until after the death of Guaicaipuro in the mid-sixteenth century. As the tough and able leader of

Sir Francis Drake, an English adventurer, attacked many Spanish settlements—including Caracas—in the late sixteenth century.

For centuries the cannons of a colonial-era fort stood ready to defend the town of Juangriego, on Margarita Island off Venezuela's northeastern coast. No longer invaded by wealth-seeking pirates, the town is now frequented by sun-seeking tourists.

Henry Morgan's daring raid on Maracaibo was only one of several entries into Spanish territory. After sacking several towns in Panama, he was recalled to Great Britain to answer accusations of breaking the Treaty of Madrid between Britain and Spain. Morgan was cleared of all charges, was knighted by King Charles II, and returned to Jamaica as lieutenant governor.

Courtesy of New York Public Library

the Teques Indians, Guaicaipuro organized a 10,000-warrior force that attacked early Spanish settlements, causing many of them to be abandoned.

## Piracy

Pirates replaced the Indians as the source of early colonial harassment. The Caribbean coast of Venezuela—and the large settlements that had developed there—were favorite points of pirate attacks. Caracas and Maracaibo were subjected frequently to siege. England's Sir Francis Drake took pleasure in plundering Spanish towns and sacked Caracas in 1585.

The seige of Maracaibo was perhaps the most famous attack on Venezuela. In 1669 Henry Morgan—a Welsh buccaneer who operated from the island of Jamaica—entered Lake Maracaibo from the Gulf of

Venezuela. Upon arriving at Maracaibo, Morgan found the city seemingly undefended and collected a large booty. When the pirate turned his ships to exit the lake, he found himself and his fleet looking into the guns of three Spanish warships. Craftily, Morgan used one of his pirate boats as a decoy. After the decoy was set on fire, it was launched into the midst of the Spanish ships and managed to sink two of the war vessels. Once free of the danger of Spanish guns, Morgan made his escape.

## Colonial Era

For many years Spain was the dominant power in Central and South America and controlled its New World empire mainly from Lima, in present-day Peru. As part of the Spanish system of governing, Spain

The Spanish pattern of colonization exploited the native groups *(left)* to provide an enslaved labor force—here panning for gold—until the Indian population was severely diminished. Thereafter, a work force of African slaves *(below)* was imported to work on agricultural estates.

established an audiencia, or administrative center, in Santo Domingo on the island of Hispaniola (shared today by Haiti and the Dominican Republic). In 1526 Venezuela's territory came under the authority of the Audiencia of Santo Domingo.

In 1550 Venezuela was combined with the territory of present-day Colombia to form the Audiencia of Santa Fe de Bogotá. This same area was later added to what is now Ecuador in 1718 to form the Viceroyalty of New Granada, though Venezuela still practiced no self-government. Finally in 1777 the provinces of Caracas, Maracaibo, Barinas, Cumaná, and the islands of Margarita and Trinidad were merged into a captaincy general (military governorship) in Venezuela. Power eventually came to rest in the colony in 1786, when Spain created the Audiencia of Caracas.

The Spanish attitude toward all of its New World colonies was to exploit their natural wealth by forcing the native groups

into slave labor. They then sent back to Spain whatever was valuable. Venezuela was no exception to this general pattern, and several events caused growing resentment among the population.

A childless royal marriage and later a war in Europe resulted in the French Bourbon dynasty taking over the Spanish throne in 1700. The French monarchs introduced several new policies concerning the Spanish colonies. One of these policies established the Royal Guipúzcoana Company of Caracas, better known as the Caracas Company. The move was particularly disagreeable to Venezuelans, since the company was granted a monopoly on all trade within the colony. The company created wealth and developed agriculture. Consequently, exports to Spain increased. But the cost of this record of achievement—ridiculously low wages for Venezuelan workers and high prices for all imported goods—sowed the seeds of discontent that eventually led to revolution and independence.

Since the conquest, the population of the territory had divided into three classes. At the top of the social and economic ladder were the Spaniards, who held the reins of government and enjoyed the privileges of their offices. Next in order came the colonial-born descendants of the Spanish—known as Creoles. This group was the richest class by virtue of its landholdings but was frustrated in its hopes to govern its own country. At the bottom were the Indians, the blacks—whose ancestors had been brought as slaves to work the land—and the people of mixed racial backgrounds.

## Independence

By the late eighteenth century, dissatisfied Venezuelans became increasingly agitated against Spain, whose methods of exploitation slowed economic development in the area. The independence movement included both the poor, overworked native groups as well as the wealthiest people in Venezuela—the Creoles. These anticolonials were influenced by the new ideas of democracy developed after the successful

**A British engraving from the period of Venezuela's independence struggles depicts Caracas as a fairly typical colonial city with Spanish-style architecture and many religious buildings.**

wars of independence in the United States and France.

The Spanish crown, on the other hand, felt that Venezuela should be controlled by officials sent from Spain. Not surprisingly, friction with the Creoles resulted and led to revolutionary movements in several parts of Venezuela. At first, the Spanish authorities put down such rebellions quickly, but the independence movement could not be halted for very long after the beginning of the nineteenth century.

April 19, 1810, marks the real beginning of Venezuela's struggle for independence. On that date a group of Caracas aristocrats and wealthy Creoles forced the Spanish governor from office and formed a junta, or revolutionary council, to take over the government. The junta described itself as loyal to the Spanish king, Ferdinand VII. A declaration of full independence, however, was issued a year later, though the fight for independence went on for many years. Before the fighting was over, Venezuela was to lose nearly one-third of its population to bloodshed.

Francisco de Miranda is known in Venezuela as *El Precursor* (the forerunner) because of his early efforts to free his native land from Spanish colonial domination.

The Venezuelan flag dates from 1806 when Miranda raised it as a symbol of the independence movement. The flag later represented the 1811 Confederation of Venezuela, which consisted of seven original provinces commemorated by the seven white stars on the middle stripe. In 1830 the design became the official flag of independent Venezuela.

Simon Bolívar was at the center of the nineteenth-century South American movement for liberation from colonialism. Born in Caracas in 1783, Bolívar was educated by private tutors in Venezuela and later in Spain. From his studies, the young Venezuelan absorbed the democratic ideals described by the French philosopher Jean-Jacques Rousseau. Bolívar's early association with Latin American independence struggles was largely unsuccessful until he united his forces with those of José Antonio Páez in 1817. Thereafter, victory followed victory, and Bolívar's long-held vision of a united South America became a reality as Gran Colombia. Within only a few years, however, the dream had collapsed, and Bolívar died defeated and disillusioned in 1830.

Courtesy of Inter-American Development Bank

Independent Picture Service

Bolívar's most-trusted subordinate officer was Antonio José de Sucre, who later served as the first president of Bolivia.

Caracas-born Francisco de Miranda was one of the most important figures in Venezuela's struggle for independence. A soldier in the Spanish army who had fought in the U.S. War of Independence, Miranda led a revolutionary expedition into Venezuela in 1806 but failed to accomplish his plan to liberate the colony. In April of 1810 he returned to Venezuela and took an important position in the rebel forces that the junta had organized. Rebel losses led Miranda to surrender to the Spanish in 1812. The Spanish broke the terms of Miranda's surrender and deported him in chains to Spain, where he died in prison four years later.

## Simon Bolívar

Simon Bolívar, however, outshines Miranda as the liberator not only of his own country—Venezuela—but also of Colombia,

Along with many other Venezuelan patriots of the period, Francisco de Miranda signed the nation's Declaration of Independence on July 5, 1811, in Caracas.

Panama, Ecuador, Peru, and Bolivia. After losing important battles in 1812, he led the rebel soldiers to win many victories in the next two years. After repeated attempts to defeat the Spanish, Bolívar devised a plan to split the Spanish forces and scored a decisive victory over them in 1819.

He was elected president of Gran Colombia (Great Colombia), a federation of the present-day nations of Ecuador, Colombia, Panama, and Venezuela established in 1819. In 1821 a victory by Bolívar at Carabobo finally ensured independence for Venezuela, and Bolívar entered Caracas in triumph. But he continued to fight for the freedom of the rest of Gran Colombia and South America.

By 1825 Bolívar had helped to free much of South America and was the most-important and most-powerful man on the continent. Soon, however, opposition to his

power arose, and, when Bolívar declared himself a dictator to enforce his rule, he was nearly assassinated. He could not halt the crumbling of Gran Colombia in 1830, and, when Venezuela and Ecuador left the federation in that year, he resigned from the presidency in despair. Bolívar died a few months later, embittered by strife and the collapse of his political dream. It was not until much later that South Americans recognized him as one of the greatest heroes of Latin American history.

## Republican Life

After Bolívar's resignation and death, José Antonio Páez dictated Venezuela's policies both through his position as president and later through his personal influence. In 1843, when José Tadeo Monagas was elected president, Páez began a revolt against Monagas and tried to have him legally removed from office. Quick to react, however, Monagas closed down the congress, quieted the revolt, and forced Páez into exile. Monagas remained in power until 1858, when he was overthrown in a surprise revolt supported by both conservative and liberal politicians. Thus began a period of 130 years during which the norm in Venezuela was either short-term rulers, who were quickly overthrown, or long-term dictators, who imposed themselves on the country through superior military strength.

### THE CAUDILLOS

The most remembered leaders of this unsettled period were the caudillos (tyrannical political leaders with their own military followings). Antonio Guzmán Blanco dominated Venezuela—though completely outside the constitutional process—from 1870 to 1888. Guzmán Blanco is today considered an example of a benevolent, if self-serving, tyrant.

With Richard Olney's flat assertion that the United States was ". . . practically sovereign on this [the South American] continent," he announced that the United States would play a vigorous role in the resolution of Venezuela's boundary dispute with British Guiana.

In his middle years, Antonio Guzmán Blanco served as advisor and vice president to Juan Falcón. After Falcón was overthrown in 1870, Guzmán Blanco ruled Venezuela for the next 18 years. He retired to Paris in 1888 and died there in 1899.

During his lengthy reign of influence, he oversaw the beginning of a system of compulsory public education, slightly reformed the operations of the government, and undertook much public construction. With an oversized sense of his own importance, Guzmán Blanco also commissioned many paintings and statues of himself.

Guzmán Blanco never legally served as president during all of the 18 years he ran Venezuela. One of his puppets was Joaquín Crespo, who overthrew Guzmán Blanco to make himself dictator. During Crespo's regime, a Venezuelan boundary dispute occurred that attracted international attention.

Great Britain and Venezuela had a long-standing disagreement over where the boundary between Venezuela and the colony of British Guiana (present-day Guyana) should be drawn. In 1895 the U.S. secretary of state, Richard Olney, applied the broadest possible interpretation of the Monroe Doctrine (a statement asserting that the United States would not allow further European colonization in the Western Hemisphere). He demanded that Great

27

Britain allow the matter to go to international resolution. Lord Salisbury, the British prime minister, politely refused, which angered U.S. president Grover Cleveland. Cleveland took the matter to Congress, where he denounced Britain's unwillingness to cooperate.

With talk of a possible war, which neither the United States nor Britain wanted, Britain allowed the dispute to be resolved by international efforts. In 1899 the new boundary line was drawn, and a new dictator—General Cipriano Castro—replaced Crespo, who had been killed in conflicts over the election of his successor.

## The Twentieth Century

Corrupt, greedy, and incompetent, Castro soon had the nation's finances in chaos and refused to honor Venezuela's financial obligations to foreign creditors. In 1902 Great Britain, Germany, and Italy sent a joint naval force to blockade and shell Venezuelan seaports as a means of collecting Venezuela's unpaid foreign debts. Only with U.S. intervention was the matter finally resolved.

### JUAN VINCENTE GOMEZ

Castro was followed by Juan Vincente Gómez—one of the longest lasting of all Latin American dictators. Gómez ruled Venezuela as an absolute dictator from 1908 until his death in 1935. To staff his repressive government, Gómez relied on relatives and trusted friends from Táchira, his rugged, Andean home-state. To maintain himself in power, Gómez modernized the army and constantly rotated its top

Photo by Organization of American States

**Surrounded by dozens of his staff members, Juan Vincente Gómez *(center)* displays his notably strong relationship with the military.**

commanders to prevent any one officer from becoming powerful enough to challenge Gómez's authority.

Gómez had the good fortune to rule Venezuela when foreign oil companies were lining up to obtain lucrative concessions from the nation's oil bonanza. With increased revenues from oil, Gómez was able to pay off Venezuela's debts—while enriching himself beyond his wildest dreams. The longer he held power, however, the more tyrannical his regime became. In the dictator's final years, information about the torture of Gómez's political enemies shocked Venezuela and the world. The anger of the nation's citizens over Gómez's active role in selling the country's oil rights to foreigners exploded after his death in 1935. Venezuelans expressed their anger in the massacre of Gómez-era officials and in attacks on oil company installations in the Lake Maracaibo area.

## Contemporary Democracy

Some historians date the origins of Venezuela's contemporary democracy to the death of Gómez, even though unsettled times still lay ahead. In 1935 Eleázar López Contreras was elected president to a five-year term and, though still a dictator, he loosened the grip of the Gómez-era organizations of repression. He was followed in office by Isaías Medina Angarita, who continued to stabilize Venezuelan politics. Political activists—who had been imprisoned or exiled—were freed or encouraged to return home.

Among those who returned was a dynamic revolutionary leader, Rómulo Betancourt, head of the Democratic Action party (AD). His party was a liberal-minded group that had helped to pressure the conservative government into increasing Venezuela's share of the profits of foreign-owned oil companies.

Betancourt's followers, drawn to their leader by his ability to describe the need for reform, demanded far-reaching changes.

Gómez's regime ignored social issues, agriculture, and industry—except for the development of petroleum. This philosophy resulted in severe hardships for most Venezuelans, while Gómez amassed a large fortune.

Petroleum found beneath Lake Maracaibo in 1913 became the source of enormous wealth for Gómez and his friends.

Born in Caracas in 1884, Rómulo Gallegos was trained to be a teacher and practiced his profession from 1912 to 1930. During this period, he published many novels—including *Doña Bárbara* in 1929, which was interpreted as an attack on the tyranny of Juan Vincente Gómez. Because of his anti-Gómez stance, Gallegos lived in and out of exile from 1931 until his final return to Venezuela in 1958.

Courtesy of Organization of American States

These new ideas frightened both the leadership of Venezuela's conservative, influential military establishment and its foreign backers—the oil companies. When Medina tried to select his successor, the civilian Betancourt and some of the more liberal junior officers within the military staged a coup d'état.

After the coup, Betancourt headed a seven-member, civilian-dominated junta, whose acknowledged purpose was to make sure elections were held. But the junta took advantage of its three-year tenure in office to undertake radical reforms. Government officials guilty of using their positions for personal gain under previous administrations were brought to trial. Under Juan

Pablo Pérez Alfonso—Betancourt's minister of development—new taxes were imposed on foreign oil companies. As a result, the profits of the Venezuelan government rose from 30 to 50 percent.

### AD PARTY IN POWER

When elections were held in 1947, Rómulo Gallegos, a novelist and candidate of Betancourt's Democratic Action party, was elected by an overwhelming majority of the Venezuelan voters. Gallegos, however, refused to bow to military demands for cabinet posts. Furthermore, there was growing agitation over the radical direction being taken by the leadership of the Democratic Action party. A conservative military coup overthrew Gallegos in November 1948, only eight months after he had taken office.

A period of repressive military rule followed—including the exiling again of Betancourt, Gallegos, and many other AD members. Eventually, one of the cruelest tyrants in all Venezuelan history—Marcos Pérez Jiménez—rose to power. Besides trampling on human rights, Pérez Jiménez increased his personal wealth—amounting to $700 million—until he was thrown out of office in 1958.

### ROMULO BETANCOURT

Rómulo Betancourt once again became the head of the Venezuelan government in 1958. This time, he was chosen as president in a democratically held, national election. A small, magnetic, tough man, Betancourt supported radically leftist political views in his early years but later became a social reformer with great faith in the democratic process.

A man of vision, Betancourt demonstrated that overdue social changes could be brought about by democratic means. Personally beyond corruption, Betancourt could see that attention had to be paid to a Venezuelan economy that would be bankrupted when the oil ran out, unless new industries were created.

Throughout his time in office, Betancourt faced opposition within Venezuela,

In the 1950s Marcos Pérez Jiménez presided over one of Venezuela's most repressive regimes. He authorized, for example, the establishment of an elaborate police network, which hunted students, intellectuals, and politicians who disagreed with his policies. These poorly devised policies tended to emphasize development of the petroleum industry at the expense of the agricultural sector. A coalition forced Pérez Jiménez from office in 1958, and a later constitutional amendment barred him from seeking the presidency again.

Courtesy of Organization of American States

31

both from left-wing groups and from strongly conservative sections of the military. Betancourt used his growing personal popularity with the Venezuelan people to enact programs of agrarian reform and to improve standards of housing, health, and education. He furthered the notion of "sowing the petroleum"—using the profits from oil to better the lives of Venezuelans.

Betancourt's most important contribution, however, was to lay the foundations of democracy in Venezuela. Since this achievement, power has alternated between the liberal Democratic Action party and the conservative Social Christian party.

## After Betancourt

By working together within the framework of democracy, these two main parties, along with smaller political parties, have provided Latin America with a rare example of democracy in action. During the last quarter of a century, Venezuela has successfully weathered threats to its stability. In the late 1960s and early 1970s, for example, guerrilla groups tried to disrupt the country's election process through robberies, kidnappings, and threats.

Venezuela also has had to cope with continuing governmental corruption. In the 1970s, when Venezuela's income from oil suddenly quadrupled because of actions taken by the Organization of Petroleum Exporting Countries (OPEC), the incumbent government of Carlos Andrés Pérez proved quite prone to corruption. Pérez's administration had more revenue to spend from oil earnings than all previous Venezuelan administrations since independence. During Pérez's administration, some high-ranking government officials were guilty of dishonesty. These offenses took the form of bribes and secret commissions.

In 1983 Jaime Lusinchi—an AD party member—was elected to the Venezuelan

Courtesy of Inter-American Development Bank

**Betancourt's administration enacted an agrarian reform law in 1960 that aimed to broaden and modernize Venezuela's agricultural production.**

**Rómulo Betancourt** *(left)* **was president of Venezuela from 1959 to 1964.**

## Government

Under the Constitution of 1961, Venezuela is a federal republic with executive, legislative, and judicial branches of government. The president is elected to a five-year term of office and may not immediately have a second term, though the president is eligible for reelection after an interval of 10 years. The president and the legislature are directly elected by the people in national elections, in which voting is obligatory for all Venezuelans 18 years of age or older.

For advice in official matters, the president turns to a 24-member, presidentially appointed council of ministers. Venezuela has a bicameral (two-house) elected congress, comprising a 203-member chamber of deputies and a 49-member senate. Former presidents automatically become life members of the senate. Judicial power is exercised by a supreme court, whose nine members are appointed by the congress to nine-year terms.

Administratively, Venezuela is subdivided into 20 states, the federal district of Caracas, and two territories. Some of these local administrative units include nearby islands.

presidency with the largest majority in 25 years of democracy. Lusinchi initiated measures to counter Venezuela's depressed economy and tried to provide social welfare.

In 1988 the people again elected Carlos Andrés Pérez president. Soon after taking office, Pérez raised prices on items such as gasoline and public transportation. These efforts to improve Venezuela's economy provoked rioting. To restore peace, Pérez froze some prices and raised wages.

But criticism of government policies and charges of corruption continued to plague the president. After two unsuccessful government overthrows by the Bolívar Revolutionary movement and a legislative attempt to oust him from the presidency, Pérez was forced from office in May 1993 on charges of corruption and the misuse of public funds.

Interim president Ramon Velasquez contended with a sluggish economy and a widening budget deficit before turning over the office to Rafael Caldera in February 1994. Elected on a common-people platform, Caldera vowed to continue government control of the business sector. But as the economy continued to fail, he began a harsh and painful economic adjustment in 1996 turning Venezuela toward recovery.

**Venezuela's congress meets in the domed capitol building, which is situated in a crowded section of Caracas.**

Venezuela has one of the highest birth rates in Latin America. Consequently, 40 percent of the population is under 15 years of age.

# 3) The People

From 1970 to 1985, Venezuela's population increased at the annual rate of 2.7 percent —one of the highest growth rates in South America. Presently at 22.6 million, Venezuela's population will double every 27 years at its current pace of expansion.

Besides a high birth rate, Venezuela has a young population. About 40 percent of Venezuelans are younger than 15 years of age. Recent years have witnessed a rapid movement of the population to cities and towns. Today about one-sixth of Venezuela's total population lives in the metro-

politan area of Caracas, and much of the rest of the nation's people are concentrated in cities and towns near or within the Andean highlands. In contrast, the llanos, the Lake Maracaibo Basin, and the Guiana Highlands are sparsely settled.

## Ethnic Mixture

About 67 percent of Venezuela's population is classified as mestizo, or of mixed Indian-and-Spanish bloodlines. A higher percentage of mestizos live in the rural

Middle-class *caraqueños*—citizens of Caracas—enjoy conventional pleasures on the weekends, such as walks through the city's parks with brief stops to feed the pigeons.

The moderate daytime climate in Caracas brings out fitness-minded residents of the capital.

Bright balloons attract interested customers in one of the many parks in Caracas.

35

areas than in the cities. Twenty-one percent of Venezuelans are of European—mainly Spanish—ancestry and are heavily concentrated in the cities. Traditionally, this group has controlled Venezuela's political, social, and economic life. Blacks—whose ancestors were brought to the country as slaves—represent 10 percent of the population and live mostly in coastal areas including the Maracaibo Lowlands.

Only 2 percent of the population is classified as pure Indian. Surviving Indians in Venezuela live mainly in remote highland areas of the country. Soon after the Spanish conquest, the largest Indian groups were worked to extinction. Small numbers fled to the inaccessible jungle—where some tribes already lived—and this move altered living patterns to a more restricted lifestyle. The Motilón, for example, who live along the border of Venezuela and Colombia, resist all contact with strangers—even to the point of shooting arrows to keep people away. The Goajiro are the largest native group still left in Venezuela. They live mainly in the western section of the Lake Maracaibo Basin and continue to be nomadic herders.

## Rich and Poor

The contrasts between rich and poor are clearly visible in Caracas, where wealthy families live in modern, high-rise apart-

The Motilón live in hard-to-reach areas of the Venezuelan jungles. After clearing a section of forest, the Indians build one large dwelling in which all members of the community live.

Only wealthy Venezuelans can afford to live in modern, high-rise apartment buildings. These structures line the shores of Lake Maracaibo—the site of the nation's oil riches.

ment buildings staffed by uniformed domestic servants, while the poor live in hillside ranchos. Wealthy Venezuelans shop at well-stocked supermarkets or at department stores bursting with the latest consumer products. The rich of Caracas enjoy sports cars, entertainments as diverse as those found in New York City, and frequent trips abroad.

The same Caracas that supports these comfortable lifestyles is ringed by barrios —communities of an ever-growing unemployed and impoverished population. The number of poor people has increased rapidly in recent years, partly because of the large influx of illegal immigrants from neighboring Colombia, where job opportunities are few. Despite the downturn of the Venezuelan economy, the demand for unskilled labor has remained high.

Venezuela's middle class is large and fairly active—compared to the middle-income groups of other South American nations. Moreover, about one million European immigrants—from nations such as Spain, Italy, and Portugal—have settled

In Caracas the demand for living space is intense. Some newcomers to the capital—both from the Venezuelan countryside and from nearby foreign nations—build their homes on the hills surrounding the city.

37

The scene at a public water fountain in a Venezuelan village demonstrates the vast gap between the standards of living in the country's urban and rural areas. Venezuela's wealth is concentrated in the cities, while villages exhibit the conditions of poverty common to many Latin American countries.

in Caracas since the 1950s. These immigrants have further strengthened the median-income group.

## Rural Life

The city limits of Caracas mark a boundary between two worlds. Beyond the capital lies a typically agricultural society, except for a handful of secondary cities that support considerable industry. Rural Venezuela is composed of quiet towns and villages, where land is in the hands of the few and where most agricultural laborers produce subsistence crops on rented or unclaimed land.

The pace of life is slower in Venezuela's villages, which were established long ago to serve the coffee growers of the highlands and the sugarcane and cacao plantations of the lower elevations. Geographically isolated, the people of rural Venezuela tend to be conservative in outlook and to cling to the preservation of traditional values.

## Art

During the twentieth century, Caracas has supported a thriving cultural and intellectual life and has become the place where

In a detail from *The Baptism,* nineteenth-century Venezuelan artist Cristóbal Rojas reflects the creative influence of his Parisian tutor Jean-Paul Laurels.

Arturo Michelena was born in 1863 and died in Caracas of tuberculosis in 1898. His work is often compared to that of Cristóbal Rojas because they studied under the same master in Paris. This example of his style—entitled *La Vara Rota* (The Broken Lance)—depicts a bullfight in which the picador (*seen climbing over the wall*) has failed to weaken the bull by thrusting his pic, or lance, into the animal's neck muscles.

Venezuelan artists must exhibit to obtain national recognition. The greatest collection of Venezuelan paintings is found in the Museum of Fine Arts in Caracas, where the works of both nineteenth-century and contemporary artists are shown. On exhibition are paintings by Arturo Michelena, Cristóbal Rojas, Martín Tovar y Tovar, Francisco Valdés, Antonio Herrera Toro, José María Ver León, and Tito Salas.

Some Venezuelan artists adopted the social themes of *indigenismo*—an early twentieth-century South American cultural movement that emphasized national pride in pre-Columbian traditions. Their works, however, reflected a greater attachment to cubism (an abstract art form) and to caricature (an exaggerated illustration technique). Later abstract ideas developed a wide appreciation beginning in

Painted in 1905 by Tito Salas, *La San Genaro* illustrates a popular festival held annually in Spain. Salas lived in Spain for a long time before returning to his native Venezuela where he died at an old age.

A self-portrait of painter Hector Poleo depicts the artist as blind and withered with age. Poleo, whose canvasses sometimes have a quality of fantasy, was known as a painter of social scenes.

Courtesy of Museum of Modern Art of Latin America

the 1970s. Their most-famous Venezuelan advocate is perhaps Jesús Rafael Soto.

Venezuelan sculptors, such as Alejandro Otero, have introduced modern geometrical forms into their works. This trend is equally true in Venezuelan architecture. Caracas has expanded greatly since the oil boom, and its public buildings—including additions to the Central University—reflect both the benefits of the oil profits and a new architectural style.

## Literature

Surprisingly, the production of Venezuelan literary works began with the British and not the Spanish. James Lamb and Matthew Gallagher published the *Gaceta*

*de Caracas* in 1808 as well as the first Venezuelan book, *Calendario manuel y guía universel de forasteros en Caracas para 1810,* which contained a history of Venezuela by the noted classical scholar Andrés Bello. Bello later wrote "On the agriculture of the Torrid Zone," and in 1843 he produced the sentimental *Prayer for All.* Another early printing press was set up on Margarita Island for Simon Bolívar. The press issued his proclamations and other historic documents.

In the nineteenth century, romanticism —a movement that glorified events in sentimental language—became extremely popular in much of South America. In Venezuela this style focused on the independence era. Representative of the romantic

*Delta Solar* by Venezuelan artist Alejandro Otero stands in the garden of the National Air and Space Museum in Washington, D.C. The sculpture has dozens of lightweight, reflective steel reels that move with the slightest breeze. The people of Venezuela donated the artwork to the people of the United States to commemorate the U.S. bicentennial in 1976.

school were the works of José Antonio Maitín, José Antonio Calcaño, Abigaíl Lozano, and Juan Antonio Pérez Bonalde.

One of the best known South American novelists at the beginning of the twentieth century was Manuel Díaz Rodríguez. Another leading twentieth-century literary figure was the talented novelist and former president, Rómulo Gallegos, author of *La trepadora, Canaima,* and *Pobre negro.* His best-known work is *Doña Bárbara,* whose heroine struggles to impose civilization on the wilderness of the plains.

A lesser-known movement called *costumbrismo* also thrived in Venezuela. In sharp contrast to romanticism, this style was noted for its realism and its focus on less-sentimental, rural scenes. *Peonía,* a novel by Manuel Vicente Romero García, was at the forefront of this style, which later developed a critical side. A few current writers have abandoned the pastoral settings for more urban backgrounds.

As a young man the Venezuelan poet and scholar Andrés Bello was a dedicated educator.

Venezuelan folk music has strong ties to homemade instruments, which are fashioned from a wide variety of materials. Here, a decorative keg and a long stick produce a percussive sound.

Independent Picture Service

Independent Picture Service

During an annual festival in the state of Miranda along Venezuela's northern coast, a musician tunes his *cuatro,* or four-stringed guitar, before his performance.

42

Venezuela's high fertility rate—3.6 children for each woman of childbearing age (15 to 49)—has resulted in a vigorous attempt to educate women about methods of planning the growth of their families. Only a small percentage of the female population, however, uses any form of birth control.

Their works depict the effects of oil profits on a once largely agricultural land.

## Music

Better known than its literature and art is Venezuela's music, especially its distinctive folk and popular songs. Much of the folk music comes from the llaneros (people of the plains), who sing songs about the wide, open spaces of Venezuela.

The Popular Music School is a unique institution that teaches the playing of musical instruments only to amateurs who are interested in music as a hobby. While other schools teach classical instrumentation, this school teaches techniques for playing the most popular Venezuelan musical instruments—the guitar, the harp, and a small, four-stringed guitar called a *cuatro*. These instruments are used in playing most Venezuelan folk music, including the joropo—the national dance—the *carite,* and the *gaita zuliana.*

## Health

The average lifespan of a Venezuelan born in 1997 is about 72 years of age, which is an improvement over past figures, though it falls short of life expectancy figures of industrialized countries. Medical care is good but expensive and is concentrated mostly in the cities. Statistically, there is 1 doctor for every 630 people, and 1 hospital bed for every 425 Venezuelans—though figures for both statistics are better in urban than in rural areas. Authorities have not yet designed a health-care system to reach the slums or to serve the needs of people in rural areas. Nursing aides are the most frequently found medical personnel in the countryside.

Diseases caused by insects have largely been controlled by herbicides, and a vaccination campaign has also decreased the number of polio and tuberculosis cases. Government efforts to improve environmental conditions by filling disease-spreading ponds and by providing clean drinking water have also created better health conditions. The infant mortality rate is 24 deaths in every 1,000 live births—one of the lower ratios in South America.

## Sports

Two national sports—baseball and soccer—dominate Venezuela's recreational activities. Most towns and all cities have their own stadiums, and there are many professional and amateur teams. Bullfighting draws large crowds and top-ranking international matadors to the rings of the Nuevo Circo in Caracas and the Maestranza in Maracay. The events are usually organized in connection with a fair or festival.

Water sports are very popular with Venezuelans, who flock to the seaside for holidays. Swimming, diving, waterskiing, and fishing are enjoyed all year long. Good river and lake fishing, where participants angle for trout, catfish, or dorado (South American salmon), is also common.

The Andes in northwestern Venezuela provide challenges for sports enthusiasts.

Mountain climbers find many peaks and rocky crags to scale. Skiers take advantage of frequent snowfalls that cover Pico Bolívar nearly every day between May and October.

## Education

In 1992, the Venezuelan government devoted more than 23 percent of its national expenses to public education. This high percentage dramatically raised educational standards in recent decades. Today about 91 percent of all Venezuelans can read and write. Adults born before improvements in education and residents of remote rural regions that are not adequately served by public schools are often still illiterate. To erase adult illiteracy, Venezuelan authorities make special evening classes available at all school levels.

With the proceeds of oil profits, the Venezuelan government supports full scholarships annually for more than 1,000 promising young students to pursue their academic careers at universities abroad. Such support, however, is conditional—the

In a country with so much coastline, it is not surprising that Venezuelans are avid water-sports enthusiasts. Here, a beach near the capital city provides a place for people to swim, wade, and lie in the sun.

Some Andean peaks are covered with snow throughout the year. These skiers are on a mountain in the Cordillera Mérida.

students pledge to return to Venezuela to practice their professions.

Venezuela has 18 public universities and 15 privately supported institutions of higher learning. The total enrollment at these universities is more than 600,000, which represents a 50 percent increase during the past decade. The centerpiece of higher education is the Central University in Caracas, which has a beautifully landscaped setting with modern buildings and the latest in educational equipment.

University City – on the 400-acre campus of the Central University of Caracas – has up-to-date educational facilities in a setting of modern sculptures, murals, and architecture.

45

## Religion and Festivals

Roman Catholicism is the official religion of the country. The Venezuelan government is an active participant in the selection of Church officials. Freedom of religion exists in Venezuela, although nearly 95 percent of the people call themselves Catholic. Venezuelans often do not regularly attend services, but they turn to the Church in times of crisis or to perform rites such as baptisms, marriages, and funerals. The Church has not been an active participant in political affairs but does speak out frequently in support of social reform.

Numerous festivals are held throughout the year in Venezuela. The biggest holiday is Carnival (or Mardi Gras), which is celebrated on the two days prior to the beginning of Lent. Singing and dancing are widespread in the streets of most cities and towns, and parades of colorful floats crowd the main square. Confetti, candy, and many popular amusements further contribute to the festival atmosphere.

Many holidays celebrate the feast days of local saints, and each celebration has its own costumes and customs. For example, grotesque masks and red clothes are a feature of the Dancing Devils—an Indian-inspired entertainment performed in San Francisco de Yare on the feast of Corpus Christi.

In bright red costumes, the Dancing Devils of San Francisco de Yare shake their maracas and move rhythmically through the streets until they reach the door of the local church.

Dawn breaks over the Lagoven refinery at Amuay on the Paraguaná Peninsula, just northeast of the Gulf of Venezuela.

# 4) The Economy

With per capita earnings of more than $2,500, Venezuela statistically ranks among the most economically advanced countries of Latin America. The figure, however, masks deep inequalities in the division of wealth, which is heavily concentrated in the hands of a small minority. At present 11 percent of Venezuela's work force is unemployed. Unpredictable world oil prices have created an economic uncertainty that sometimes discourages investments in new industries.

## Oil Earnings

The Venezuelan economy experienced a serious battering in the late 1980s and early 1990s because of declining earnings from its oil exports. The shortfall in oil revenues increased already-spiraling foreign debts.

47

Until the discovery of oil in the early twentieth century, Venezuela had a traditional, agriculture-based economy.

But rising oil prices and increased production in the mid 1990s led to four straight years of growth in export revenues.

Between 1995 and 1997, Venezuela pushed oil production from 2.3 to 3 million barrels per day. Petroleum production is expected to reach 6 million barrels per day by 2005.

For the near future, oil will continue to dominate the Venezuelan economy. Meanwhile, the country's government and private sector are working to develop a more varied industrial base by using oil-derived income to exploit other minerals—iron ore, for example. The government is also trying to build processing plants to convert more of Venezuela's crop and mineral production into finished products.

To assure that the country does not soon run out of oil, the government has been studying ways to develop hard-to-reach reserves in the Orinoco Basin. Researchers have discovered methods to pump and store the reserves, resulting in increased production.

Despite oil's predominance, agricultural crops—such as coffee—still contribute to export earnings.

## History of Venezuela's Oil Industry

For 400 years—before Venezuela's oil boom in the 1920s—the country was predominantly agricultural. It depended on earnings from exports of coffee, cacao, hides, fruits, sisal (a strong fiber employed in rope making), and gold. Venezuela purchased from foreign markets almost every manufactured product that the country's people used. Then, when oil was discovered in great quantities beneath the surface of Lake Maracaibo, a rapid change took place. European and U.S. companies sent people to Venezuela to drill and process the newly found petroleum. Because gasoline-driven cars had become commonplace in most industrial countries, the demand for oil rose quickly and brought vast wealth to Venezuela.

But the wealth went into the pockets of foreigners and of Venezuelan government officials. Little trickled down to the Venezuelan people. The government charged the foreign oil companies to remove the oil

Courtesy of Embassy of Venezuela, Washington, D.C.

These sturdy buildings house the Maracaibo headquarters of Venezuela's oil industry.

Independent Picture Service

Venezuela's first oil refinery was located on the mist-covered hillsides near San Cristóbal in the state of Táchira.

from Venezuela, but corrupt government leaders kept much of the money for themselves. Oil became the only real industry in Venezuela as demand for oil grew and as new deposits were found.

### POSTWAR OIL BOOM

When World War II started, the demand for petroleum immediately rose to new heights. As Venezuelan production of oil increased, new earnings were created. But, again, most of the wealth did not reach the people, though it did help other industries to begin and expand. Postwar governments were led by dictators and juntas—few of whom looked beyond the immediate wealth that the petroleum industry produced.

In 1956, during the regime of Marcos Pérez Jiménez, the Suez Canal was closed to the exportation of Middle Eastern oil, which resulted in an unprecedented expansion of Venezuelan oil production and earnings. The foreign-owned oil companies made more money, and Pérez Jiménez became one of the world's wealthiest people. He took much of the increased profits, while many Venezuelans were still poor.

### REFORMS IN THE OIL INDUSTRY

The big change in the petroleum industry came about in 1958 when Pérez Jiménez was overthrown by another military junta, which immediately held elections. Rómulo Betancourt became the democratically elected president. The attitude of the new government toward the oil industry—and toward the economy as a whole—changed dramatically. Betancourt started many social reforms and used the oil company royalties to finance them. Many Venezuelans believed that his was the first basically honest government in Venezuela since the nation had gained independence.

Under the administration of Rómulo Betancourt, oil profits were used to modernize the agricultural sector.

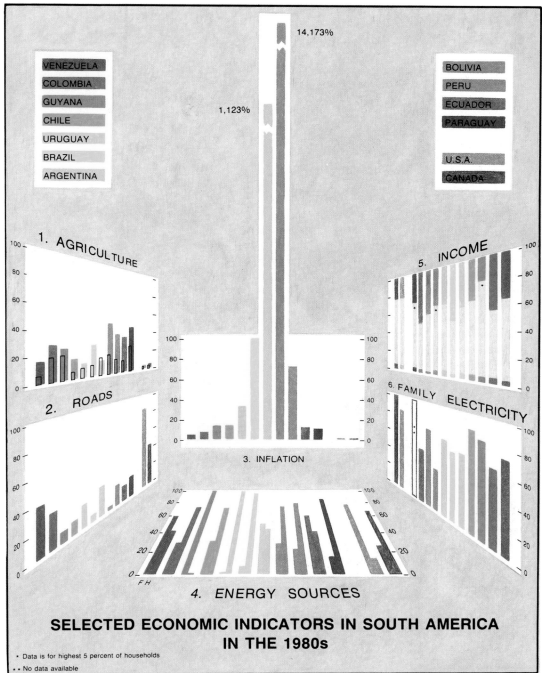

14,173%

1,123%

VENEZUELA
COLOMBIA
GUYANA
CHILE
URUGUAY
BRAZIL
ARGENTINA

BOLIVIA
PERU
ECUADOR
PARAGUAY

U.S.A.
CANADA

1. AGRICULTURE

5. INCOME

2. ROADS

3. INFLATION

6. FAMILY ELECTRICITY

4. ENERGY SOURCES

## SELECTED ECONOMIC INDICATORS IN SOUTH AMERICA IN THE 1980s

• Data is for highest 5 percent of households
•• No data available

Artwork by Carol F. Barrett

This multigraph depicts six important South American economic factors. The same factors for the United States and Canada are included for comparison. Data is from *1986 Britannica Book of the Year, Encyclopedia of the Third World, Europa Yearbook,* and *Countries of the World and their Leaders, 1987.*

In GRAPH 1—labeled Agriculture—the colored bars show the percentage of a country's total labor force that works in agriculture. The overlaid black boxes show the percentage of a country's gross domestic product that comes from agriculture. In most cases—except Argentina —the number of agricultural workers far exceeds the amount of income produced by the farming industry.

GRAPH 2 depicts the percentage of paved roads, while GRAPH 3 illustrates the inflation rate. The inflation figures for Colombia, Guyana, and Brazil are estimated. GRAPH 4 depicts two aspects of energy usage. The left half of a country's bar is the percentage of energy from fossil fuel (oil or coal); the right half shows the percentage of energy from hydropower. In GRAPH 5, which depicts distribution of wealth, each country's bar represents 100 percent of its total income. The top section is the portion of income received by the richest 10 percent of the population. The bottom section is the portion received by the poorest 20 percent. GRAPH 6 represents the percentage of homes that have electricity.

Multiple pipelines move crude oil from tanks to the shipping terminal at La Salina on the shores of Lake Maracaibo.

"Pigs" *(left and above)* are large rotating brushes that clean sludge deposits from the inside of the oil pipelines.

Betancourt also insisted that Venezuelans themselves should benefit from the mineral wealth of Venezuela. Almost every oil company in Venezuela was foreign-owned when Betancourt came to power, and almost every company used employees from its home country to work in Venezuela. Betancourt directed the companies to hire and train Venezuelans for increasingly more important jobs. The oil companies eventually agreed, and many foreigners and their families were sent home.

Betancourt further demanded that the oil companies pay Venezuela 65 percent of the profits as a royalty rather than the 50 percent they had been paying. In addition, Betancourt stopped granting oil concessions to private companies. The newly formed, government-owned Corporación Venezolana de Petróleo (CVP) was put in charge of exploiting further oil production.

Independent Picture Service

A worker fills drums with lubricating oil at an Amuay refinery.

Independent Picture Service

Most underground oil contains large amounts of liquid natural gas, which helps to force the petroleum to the surface. This injection plant returns the natural gas to the oil reservoir to preserve it for later use.

In 1960 Venezuela became a founding member of OPEC. This multi-national organization sets prices and establishes production quotas for member-countries.

### THE INDUSTRY IN RECENT TIMES

Betancourt realized that petroleum was a nonrenewable resource and that complete dependence on it could lead to disaster when the supply dwindled. Experts advised Betancourt that such a reduced supply could occur in less than 20 years. With this in mind, Betancourt's government—and those that have followed—have diversified the economy through development plans that emphasize the growth of manufacturing and agriculture.

During the early 1970s, the oil companies paid Venezuela over $1 billion a year in royalties. Most of this money was for oil removed from the Maracaibo area and accounted for over 70 percent of the crude oil production. Eastern Venezuela's deposits accounted for almost all the rest.

Approximately 21 companies—most of them U.S. owned—were engaged in the production of crude oil.

In 1974 Venezuela announced that the country's iron industry would be nationalized—converted from private to government ownership—on January 1, 1975, and that nationalization of the oil industry would follow. In 1976 Petróleos de Venezuela (Petroven), the federally owned oil monopoly, assumed control of the nation's oil industry. The company continues to rely on foreign firms for needed technical help.

When the Venezuelan government took over the foreign-owned oil operations, the foreign companies received $1.1 billion in compensation. Of this amount, 10 percent was in cash and the rest was in government bonds. The nationalization process was achieved on friendly terms, and many of the foreign companies contracted with Petroven to provide it with technical assistance and marketing outlets.

The Lagoven Amuay Refinery has the largest flexi-coking (specialized distillation) unit in the world. In an attempt to get more oil from the distillation process, the unit heats petroleum-filled sludge taken from the basin of Lake Maracaibo to high temperatures. This process allows the lighter and heavier substances in the sludge to separate. The heavier portions collect at the bottom of the stills in the form of coke—a dry fuel.

Courtesy of Colonial Pipeline Company

The United States is one of the largest importers of Venezuelan oil. Here, a tanker unloads refined petroleum products from Venezuela at New York Harbor.

Before the 1960s most Venezuelan oil was refined abroad, and natural gas was burned off or wasted. Domestic oil refineries have now been established, and gas is distributed by pipeline for use as fuel, as raw material for the petrochemical industry, and as part of the manufacturing of liquid gas. The Maracaibo area in the state of Zulia operates most of the nation's eight refineries.

Courtesy of Inter-American Development Bank

Improvements in oil production have enabled the petrochemical industry to expand greatly. Petrochemicals, which are derived from petroleum and from the by-products of oil production, are made into such items as synthetic rubber, fertilizers, plastics, nylons, polyesters, and detergents.

The state of Bolívar has become important in the mining and refining of iron ore. After the ore has been dug out of the earth, it is transported to plants for further refinement into steel or crude iron.

## Other Minerals

Most of the growth in the mining sector of the economy has been in the production of iron ore. About 10 million tons are produced annually. Venezuelan reserves of iron ore are estimated at more than one billion tons. Iron ore is produced in Bolívar state by two companies that are owned by U.S. steel manufacturers. Most of the ore is mined for export.

Bauxite—from which aluminum is made —is exploited in the Guiana Highlands by Bauxien, a state agency. Bauxite reserves are known to total at least 200 million tons. Important gold mines are located southeast of Bolívar state, and new deposits were discovered in the early 1960s near El Callao in the Guiana Highlands.

Diamonds are found in Venezuela's Amazonas territory, and high-grade phosphate rock has been found in Falcón state. Sulfur deposits are located in the state of Sucre, and nickel mines are sited near Las Tejerías. Venezuela is also known to have deposits of manganese, copper, and asbestos. Coal is mined in the states of Táchira, Aragua, and Anzoátegui. Proven coal reserves in the state of Zulia amount to 160 million tons.

## Agriculture and Livestock

Profits from agriculture contribute only a small percentage to Venezuela's total national income, and agricultural activities provide work for only about 18 percent of the labor force. Over 50 percent of all farmers are engaged in subsistence production —growing crops for their own needs—and growth rates in agricultural output have not kept pace with population expansion. Despite more than two decades of agrarian reform in Venezuela, the rural population has continued to decline. Only about 20 percent of the land is cultivated for crops or for pastureland, and, consequently, imported food makes up about 40 percent of the country's total consumption. Farm workers are in demand, and illegal immigrants continue to enter the agricultural sector from Colombia and other countries.

These storage facilities for corn and rice help to preserve Venezuela's grain crop. The complex is at Urachiche, a village in a productive farming region between Barquisimeto and Valencia.

Subsistence farming still forms a large proportion of all agricultural activity in Venezuela, especially in the Andes where there are few stretches of level land.

Only 30 percent of Venezuela's land is used for farming or grazing. Nineteen percent of all farmland is planted with permanent crops, such as citrus groves, while the remainder either is left unused or under temporary cultivation.

Horses splash across a waterway as they are herded to better pastureland.

Venezuela's agricultural and pasture-land zones contribute in different ways to food production. Principal crops in the agricultural zone are coffee, cacao, sugarcane, maize (corn), rice, wheat, tobacco, cotton, beans, and sisal. There are more than 62,000 coffee plantations covering about 500,000 acres. High-quality cacao comes from 13,000 plantations, chiefly in the states of Sucre and Miranda. Sugarcane is processed at 6 government-owned and 20 privately owned mills. About five million acres of sugarcane are under cultivation.

The pastureland areas, mostly in the llanos, afford grazing for 14 million cattle and 500,000 horses. In the 1990s, the livestock count for the nation showed 2.3 million pigs, 1.5 million goats, 525,000 sheep, and 52 million poultry. Over half of the land used in farming is pastureland.

## Fishing

The waters of Venezuela are rich in fish resources, and production of canned and fresh fish has doubled in the last 10 years.

Courtesy of Inter-American Development Bank

**Recent government programs have aimed to increase Venezuela's production of food—including tropical fruits.**

Courtesy of Embassy of Venezuela, Washington, D.C.

Oysters are unable to move and, therefore, attach themselves to rocks or other stationary materials along the sea bottom, where Venezuelan fishermen can easily collect them.

In the state of Sucre, a heavily laden fishing boat unloads its day's catch of small fish taken from Venezuela's northeastern waters.

Most fishing activities are clustered around large port cities, such as Maracaibo, and on the Paraguaná Peninsula. Porlamar on Margarita Island is noted for its pearl fisheries, but shrimp and sardines are the most important national fish catches. The total fish take is about 250,000 tons each year. The government is trying to develop this industry through loans from international financial agencies, such as the Inter-American Development Bank.

## Industry

Perhaps most important for continuous stability in Venezuela's economy is the development of manufacturing industries. At present, manufacturing accounts for about 16 percent of the country's total employment and 28 percent of the gross domestic product.

Until the 1960s, manufacturing was largely concentrated in Caracas. Since then, the government has promoted the distribution of heavy industry to other parts of the country. Ciudad Guayana, at the junction of the Caroní and the Orinoco rivers, has been developed as an industrial complex to process iron ore mined in the Guiana Highlands. A government-owned steel plant turns out structural steel, reinforcing rods, rails, steel sheets and tubes, and seamless steel pipes for the petroleum industry.

Several electric furnaces, using power generated by the hydroelectric plant at Guri on the Caroní River, manufacture iron into products needed by industry. The Guri dam is 500 feet high and supplies water to 24 generators. In addition to its use in steel manufacturing, electric power helps fuel the area's two aluminum complexes, which receive bauxite from two mines in the Guiana Highlands. More than 417,000 tons of aluminum were manufactured in the early 1990s. An oil refinery and a petrochemical complex have also been installed at Ciudad Guayana.

Morón, situated about 100 miles west of La Guaira, is the center of Venezuela's petrochemical industry. Products include fertilizers, insecticides, explosives, soda, and other chemicals. Fertilizer production alone exceeds 900,000 tons annually.

The processing of foods, the rebuilding of heavy machinery, and the production of paper, electrical equipment, and pharmaceuticals are concentrated in the Maracaibo area. At the present time, Venezuela fills about 90 percent of its domestic demand for processed foods, beverages, tobacco, clothing, and textiles. Paper and cardboard production amount to about 612,000 tons annually, and factories assemble about 68,000 automotive vehicles each year.

Courtesy of Inter-American Development Bank

Since Venezuela nationalized its oil industry in 1975, the country has extensively developed its petrochemical manufacturing facilities—including a new complex at Morón.

Independent Picture Service

Independent Picture Service

Among the items on Venezuela's list of manufactured goods are tires (left) and textiles (right).

61

Venezuela's greatest economic progress since the 1960s has been in developing a framework of highways, pipelines, power lines, and hydroelectric plants to serve the expanding needs of the nation's mineral producers. As proven reserves of oil, gas, iron ore, and bauxite have expanded, the government has encouraged the installation of the equipment needed to process these materials.

## Transportation

In the mid-twentieth century, Venezuela developed an excellent highway network, especially in the northern and western parts of the country, where three well-paved roads exist. A section of the Pan-American Highway runs southwest from Caracas to Cúcuta, Colombia. Another highway runs along the Andean foothills from Valencia to San Cristóbal. The highway in the llanos extends east from Caracas to Ciudad Bolívar. Several branch roads supplement these main thoroughfares. Highways bear a particularly heavy burden, since there is only one 100-mile commercial rail line in service, which links Barquisimeto with Puerto Cabello.

Heavy goods are moved by coastal shipping routes and inland waterways. Most of the nation's foreign commerce is carried by sea. Eight ports are operated by the government. The principal ports are at La Guaira, Maracaibo, Puerto Cabello, Puerto La Cruz, and Amuay. The Orinoco River and Lake Maracaibo are heavily traveled inland waterways. A frequently dredged channel keeps Lake Maracaibo open to seagoing vessels.

Two national airline companies—Línea Aéropostal Venezolana (LAV) and Aerovías Venezolanas (AVENSA)—serve numerous domestic airports. Venezolana

Constructed at a cost of $71 million, the *autopista* that connects Caracas with La Guaira streamlines the traffic flow between the capital and its port city.

Until Venezuela broadens its manufacturing capabilities, the nation's economic prosperity will continue to rely on the oil deposits that lie beneath the placid waters of Lake Maracaibo.

Internacional de Aviación (VIASA) operates international routes in conjunction with KLM, a Dutch airline. International air traffic uses Venezuelan airports as stopovers on flights between North and South America.

## Trade

Venezuela continues to maintain a favorable balance of trade by exporting more than it imports in terms of monetary value. Petroleum remains its principal export, and the major destinations for this commodity are the United States, the Netherlands Antilles (because of its nearby oil-processing facilities off the coast of Falcón), Canada, and Great Britain.

Venezuela's principal imports are electrical and automotive machinery, manufactured goods, chemical products, and grains. Almost half of all imports come from the United States. Other suppliers are Germany, Japan, Italy, Brazil, and Great Britain.

## Future Prospects

Increased oil production, short-term loans, and international investors are enabling Venezuela to make marked progress toward economic recovery. The unfair distribution of wealth and the memory of recent economic collapse, however, continue to concern much of the population.

Most Venezuelans realize that jumpstarting the economy will require some concessions, but they will not tolerate for long a government that asks so much of those with so little. President Caldera will need to continue economic reform through free markets and privatization while providing social programs that help support the citizens through this time of high unemployment and outrageous inflation.

In addition, Venezuelans must break their total dependence on oil by continuing to develop other resources and industries. In this way, the nation's fortunes will not be affected by unreliable foreign oil prices, and Venezuela will be prepared for the day when its oil reserves run out.

# Index